©Master Key
to the
GRE

| Volume 4 |

Statistics &
Data Interpretation

Made by
Sherpa Prep

Master Key to the GRE: Statistics & Data Interpretation.

ISBN: 978-0-9966225-2-3

© 2017 Sherpa Prep.

Register Your Book!

To access the online videos that come with this book, please go to:

www.SherpaPrep.com/Activate

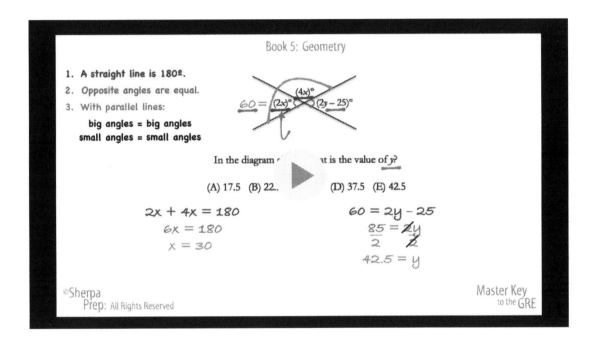

When registering:

Be sure to provide the **same** last name and shipping address that you used to purchase this book or to enroll in your GRE course with Sherpa Prep!

Register @ www.SherpaPrep.com/Activate

Master Key by
Sherpa Prep

Dear Student,

Thank you for purchasing Sherpa Prep's guide to <u>Statistics & Data Interpretation</u>. We know that preparing for the GRE can be a grueling and intimidating process. The fact that you've chosen us to assist you is deeply appreciated.

This series of books is the culmination of nearly three decades of experience teaching the GRE on a daily basis. We think you'll find that experience and expertise reflected in the pages that follow.

As with any undertaking of this size, there are a number of people who deserve special recognition. First among them is Nasheed Amin, who critiqued <u>Master Key to the GRE</u> in its entirety and whose insightful recommendations significantly enhanced all five volumes. We would also like to recognize the contributions of Seth Alcorn, Shawn Magnuson, Bronwyn Bruton, and Jessica Rider Amin. Without their assistance, this project would not have been possible. Finally, we would like to extend our gratitude to the students and instructors of Sherpa Prep, whose feedback, questions, and experiences lie at the heart of these materials.

Good luck with your preparation! If we can be of further assistance, please reach out to us at <u>jay@sherpaprep.com</u> or <u>nafeez@sherpaprep.com</u>. **We'd love to hear from you.**

On behalf of everyone at Sherpa Prep,

Jay

Nafeez

Jay Friedman
Founder
Sherpa Prep

Nafeez Amin
President
Sherpa Prep

Table of Contents

Volume 4

Statistics &
Data Interpretation

Chapter 1

Introduction to the GRE

Introduction

To be discussed:

Master Key to the GRE

Get a sense of how to use our books, how to study properly for the GRE, and how to access our online video content.

1	Choosing the Right Guide	**4**	Proper Study Habits
2	Why Master Key is Special	**5**	The App
3	How to Use Our Guides	**6**	Register Your Book!

The Structure & Scoring System

Read about the structure and scoring system of the GRE. Learn how to sign up for the exam and report your scores.

7	The Structure of the GRE	**9**	Registering for the GRE
8	The Scoring System	**10**	Reporting & Canceling Scores

Navigating the Exam

Get an in-depth sense of how the GRE's scoring system works and what you can do to maximize your performance on test day.

11	How the Exam Works	**13**	Strategy & Time Management
12	The Scoring Algorithm	**14**	Practice Tests

Intro to Quantitative Reasoning

Before you get started, educate yourself about the sort of math you'll find on the GRE and the four ways in which the exam formats its math questions.

15	Content Overview	**18**	Numeric Entry Questions
16	Problem Solving Questions	**19**	Quantitative Comparisons
17	"Select One or More" Questions	**20**	Before You Get Started

Master Key to the GRE

(1) Choosing the Right Guide – If you're like most people preparing to take the GRE, you probably have little sense of what differentiates one GRE guide from another.

• You may think that all GRE guides are more or less the same, or that the guides you see in bookstores are the most comprehensive on the market.

> ➢ The basic story is that most guides fall into one of two categories: "strategy-based" or "content-based".

• **The guides that you find in bookstores are almost always strategy-based.** In general, strategy-based guides provide:

> 1. A brief discussion of each question type that you find on the GRE.
> 2. A small set of suggestions for approaching these question types.
> 3. A collection of one hundred or so practice questions with some brief solutions.

• You also tend to find instructions on how to register for the GRE and report your scores; advice for the test day experience; and a few appendices that review vocabulary and elementary math principles.

> ➢ You won't find a lot of "know-how", however, in strategy-based guides. **The focus of such books is test-taking advice, not education.**

• The latest "premier" guide of one well-known test-prep provider, for example, devotes just nineteen pages to explaining math concepts.

• This said, you will find some useful ideas for taking the exam strategically, among them: ways to use the answer choices to your advantage; advice on how to pace yourself; and recommendations on how to read.

> ➢ In our experience, learning these sorts of strategies is helpful for most test-takers. Unfortunately, **they will not help you attain a strong GRE score, on their own**.

• If you do not know how to solve the problems you find on your exam, you will not do well, regardless of how well you can eliminate irrational answers, pace yourself, or otherwise "game" the exam.

> In contrast, **content-based guides teach the "know-how" you need** to solve exam questions without guessing.

• Such guides generally devote several pages of discussion to most of the major topics tested by the GRE.

• At the end of each discussion, you tend to find a set of section-ending exercises that allow you to practice what you've studied. As a result, content-based guides almost always have far more practice questions than their strategy-based counterparts.

> In our view, **this sort of approach is critical to success on the GRE**. It may not be the only thing you need to succeed, but it is the most important.

• Think about it logically for a moment. Is there any other exam you would dare take without learning its content beforehand?

• Of course not. Yet students regularly "prep" for the GRE using books that do not review the content of the exam. It takes years to graduate from college, and some admissions committees weigh GRE scores more heavily than grade point averages. Isn't an exam that means so much worth preparing for properly?

> Unfortunately, there a number of drawbacks to the content-based guides currently available for the GRE.

• For starters, **these guides almost always ignore the tactics recommended by strategy-based guides**, tactics that we believe are an asset to any test taker.

• What's more, such guides rarely tell you how frequently a particular topic is tested. Knowing which topics to study is important if you only have limited time to prepare for the GRE!

> Most importantly, none of the guides actually teach you EVERYTHING tested by the GRE.

• While most cover the major topics found on a typical exam, **none cover the vast array of rare and advanced concepts that you need to grasp if you're hoping to score <u>above</u> the 90th percentile.**

(2) Why Master Key Is Special – <u>Master Key to the GRE</u> is the only guide to the GRE that will teach you everything you need to attain a perfect score.

• Whether you're looking for help with advanced concepts, or are starting from scratch, our materials will have what you need.

> **We start by assuming you know NOTHING.** Everything is laid out for you as if you haven't done math in years.

• Each chapter focuses on a specific topic, such as Fractions, Rates, or Triangles, and opens with a thorough discussion of its simplest, most fundamental concepts.

• Bit by bit, we gradually explore ALL the wrinkles associated with that topic, so that you can solve problems involving sophisticated nuances, not just easy problems.

> At the ends of our chapters, you'll find a treatment of **every RARE and ADVANCED concept tested by the GRE**.

• You won't find these topics discussed anywhere else. <u>Master Key to the GRE</u> is the only resource that covers them.

• We know that some of you only need help solving the most difficult questions — the questions that determine who scores ABOVE the 90th percentile. We've made sure that our guides teach <u>everything</u>, so that students in your position get all the support they need.

> To keep things simple, we discuss math in **language that's EASY to understand** and focus on **SMART strategies for every level of material**.

• In writing <u>Master Key to the GRE</u>, we were determined to make our guides helpful for everyone, not just math geeks.

• We are GRE specialists who have spent our entire professional careers making math ACCESSIBLE to students who hate it. **These books are the culmination of over three decades of daily classroom instruction.** No matter how difficult a topic may be, we walk you through each concept, step by step, to ensure that everything makes sense.

> Along the way, **we sprinkle in hundreds of SHORTCUTS and TRICKS** that you won't find in any other guide.

• We know that TIME is a major concern for many test-takers, so we've included every time-saving strategy out there to help you "beat the clock".

- We don't care how well you think you know math. These shortcuts will save you valuable minutes, no matter what your current skill level may be.

  ➢ To complement our content-oriented approach, the first volume of <u>Master Key to the GRE</u> devotes **an entire chapter to something we call "Plan B" strategies**.

- A "Plan B" strategy is a strategy that can help you deduce a correct answer when you don't know how to solve a problem.

- Such "tricks of the trade" are sometimes encountered in mainstream strategy-based guides. No other guide, however, features a collection like the one we've put together here. We've got all of the tricks, not just a few.

  ➢ We also complement our content-oriented approach by telling you **how FREQUENTLY the GRE tests every concept** — something no other guide does.

- We know that most people don't have the time to study everything and aren't looking for a perfect score — just a score that's good enough to get them into the school of their choice.

- So, we let you know which topics are <u>commonly tested</u> and which ones are not so that you can determine for yourself which topics are worth your time.

  ➢ Additionally, **we organize our discussions by level of DIFFICULTY**, as well as by topic.

- As we see it, test-takers deserve to know which topics they need to master in order to get elite scores and which topics they can afford to skip if they're only looking for above average scores.

- Our hope is that by organizing our material in this way, you'll be able to limit your efforts to material that is right for you.

  ➢ In total, <u>Master Key to the GRE</u> includes **nearly ONE THOUSAND practice questions**. That's more than any other resource out there.

- Like our teaching sections, our practice questions are sorted by difficulty, as well as by topic, so that you can focus on any level of material and on any topic that you like.

- Moreover, nearly a quarter of these questions involve the most rare or advanced topics tested by the GRE. So if you're looking for a lot of help with diabolical fare, you'll find it here.

➤ Most of the solutions to these questions come in the form of **ANIMATED VIDEOS, which you can play on any computer, tablet, or smart phone**.

• We understand that the short, written explanations found in other GRE handbooks are often insufficient for students who find math challenging.

• By providing you with video solutions, we are able to talk you through our practice problems, every step of the way, so that you can follow along easily and see where your solution went wrong.

➤ In many cases, you'll find that our animated videos discuss **multiple ways to solve a question**.

• In math, there is often more than one way to solve a problem. Not all of these approaches, however, are equally efficient.

• Our videos discuss the best of these approaches to ensure that you're exposed to a solution that's not only fast and simple, but also works well with your way of thinking.

➤ We know that Master Key to the GRE is the most expensive GRE guide on the market.

• It's anywhere from $60 to $100 dollars more expensive than most of the alternatives out there. That's a lot of money.

• But let us ask you this. Which would rather have: an extra $60 to $100 dollars or the GRE scores that you need?

➤ Remember, it took you years to graduate from college, and many admissions committees weigh GRE scores more heavily than your grade point average.

• Isn't an exam that means so much worth the cost of a college textbook? Of course it is.

• If you're still not certain, **we encourage you to compare our materials to anything else** that you can find. Whether you're looking for help with advanced material or something a little less extreme, we have no doubt that you'll see why Master Key to the GRE is worth the difference.

(3) How to Use Our Guides – As mentioned, <u>Master Key to the GRE</u> has been designed to help you solve EVERY question on the GRE.

• It explains ALL of the TOUGH concepts that no other GRE prep book attempts to cover, not just the easy ones.

  ➤ Depending on your goals, however, you may NOT need to master everything. Not every program requires a perfect score. In fact, most don't require anything close.

• If you've yet to do so, we strongly encourage you to contact the programs you're interested in to see what sort of scores they require.

• Knowing "how high" to set the bar will give you a sense of whether you need to cover everything or just the core material. (Remember, we'll tell you how frequently each topic is tested!)

  ➤ Every volume of <u>Master Key to the GRE</u> has been designed to help someone starting from SCRATCH to build, step by step, to the most challenging material.

• Thus, Chapter 1 is intended to precede Chapter 2, and the same is true for each volume: <u>Arithmetic & "Plan B" Strategies</u> (Vol. 1) is intended to precede <u>Number Properties & Algebra</u> (Vol. 2).

• The chapters, however, are largely independent of one another, as are the books, so you're welcome to skip around if you only need help with a few key topics or are short on time.

  ➤ As you study, bear in mind that you DON'T have to master one topic before studying another.

• If you have a hard time with something, put it aside for a day or two. It can take one or two "exposures" for a concept to "click" – especially if it's new or tricky.

• You also don't need to solve all 1,000 of our practice problems. If you're comfortable with a topic, feel free to skip the questions marked "fundamental" to save time.

  ➤ Finally, remember that our ADVANCED materials are intended for students in need of PERFECT scores.

• If that's not you, don't waste your time! Questions involving advanced topics are generally rare for the GRE, so if you'd be thrilled with a score around the 90th percentile, you're more likely to achieve it by focusing on questions and materials involving core concepts.

(4) Proper Study Habits – Whatever your goals may be for the GRE, it's important that you work consistently.

• Studying a little EVERY DAY is the best way to retain what you're learning and to avoid the burn out that comes with studying too intensely for too long.

> ➤ In a perfect world, we'd have you study about an hour a day during the workweek and one to two hours a day on the weekends.

• Unfortunately, we know that such a schedule is unrealistic for some people. If you can't find an hour each day, at least DO SOMETHING!

• Even 5 minutes a day can help you stave off rust and prevent the cycle of guilt and procrastination that comes from not studying.

> ➤ If you can, do your best to AVOID CRAMMING. Much of what you'll be studying is boring and technical. It will take "elbow grease" to master.

• We truly question how much of this information can be absorbed in a few short weeks or in study sessions that last three or four hours.

• In our experience, most students who do too much too rapidly either burnout or fail to absorb the material properly.

> ➤ To avoid "study fatigue", SWITCH things up. Spend part of each day studying for the math portion of the exam and part for the verbal portion.

• And do your best to incorporate at least part of your study routine into your daily life.

• If you can study 30 minutes out of every lunch break and a few minutes out of every snack break, we think you'll find that you have more time to prepare than you might believe. We also think you'll find the shorter study sessions more beneficial.

> ➤ As you study, be sure to bear in mind that QUALITY is just as important as QUANTITY.

• Many test-takers believe that the key to success is to work through thousands of practice questions and to take dozens of exams. This simply isn't true.

- While working through practice questions and taking exams are important parts of preparing for the GRE, doing so does not mean that you are LEARNING the material.

  ➢ It is equally important that you LEARN from your MISTAKES. Whenever you miss a practice question, be sure to watch the video explanation that we've provided.

- Then, redo the problem yourself. Once you feel that you've "got it", come back to the problem two days later.

- If you still get it wrong, add the problem to your "LOG of ERRORS" and redo it every few weeks. Keeping track of tricky problems and redoing them MORE THAN ONCE is a great way to learn from your mistakes and to avoid similar difficulties on your actual exam.

  ➢ As you prepare, keep the REAL exam in mind. The GRE tests your ability to recognize concepts under TIMED conditions. Your study habits should reflect this.

- If it takes you 3 minutes to solve a problem, you may as well have missed that problem. 3 minutes is too much time to spend on a problem during an actual exam. Be sure to watch the video solutions for such problems and to redo them until you can solve them quickly.

- Likewise, bear in mind that you will take the GRE on a COMPUTER, unless you opt to take the paper-based version that is administered only three times a year.

  ➢ So adopt GOOD HABITS now. Whenever you practice, avoid doing things you can't do on a computer, such as writing atop problems or underlining key words.

- And make a NOTECARD whenever you learn something. The cards don't have to be complicated – even a sample problem that illustrates the concept will do.

- As your studying progresses, it can be easy to forget concepts that you learned at the beginning of your preparation. Notecards will help you retain what you've learned and make it easy for you to review that material whenever you have a few, spare minutes.

  ➢ Finally, do your best to keep your emotions in check. It's easy to become overconfident when a practice exam goes well or to get down when one goes poorly.

- The GRE is a tough exam and improvement, for most students, takes time.

- In our experience, however, test-takers who prepare like PROFESSIONALS — who keep an even keel, who put in the time to do their assignments properly, and who commit to identifying their weaknesses and improving them – ALWAYS achieve their goals in the end.

(5) The App – <u>Master Key to the GRE</u> is available in print through Amazon or through our website at **www.sherpaprep.com/masterkey**.

• It's also available as an app for iPhones and iPads through Apple's App Store under the title <u>GRE Math by Sherpa Prep.</u>

  ➢ Like the printed edition, the app comes with access to all of our LESSONS, practice QUESTIONS, and VIDEOS.

• And, like any book, it allows you to BOOKMARK pages, UNDERLINE text, and TAKE NOTES.

• Unlike a book, however, it also allows you to design practice quizzes, create study lists, make error logs, and keep statistics on just about everything.

  ➢ The ⟦**DESIGN a PRACTICE QUIZ**⟧ feature lets you make quizzes in which you select the TOPICS, the NUMBER of questions, and the DIFFICULTY.

• It also allows you to SHUFFLE the questions by topic and difficulty and to SET a TIMER for any length of time.

• For example, you can make a 30-minute quiz comprised of fifteen intermingled Ratio, Rate, and Overlapping Sets questions, in which all the questions are advanced. Or you can make a 10-minute quiz with just ten Probability questions, of which some are easy and others are intermediate. You can pretty much make any sort of quiz that you like.

> ➤ AFTER each quiz, you get to REVIEW your performance, question by question, and to view video solutions.

• You also get to see the difficultly level of your quiz questions, as well as the time it took you to answer each of them.

• You even get to COMPARE your performance to that of other users. You see how frequently other users were able to solve the questions on your quiz and how long it took them, on average, to do so.

> ➤ As you read through our lessons, the MAKE a STUDY LIST feature allows you to form a personalized study list.

• With the tap of a button, you can add any topic that you read about to an automated "to do" list, which organizes the topics you've selected by chapter and subject.

• From your study list, you can then access these topics instantly to revisit them whenever you need to.

> ➤ Similarly, the CREATE an ERROR LOG feature allows you to compile a list of practice problems you wish to redo for further practice.

• Every time you answer a question, you can add it to this log, regardless of whether you got the question right or wrong, or left it blank.

• By doing so, you can keep track of every problem that you find challenging and redo them until they no longer pose a challenge.

> ➤ Finally, the app TRACKS your PERFORMANCE at every turn to help you identify your strengths and weaknesses.

• In addition to the data from your practice quizzes, the app provides key information on how you're performing, by TOPIC and across DIFFICUTLY LEVELS.

• So if you want to know what percentage of advanced level Algebra questions you're answering correctly, the app can tell you. Likewise, if you want to know what percentage of intermediate level Triangle questions you're answering correctly, the app can tell you that too.

> ➤ The app offers the first volume of Master Key to the GRE for FREE. The other four volumes retail for $9.99 apiece.

(6) Register Your Book! – Every volume of <u>Master Key to the GRE</u> comes with six months of free access to our collection of video solutions.

- If you have a print edition of <u>Master Key</u>, you'll need to ⌐Register⌐ your book(s) to access these videos.

  ➢ To do so, please go to **www.sherpaprep.com/activate** and enter your email address, last name, and shipping address.

- **Be sure to provide the SAME last name and shipping address that you used to purchase your copy of <u>Master Key to the GRE</u>.**

- If you received your books upon enrolling in a GRE prep course with ⌐Sherpa Prep⌐, be sure to enter the same last name and shipping address that you used to enroll.

  ➢ Once you've entered this information, you will be asked to create an account password.

- Please RECORD this password! You will need it to login to our website whenever you choose to watch our videos.

- Our login page can be found at **www.sherpaprep.com/videos**. We recommend that you BOOKMARK this page for future visits.

  ➢ If your registration is ⌐Unsuccessful⌐, please send your last name and shipping address to **sales@sherpaprep.com**.

- We will confirm your purchase manually and create a login account for you.

- In most cases, this process will take no more than a few hours. Please note, however, that requests can take up to 24 hours to fulfill if you submit your request on a U.S. federal holiday or if we are experiencing extremely heavy demand.

  ➢ Six months after your date of registration, your video access to <u>Master Key to the GRE</u> will come to an end.

- An additional six months of access can be purchased at a rate of $9.99 per book. To do so, simply login at **www.sherpaprep.com/videos** and follow the directions.

About the GRE

(7) The Structure of the GRE – Before examining the content of the GRE, let's take a moment to discuss how the exam is structured and administered.

• The GRE is a computer-based exam that is offered world-wide on a daily basis.

> ➤ The test consists of six sections and takes around 3 hours and 45 minutes to complete (not including breaks).

• These sections are as follows:

    I.   An Analytical Writing section containing two essays.
    II. Two Verbal Reasoning sections.
    III. Two Quantitative Reasoning sections.
    IV. One Unidentified Research section.

• The Analytical Writing section is always first, while **the other five sections may appear in ANY order**. You get a 10-minute break between the third and fourth sections, and a 1-minute break between the other test sections.

> ➤ The Unidentified Research section **does NOT count towards your score** and is either a Verbal Reasoning section or a Quantitative Reasoning section.

• Unfortunately, the Unidentified Research section is designed to look exactly like the other sections — there is no way to spot it.

• As such, you must take all five sections seriously. Even though one of them will not count towards your score, there is no way of knowing which section that is.

> ➤ Finally, some exams have an **Identified Research section** in place of the Unidentified Research section.

• This section is marked "For Research Purposes" and does not count towards your score. If your exam has an Identified Research section, it will appear at the end of the test.

• On the following page, you'll find a breakdown of all six sections. Notice that every Quantitative Reasoning section has 20 questions and is 35 minutes long.

• Similarly, notice that every Verbal Reasoning section also has 20 questions but is only 30 minutes long.

➤ When viewing the table below, remember that **the order of sections 2 through 6 is RANDOM**. These sections can occur in any order.

• This means that the Unidentified Research section can be ANY section after the first and that you might get two Quantitative sections in a row (or two Verbal sections)!

Section	Task	Number of Questions	Time	Note
1	Analytical Writing	Two Essays	30 minutes per essay	
2	Verbal Reasoning	20	30 minutes	
3	Quantitative Reasoning	20	35 minutes	
10-minute break				
4	Verbal Reasoning	20	30 minutes	
5	Quantitative Reasoning	20	35 minutes	
6	Unidentified Research	20	30 or 35 minutes	Not scored

• Also remember that that Unidentified Research section may be replaced with an Identified Research section. If so, the Identified Research section will appear at the end of the test.

(8) The Scoring System – After your GRE has been completed and graded, you will receive three scores:

1. A Verbal Reasoning score.
2. A Quantitative Reasoning score.
3. An Analytical Writing score.

• **Both the Verbal Reasoning and Quantitative Reasoning scores are reported on a scale from 130 to 170, in one-point increments**.

➢ The Analytical Writing score is reported on a scale from 0 to 6, in half-point increments.

• A score of NS (no score) is given for any measure in which no questions (or essay prompts) are answered.

• In addition to these scaled scores, you will also receive percentile rankings, which compare your scores to those of other GRE test-takers.

➢ Before applying to graduate school or business school, you should have a basic sense of what constitutes a good score and what constitutes a bad score.

• Currently, **an average Verbal Reasoning score is 151, an average Quantitative Reasoning score is 152, and an average Analytical Writing score is approximately 3.5**.

• Roughly two-thirds of all test-takers receive a score within the following ranges:

1. Verbal Reasoning: 142 to 159
2. Quantitative Reasoning: 143 to 161
3. Analytical Writing: 3 to 4.5

➢ As a loose guideline, these ranges suggest that any score in the 160s is fairly exceptional and that any score in the 130s may raise a red flag with an admissions committee.

• The same goes for Analytical Writing scores higher than 4.5 or lower than 3. In fact, only 7 percent of test-takers receive a score above 4.5 and only 9 percent receive a score below 3.

• You can find a complete concordance of GRE scores and their percentile equivalents on page 23 of this document: **http://www.ets.org/s/gre/pdf/gre_guide.pdf**.

➢ As you prepare for the GRE, we strongly encourage you to research the programs to which you plan to apply.

• Get a general sense of what sorts of scores your programs are looking for. See whether they have "cutoff" scores below which they no longer consider applicants.

• Knowing what you need to achieve is important. If your program needs an elite math score, it's best to know immediately so that you can make time to prepare properly!

➢ In some cases, you'll find the information you need online. In many cases, however, you'll need to contact your program directly.

• If you are reluctant to do so, bear this in mind: many programs are more forthcoming about scores in person or over the phone than they are by email or on the internet.

• Moreover, it never hurts to make contact with a prospective program. Saying "hi" gives you a chance to ask important questions and — if you can present yourself intelligently and professionally — to make a good impression on a potential committee member.

➢ If a school tells you they are looking for applicants with an average score of 160 per section, remember that such quotes are only averages!

• Some applicants will be accepted with scores below those averages and some will be turned down with scores above them.

• An average is simply a "ballpark" figure that you want to shoot for. Coming up short doesn't guarantee rejection (particularly if the rest of your application is strong), and achieving it doesn't ensure admission.

➢ Unfortunately, not all programs are willing to divulge average or "cutoff" GRE scores to the public.

• If that's the case with a program you're interested, here are some general pointers to keep in mind:

1. Engineering, Economics, and Hard Sciences programs are likely to place far more emphasis on your Quantitative Reasoning score than your other scores.

2. The more prestigious a university it is, the more likely its programs will demand higher scores than comparable programs at other schools.

3. Public Health, Public Policy, and International Affairs programs likely require very strong scores for all three portions of the GRE.

4. Education, Sociology, and Nursing programs are less likely to require outstanding scores.

➢ Should you wish to get a sense of average GRE scores, by intended field of study, you can do so here: **http://www.ets.org/s/gre/pdf/gre_guide_table4.pdf**.

• When viewing these scores, remember that these are the scores of INTENDED applicants!

• The average score of ACCEPTED applicants is likely to be higher for many programs — in some cases, much higher.

➢ Finally, it's worth noting that many programs use GRE scores to determine which applicants will receive SCHOLARSHIPS.

• When contacting programs, be sure to ask them about the averages or "cutoffs" for scholarship recipients.

• And if you find it difficult to study for an exam that has little to do with your intended field of study, just remember: strong GRE scores = $$$!

(9) Registering for the GRE – The GRE is administered via computer in over 160 countries on a near daily basis.

- This means that you can that you take the GRE almost ANY day of the year.

  ➤ To register, you must create a personalized GRE account, which you can do online at **http://www.ets.org/gre/revised_general/register/**.

- When creating your account, the NAME you use must MATCH the name you use to register for the GRE.

- **It must also match the name on your official identification EXACTLY**! If it doesn't, you may be prohibited from taking the exam (without refund).

  ➤ We encourage you to schedule a date that gives you ample time to prepare properly. Don't choose a random date just to get it over with!

- If possible, wait until you score a few points higher than your target score at least TWO TIMES in a row on practice exams. Doing so will ensure that you're ready to take the exam.

- When scheduling the time of day, **don't schedule an 8 a.m. exam if you are not accustomed to waking up at 6:30 a.m. or earlier**. The exam is challenging enough. Don't take it when you're likely to be groggy or weary!

  ➤ If you plan to take the exam on a specific date, register at least one month in advance. Exam centers have limited capacity, so dates can fill up quickly, especially in the fall.

- On the day of the test, be sure to bring your official identification and your GRE admission ticket.

- Once you register for the exam, your admission ticket can be printed out at any time through your personalized GRE account online.

  ➤ Finally, if you need to reschedule or cancel your exam date, you must do so no later than FOUR days before your test date. (Ten days for individuals in mainland China.)

- This means that a Saturday test date must be canceled by Tuesday and that an April 18th test date must be canceled by April 14th.

- You can find more information on canceling or rescheduling a test date here: **http://www.ets.org/gre/revised_general/register/change**.

(10) Reporting & Canceling Scores – Immediately upon completing your exam, you will be given the opportunity to cancel your scores or to report them.

• If you choose to cancel your scores, they will be deleted irreversibly.

➢ Neither you nor the programs to which you're applying will see the numbers. Your official score report, however, will indicate a canceled test.

• In general, there's almost no reason to cancel your scores.

• **The GRE has a Score Select option that allows you to decide which scores to send if you've taken the GRE more than once.** Thus, if you take the exam a second time (or a third time), you can simply choose which set of scores to report.

➢ If you choose to report your scores, you will immediately see your unofficial Quantitative Reasoning and Verbal Reasoning scores.

• Roughly 10 to 15 days after your test date, you will receive an email notifying you that your official scores and your Analytical Writing score are available.

• To view them, simply go to the personalized GRE account you created to register for the exam.

➢ You won't need to memorize any school CODES to send your scores while at the test center.

• Such codes will be accessible by computer, should you wish to report your scores when you're there. To get the code for a particular program, you'll need:

1. The name of the college (e.g. College of Arts & Sciences).
2. The name of the university.
3. The city and state of its location.

• As long as you have this information for each of your programs, you'll have everything you need to send out your score reports on the spot.

➢ **Your OFFICIAL and UNOFFICIAL scores are unlikely to differ.** If they do, the difference will almost surely be a single point.

• For example, your Verbal Reasoning score may rise from a 157 to a 158 or your Quantitative Reasoning score may dip from a 162 to a 161.

- The scores you receive on test day are an estimate comparing your performance with previous data. The official scores compare your performance with those of everyone who took that particular exam – hence the potential discrepancy.

  ➢ **Your official scores will be valid for FIVE years**. For example, a test taken on August 2nd, 2015 will be valid until August 1st, 2020.

- Over the course of those five years, your scaled scores will never change. The percentiles, however, may shift marginally.

- Thus, a scaled Verbal Reasoning score of 162 may equate to the 89th percentile in 2015. Come 2018, however, that 162 may equate to a 91st percentile.

  ➢ On test day, after viewing your unofficial scores, you will be given a choice at the test center.

- You can choose NOT to send your scores at that time or to send **free score reports** to as many as FOUR graduate programs or fellowship sponsors.

- If you choose to send out score reports at the test center, you will be given two further options:

  1. The **Most Recent** option – send your scores from the test you've just completed.
  2. The **All** option – send the scores from all the GREs you've taken in the last five years.

  ➢ After your test date, you can send additional score reports for a fee. **For each report**, you will be given the options above.

- **You will also be given the option to send your scores from just one exam OR from ANY exams you've taken over the last five years.**

- You cannot, however, choose your best Quantitative Reasoning score from one exam and your best Verbal Reasoning score from another. When sending scores, you must send all the scores you receive on a particular exam date.

> ➢ Given all of these options, **here's our advice**. First, NEVER cancel your scores. There's no point.

• Even if you believe you've had a bad performance, you may as well learn how you did. You never know — you might even be pleasantly surprised.

• If your scores are great, you're done. Send out your scores on test day to take advantage of the four free score reports.

> ➢ If you feel you can do better, retake the exam as soon as possible. Don't let your hard work go to waste.

• Anyone can have a bad day, misplay their time, or make an uncharacteristic number of careless errors.

• **You can retake the exam every 21 days** and up to 5 times within any 12-month period, so you won't have to wait long.

> ➢ Upon receiving your second set of scores, use the Score Select option on test day to determine which set of scores to send for free (or to send both sets).

• In the unpleasant event that you take the exam more than twice, consider utilizing the Score Select option the day after your last exam.

• This will allow you to send the single set of scores (or pair of scores) that puts you in the best possible light. Of course, if that last score is awesome, use the four free score reports to send out your most recent scores while you're at the test center!

Navigating the Exam

(11) How the Exam Works – Although the GRE is administered on computer, the exam has been designed to mimic the experience of a traditional, paper-based standardized test.

• This means that you can:

    ☑ Skip questions and return to them later.
    ☑ Leave questions blank.
    ☑ Change or edit an answer.

• You can even "flag" questions with a check mark as a reminder to revisit them before time expires. (As with a paper-based exam, however, you cannot return to a section once that section ends.)

    ➢ If you took the GRE before 2011, you'll notice that this format differs dramatically from the one you remember.

• **The exam is no longer adaptive on a question-by-question basis**, so the problems don't get harder if you answer a prior problem correctly.

• In fact, you can now preview every question within a section the moment that section begins. (If you like, you can even do the problems in reverse order.)

    ➢ There are, however, a few differences between the way the GRE works and that of most paper-based standardized tests.

• First, the questions in each section do NOT get progressively harder.

• Unlike, say, the SAT, where the first questions within a section are generally easy and the last questions within a section are generally hard, **the difficulty of GRE questions varies throughout a particular section**. In other words, a section might start with a hard question and end with an easy question.

    ➢ Furthermore, the GRE has a "Review Screen" that allows you to see which questions you've answered and which ones you haven't.

• The Review Screen can also be used to see which questions you've flagged for further review. (A very helpful feature!)

> ➤ **Finally, the GRE adapts on a section-by-section basis**. If you perform well on your first quantitative section, your second quantitative section will be harder.

• Likewise, if you do not perform well on your first quantitative section, your second quantitative section will be easier.

• The verbal sections work this way, too. The quantitative and verbal sections, however, are independent of one another. A strong performance on a verbal section will not result in more difficult quantitative sections, or vice versa.

> ➤ According to our experiments with the GRE's official test software, **how you perform on your first quantitative section can produce 1 of 3 results.**

• The same is true of your performance on the first verbal section:

Approximate # of Correct Questions on First Section	Difficulty Level of Second Section
0 to 6	Easy
7 to 13	Medium
14 to 20	Hard

• In some exams, it might take 15 correct answers to end up with a hard second section. In others, it might take 13. The correlation between the number of questions you get right and the difficulty level of your second section, however, generally matches the chart above.

> ➤ Our experiments also indicate that **the difficulty of the questions that you get right has no bearing on the difficulty level of the second section**.

• In other words, getting any 14 (or so) questions correct will give you a hard second section — it doesn't matter whether those questions are the hardest 14 or the easiest 14.

• It also doesn't matter how quickly you answer anything. There are no bonus points for solving problems quickly.

> ➤ It should, however, be noted that **a hard second section is not comprised entirely of hard questions**, nor an easy second section entirely of easy questions.

• The questions in ANY section span a range of difficulties. A hard second section simply has a greater number of hard questions than an easy one. Thus, if you receive easy questions in your second quantitative section, it does not mean that you've done poorly!

(12) The Scoring Algorithm – Exactly how the GRE is scored is a closely guarded secret.

• From the official practice test software, however, it's clear that Quantitative Reasoning and Verbal Reasoning scores are essentially the byproducts of two factors:

    1. How many questions you answer correctly.
    2. Whether your second sections are easy, medium, or hard.

• As you may recall from our discussion of the structure of the GRE, every exam has two Quantitative Reasoning sections and two Verbal Reasoning sections that count.

> ➢ Since each of these sections has 20 questions, every GRE has 40 Quantitative Reasoning questions and 40 Verbal Reasoning questions.

• As you may also recall, each of these measures is scored on a 41-point scale (from 130 to 170). This means, that **each question is essentially worth 1 point**.

• Thus, to get a Quantitative Reasoning score of 170, you likely need to answer all 40 questions correctly. Each question that you get wrong more or less subtracts 1 point from your score.

> ➢ In analyzing the practice test software, however, it's also apparent that there are deductions for failing to achieve a hard or medium second section.

• In general, these deductions range from 1 to 3 points.

• For example, if you were to get 11 questions correct on your first Quantitative Reasoning section, your score would be lowered 9 points on account of the 9 questions you got wrong or left blank since the exam treats blank and incorrect answers equally. (**There is NO PENALTY for getting problems wrong, so always GUESS when you're stuck!**)

> ➢ Your 11 correct answers, however, would also result in a second section of medium difficulty.

• Thus, your score would be lowered an additional 1 to 3 points for failing to make it to the hard section.

• Likewise, if you were to answer only 4 questions correctly in your first Quantitative Reasoning section, your score would be lowered 16 points for the blank or incorrect answers, 1 to 3 points for failing to make it to the hard section, and another 1 to 3 points for failing to make it to the medium section.

> ➤ Thus, a test taker who gets 10 questions right in each of his or her Quantitative Reasoning sections would likely receive a score from 147 to 149.

• The 20 questions left blank or answered incorrectly would deduct 20 points from the total score.

• Failing to make it to the hard section would deduct an additional 1 to 3 points. Subtracted from 170 (a perfect score), this would leave a final score of 147 to 149:

170	A perfect score
10	10 missed questions in section 1
10	10 missed questions in section 2
− 1 to 3	The penalty for not reaching the hard section
147 to 149	

> ➤ In all likelihood, the scoring algorithm considers a few other factors as well.

• For example, when exam-makers opt to include a greater number of difficult questions on a particular exam, they likely slide the scale for that exam 1 to 2 points in order to normalize its data with past exams that contain fewer difficult questions.

• From what we've seen, however, the dynamics described above will predict your score perfectly in most instances.

(13) Strategy & Time Management – Given the factors we've just discussed, there are several tactics that we recommend when taking the GRE.

1. SKIP around.

• It doesn't matter which questions you get right, so you may as well work on the questions that are easiest for you first.

> **Don't waste your time on a question that you don't understand or that confuses you.**

• Engaging such questions will only take time from questions that may be easier for you. If you come across something that makes you nauseous, FLAG IT and double back after you've solved the questions that you know how to solve.

2. FOCUS on your FAVORITE 15.

• As we've seen, there are potentially harsh deductions for failing to achieve a hard or medium second section.

> Since reaching the hard second section generally demands a minimum of 13 to 15 correct responses, we encourage you to focus your efforts on the 15 easiest questions.

• You shouldn't ignore the hardest 5 questions, but you should save them for last. **If you don't think you can answer 15 questions correctly, focus your efforts on the easiest 10 questions.** Landing in the lowest tier can devastate your score.

3. GUESS on questions that you don't understand.

• We've also seen that an incorrect answer is no worse than a blank answer, so you may as well <u>guess</u> on anything that you don't understand and flag it for further review. Remember, there's no penalty for guessing!

> As you'll see, **there's either a 1 in 5 chance or a 1 in 4 chance of guessing most GRE questions correctly.**

• Those chances increase if you can eliminate a couple of answer choices through logic. If you have time left over, you can return to the questions you've flagged after you've answered everything else.

4. REMEMBER the "Two-and-a-Half Minute Rule".

• Over the years at Sherpa Prep, we've noticed that test-takers who take more than 2.5 minutes to solve a question do so correctly only 25% of the time.

> Given that there are usually five answers to choose from, the odds of guessing correctly are 20%. If you can eliminate bad answer choices, those odds rise further!

• We know that it's tempting to battle questions to the end, especially if you "think" you can solve them. **Stubbornly hanging on, however, is a sure way to MANGLE your score.**

• Doing so wastes time (time that could be used to solve other problems) and is no more likely to result in a correct answer than guessing.

> So, if you find yourself stuck on a particular question, do yourself a favor: flag the question, then guess.

• If you can eliminate answer choices before doing so, great. Obeying the "2.5 minute rule" will help you save time for the questions at the end of the exam and avoid the debilitating panic that comes upon realizing that you've squandered your time.

5. Don't work TOO QUICKLY.

• We know that time is a critical factor on the GRE and that the exam-makers don't give you much of it.

> **Working at a frenzied pace, however, will only result in one thing — careless errors. A lot of them.**

• The key to saving time is obeying the "2.5 minute rule" and learning the right way to solve each type of problem – not working at breakneck speeds.

• If you know how to solve a problem, take the time to do so properly. You may not have time to triple check your work, but you do have time to work through any problem with care.

> **Watch out, however, for any question that you can solve in 10 seconds or fewer.**

• While there are plenty of GRE problems that can be solved in 10 seconds, exam-makers often design questions to take advantage of quick assumptions. Taking an extra 10 seconds to ensure that you haven't missed something is a great way to catch potential traps!

<u>**(14) Practice Tests**</u> – As you work through <u>Master Key to the GRE</u>, we strongly encourage you to take a practice exam every week or two.

• Success on the GRE is not just the byproduct of mastering its content — it also demands good test-taking skills.

> ➤ **Taking practice exams will help you build stamina and improve your time management.**

• Remember, the GRE takes nearly four hours to complete. Learning how to deal with the fatigue you'll encounter is part of the battle!

• The same is true of the pacing of the exam. If you don't master the speed at which you need to work, you can easily sabotage your score by working too quickly or too leisurely.

> ➤ Before you take the GRE, we encourage you to **take a minimum of SIX practice exams**.

• If you're like most test-takers, you'll need anywhere from six to eight practice exams to properly familiarize yourself with the GRE.

• For the first few — don't bother with the essays. As you begin your preparation, your time is better spent studying new material and reviewing what you've learned. Towards the end of your preparation, however, your practice exams should be full-blown dress rehearsals.

> ➤ **There are a number of different practice exams available online. Of these, only two are produced by the ETS, the company that designs the GRE.**

• At no cost, you can download the software that runs these exams from the following address: **http://www.ets.org/gre/revised_general/prepare/powerprep2/**.

• These exams have been designed to work on both Macs and PCs. As long as your computer's operating system and software are reasonably up to date, you should be able to use them on any computer.

> ➤ For additional exams, almost any of the available options will do. While they all have issues of one sort or another, most are reasonable facsimiles of the GRE.

• When taking such exams, however, please bear in mind that they are NOT the real thing. Some of their questions are unrealistic and their score predictions, though roughly accurate, are best taken with a grain of salt.

Chapter 1: Introduction

➢ Whenever you take a practice exam, it's important that you **make the experience as REALISTIC as possible**.

• Doing things you can't do on test day will only corrupt your practice results and prevent you from adopting helpful habits.

• If you can, take each exam in one sitting and resist the urge to pause the test or to use outside help. Likewise, refrain from drinking or eating during your tests. No coffee, no water, no snacks. Save these things for your 10-minute break between sections 3 and 4.

➢ Remember, you're preparing for a stressful "brain marathon" that's essentially 4-hours long. You'll need STAMINA to be successful.

• Figure out how much you need to eat and drink before your test. Figure out what to eat during your break. Identify the kind of foods that suit you best.

• The same goes for your bathroom habits. At the exam center, you can't pause the test to go to the bathroom. So, use your practice exams to learn how your eating habits affect your bodily needs! "Holding it in" for over an hour is a brutal way to take this test.

➢ As you take your practice exams, do your best to **stay off the "emotional rollercoaster"**. Don't get too high when things go well.

• And don't get too down if your scores don't shoot up instantly. Improving GRE scores is hard work.

• For some people, progress is a slow, steady crawl. For others, it's an uneven process, filled with periods of stagnation, occasional drops, and dramatic increases.

➢ However your exams may be going, keep grinding away! Stay focused on your goals and keep up the hard work.

• Test-takers who prepare like professionals — who keep an even keel, who do their assignments properly, and who commit to improving their weaknesses — ALWAYS achieve their goals in the end.

• As we tell our students, preparing for the GRE is like going to the gym. It may take you a while to get in shape, but ANYONE can do so if they put in the time and train properly.

> ➤ **After you complete each practice exam, go through it carefully and learn from your mistakes**.

• See whether you can identify any trends in your performance. Are you working too quickly and making careless errors? Are you struggling with the same topics repeatedly?

• Are you running out of time because you're violating the "2.5 minute rule"? Do you start off strong and then taper off as the test goes along? Does it take you half an hour to get "locked in" and then get better as you go?

> ➤ A lot of people believe they are "bad test-takers". This is nonsense. The reality is that people get questions wrong for tangible reasons.

• Analyzing your mistakes when the "game is real" will allow you to PINPOINT those reasons so you can ADDRESS them.

• To help you become a more "self-aware" test-taker, we encourage you to fill out the following table every time you complete an exam:

	Knew How to Solve	Didn't Know How to Solve
Correct	Bravo!	Luck
Incorrect	Carelessness?	**Expected**

> ➤ If you get a question wrong because you don't know how to solve it, see whether you can identify its TOPIC or notice any TRENDS.

• For example, you might notice that a lot of your mistakes involve Algebra. If so, that's a clear indication that you need to improve your Algebra skills.

• If you get a question wrong despite knowing how to solve it, see whether you can figure out how it happened. Did you misread the question? Did you write down information incorrectly? Did you make a silly math error?

> ➤ Mistakes such as these are often the result of RUSHING, which in turn is generally the byproduct of poor time management elsewhere.

• So keep track, to the best of your abilities, of whether you are finishing your sections too quickly or are making frantic efforts to finish because you're violating the "2.5 minute rule" too frequently. Both scenarios generally lead to a host of careless mistakes that will sabotage your progress.

Intro to Quantitative Reasoning

(15) Content Overview – The quantitative portion of the GRE is designed to measure your ability to think <u>smartly</u> about math — to find simple solutions to problems that seem complicated.

• The problems that you'll encounter may appear difficult or time-consuming, but there's ALWAYS a straightforward way to solve them.

  ➤ In terms of content, the GRE solely tests concepts that you learned in high school or use in everyday life.

• These concepts fall into four categories:

    1. Arithmetic, Algebra, and Number Properties
    2. Word Problems
    3. Data Interpretation
    4. Geometry

  ➤ You won't find any Calculus or Trigonometry on the GRE, nor will you find some of the more sophisticated forms of Algebra typically taught in an Algebra II course.

• That's because the emphasis of this exam is on your ability to reason.

• By limiting the content to the topics listed above, the GRE becomes less about "what you know" (everyone studied those topics in high school) and more about your ability to APPLY commonly known information and to think logically.

  ➤ This said, don't be fooled into thinking that GRE math can't be sophisticated. The exam demands that you know these topics EXTREMELY well.

• To be successful on the GRE, you'll need to relearn everything you learned about them (or were supposed to learn) back in high school.

• And, if you want to solve the most advanced questions, you'll need to learn a few intricacies that you almost surely were never taught.

➢ Based on our analysis of the official exam materials released to the public, roughly one-third of GRE questions focus on Arithmetic, Algebra, and Number Properties.

• Approximately 33% are Word Problems and a little more than a third involve Geometry or the interpretation of Charts and Graphs:

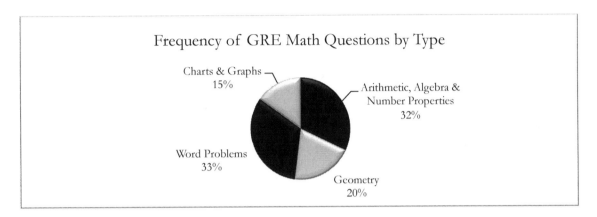

Frequency of GRE Math Questions by Type

• When viewing the diagram above, bear in mind that Word Problems and problems involving Geometry or Charts and Graphs often demand the use of Algebra and Arithmetic. Thus, in many ways, Algebra and Arithmetic are even more critical to your success than the diagram above suggests.

➢ Volume 1 of Master Key to the GRE is devoted to **Arithmetic & "Plan B" Strategies**.

• Here, you'll find discussion of such topics as:

Arithmetic Shortcuts	Strategies for "Smart Math"
Essential Number Lists	Strategies for Using the Answer Choices
Fractions	Number Picking Strategies
Decimals	Strategies for Guessing
Digit Problems	

➢ Volume 2 is dedicated to **Number Properties & Algebra**. Among the topics you'll find covered are:

Factors & Multiples	Exponents & Roots
Prime Factorization	The Properties of Evens & Odds
Number Line Problems	Algebra
Absolute Value	Functions, Sequences & Symbolism
Remainder Problems	

➤ Our discussion of **Word Problems** is divided between Volumes 3 and 4. Volume 3 focuses on topics such as:

Percents	Algebraic Word Problems
Mixtures	Age Problems
Alterations	Overlapping Sets
Ratios & Proportions	Exponential & Linear Growth
Rate Problems	

• Volume 4 examines **Statistics & Data Interpretation**.

➤ Among the various chapters of Volume 4, you'll find discussions of a wide range of topics, including:

Means, Medians & Modes	Probability
Weighed Averages	Combinatorics
Standard Deviation	Bar Graphs & Line Graphs
Quartiles & Boxplots	Pie Charts & Data Tables
Normal Distributions	Multi-Figure Data Sets
Equally Spaced Number Sets	

• Finally, Volume 5 is devoted to **Geometry**.

➤ Here, you'll find a detailed treatment of everything you may have been taught in high-school but have probably forgotten.

• The major topics include:

Lines & Angles	Rectangular Solids
Triangles	Cylinders
Quadrilaterals	Coordinate Geometry
Polygons	
Circles	

• If all of this seems intimidating, don't worry! We promise you: <u>Master Key to the GRE</u> will show you just how simple these concepts can be.

(16) Problem Solving Questions – Before we get started, let's take a few pages to discuss the ways in which the GRE formats its math questions.

• As you may recall, every GRE has two Quantitative Reasoning sections. Since each of these sections has 20 questions, your exam will feature a total of 40 math questions (that actually count).

> ➤ 25 of these will be "Problem Solving" questions and 15 will be "Quantitative Comparison" questions.

• If you've taken standardized tests before, Problem Solving questions will be familiar to you. Here's an example:

If $x + y > 14$ and $x = 2y + 8$, then which of the following must be true?

(A) $y < -3$ **(B)** $y < -2$ **(C)** $y = 0$ **(D)** $y > 2$ **(E)** $y > 4$

Answer: D. To answer questions in this format, you simply need to select the answer choice that represents the correct answer.

> ➤ Here, for example, we've been told that $x = 2y + 8$. Thus, we can rewrite $x + y > 14$ as follows, by substituting $2y + 8$ for x:

Replace x with $2y + 8$

$$(2y + 8) + y > 14$$

• To simplify the Algebra, we can drop the parentheses and subtract 8 from both sides of the inequality. Doing so proves that the correct is (D), since:

$2y + 8 + y > 14$	Drop the parentheses.
$2y + y > 6$	Subtract 8 from both sides.
$3y > 6$	Add $2y + y$.
$y > 2$	Divide both sides by 3.

• If the math doesn't make sense here, don't worry! This question is simply intended to show you what a Problem Solving question looks like. The math behind it is covered in our book on Number Properties & Algebra.

(17) "Select One or More" Questions – From time to time, Problem Solving questions will prompt you to select one or more answer choices.

• On a typical exam, each quantitative section will contain (at most) one or two of these questions.

> ➤ "Select One or More" questions are easy to spot — they always ask you to "indicate <u>all</u> such values".

• What's more, **the answer choices are always in square boxes**. In regular Problem Solving questions, the answer choices are circled.

• According to the Official Guide to the GRE revised General Test, the directions for such questions are always as follows:

> <u>Directions</u>: **Select ONE or MORE answer choices according to the specific directions.**

• If the question does not specify how many answer choices to select, you must select ALL that apply. The correct answer may be just one of the choices or as many as all of the choices. **There must, however, be at least one correct answer**.

> ➤ The exam-makers further specify that no credit is given unless you select all of the correct answers and no others. In other words, there is NO PARTIAL credit.

• Thus, if there are two correct answers, and you only select one, the GRE gives you zero credit. The same is true if there are three correct answers and you select four.

• Let's take a look at a sample question:

If $-2 \leq x \leq 8$ and $-4 \leq y \leq 3$, which of the following could represent the value of xy?

Indicate <u>all</u> such values.

$\boxed{A}$ −40 $\boxed{B}$ −32 $\boxed{C}$ 7 $\boxed{D}$ 15 $\boxed{E}$ 32

Answer: B, C, and D. Notice that there are two clues indicating that we may need to select more than one answer here.

- First, the question asks us to "indicate all such values". **Additionally, the answer choices are in boxes.**

  ➤ To answer this question, we first need to determine the range of possible values for xy.

- We can do so by identifying the greatest and smallest possible values for x and y.

- According to the problem, $-2 \leq x \leq 8$ and $-4 \leq y \leq 3$. Thus, the greatest and smallest values for each variable are:

$$x = -2 \text{ and } 8 \qquad\qquad y = -4 \text{ and } 3$$

  ➤ Next, we can **test all four combinations** of x times y to determine the largest and smallest values of xy.

- If x can be as small as -2 and as large as 8, and y can be as small as -3 and as large as 4, then those combinations would be:

Combo #1	Combo #2	Combo #3	Combo #4
$(-2)(-4) = 8$	$(-2)(3) = -6$	$(8)(-4) = -32$	$(8)(3) = 24$

  ➤ As we can see from these combinations, the greatest possible value of x times y is 24 and the smallest possible value is -32.

- Thus, the range of values for xy extends from -32 to 24. Algebraically, this can be stated as $-32 \leq xy \leq 24$.

- Since -32, 7, and 15 all fall within the range of value from -32 to 24, **we must select $\boxed{B}$, $\boxed{C}$, and $\boxed{D}$, and nothing more, to get credit for this question**. If we fail to select all three answer choices, or select a fourth, our response would be considered incorrect.

  ➤ Again, if the math doesn't make sense here, don't worry! This question is simply intended to show you what a "Select One or More" question looks like.

- The math behind it is covered in our book on Number Properties & Algebra.

(18) Numeric Entry Questions – On each of your quantitative sections, anywhere from one to three of your Problem Solving questions will ask you for a "Numeric Entry".

• Numeric Entry questions prompt you to **type a numeric answer into a box** below the problem.

> ➤ Such questions tend to be more difficult than other Problem Solving questions since you can't use the answer choices to determine whether you're on the right track.

• Further, it's almost impossible to guess the correct answer. With regular Problem Solving questions, you at least have a 1 in 5 chance of getting lucky.

• Let's take a look at a sample question:

When walking, a person takes 24 complete steps in 15 seconds. At this rate, how many steps does this person take in 5 seconds?

• There are several ways to solve a problem like this. Perhaps the easiest way is to set up a proportion:

$$\frac{24 \text{ steps}}{15 \text{ seconds}} = \frac{x \text{ steps}}{5 \text{ seconds}}$$

• When comparing the bottoms of the two fractions, notice that "15 seconds" is exactly three times as large as "5 seconds".

> ➤ With proportions, the relationship between the tops of the fractions is the same as that between the bottoms.

• In other words, "24 steps" must be three times as large as "x steps", since "15 seconds" is three times as large as "5 seconds".

• Thus, $x = 8$, because 24 is three times as large as 8. To solve this problem, therefore, **we would need to type 8 into the numeric entry box** beneath the question.

> ➤ As with the previous sections, don't worry if the math doesn't make sense here! This question is simply intended to show you what a Numeric Entry question looks like.

• The math behind it is covered properly in our book on Word Problems.

(19) Quantitative Comparisons – The rest of your math questions will prompt you to compare two quantities.

• Such questions, commonly known as "Quantitative Comparisons", consist of two quantities, labeled Quantity A and Quantity B, and, in many cases, some additional information.

➤ Beneath the two quantities you'll find four answer choices, asking which of the two quantities is LARGER. The answer choices are always the SAME.

• **MEMORIZE them IMMEDIATELY**. 15 of your 40 math questions will be in this format. If you spend 10 seconds wading through the answer choices on each of these questions, you'll be wasting 2.5 minutes of your exam!

• Let's take a look at a sample problem:

$$xy \geq 1$$

Quantity A	**Quantity B**
xy	$(xy)^3$

    (A) Quantity A is greater.
    (B) Quantity B is greater.
    (C) The quantities are equal.
    (D) The relationship cannot be determined
        from the information given.

Answer: D. At the top of the problem, we are told that $xy \geq 1$. This means that xy can be any value equal to or greater than one.

➤ If $xy = 1$, notice that the quantities are equal, since $(1)^3 = 1 \times 1 \times 1 = 1$. If $xy = 2$, however, notice that Quantity B is greater than Quantity A, since $(2)^3 = 2 \times 2 \times 2 = 8$.

• Because the two quantities can be equal or can be different, we cannot determine which quantity is larger from the given information. The correct answer is therefore (D).

• Any time two quantities have an INCONSISTENT RELATIONSHIP — i.e. any time that A can be greater than or equal to B or that B can be greater than or equal to A — the relationship between the two quantities CANNOT be determined.

Chapter 1: Introduction

(20) Before You Get Started – If you've read through the preceding pages, you're ready to get started.

- Before you do, we'd like to offer you a last few bits of advice. We know that many people who take the GRE are not very comfortable with math.

  ➤ If you're one of them, you may have been told at an early age that you weren't a "math person" or that your brain "doesn't work that way".

- That's total nonsense. The truth is that EVERYONE can learn the sort of math required by the GRE.

- Yes, it may require hard work — especially if you haven't done math in over a decade. But you CAN do it. Don't let the idiotic assessment of a bad teacher or a misogynist prevent you from attaining your goals.

  ➤ As you begin to practice, **DON'T try to do everything in your head**. Scratch work is an IMPORTANT part of the problem solving process.

- Taking notes will SPEED you up and help you avoid careless errors.

- Make sure, however, that your writing is organized and legible. Sloppy handwriting is a sure path to careless errors. Writing the work for one problem atop the work for another problem is even worse. (Yes, some people do this.)

  ➤ Likewise, **make sure that your handwriting is appropriately sized**. If you can solve twenty problems on a single sheet of paper, your writing is too small.

- Yes, the GRE only provides you with a few sheets of unlined scratch paper, but you can always raise your hand to trade for new sheets BEFORE you run out.

- Conversely, if you're using one sheet of paper per question, write smaller. You shouldn't need to request paper frequently. Divide your sheets of scratch paper into six equal sections. With proper penmanship, you should be able to fit the work for any problem in one of the sections.

  ➤ When solving problems, **beware of crazy decimals or fractions**. If your scratch work involves something like $0.123 \times \frac{7}{13}$, you're doing something wrong.

- In general, the GRE tends to use "smart numbers" — numbers that are designed to yield simple results under the proper analysis.

- When the GRE uses exotic numbers, the exam is almost always testing your ability to identify patterns or relationships (e.g. $0.\overline{54} = \frac{5}{9}$) or to approximate.

  ➤ If you're worried about anxiety, preparing THOROUGHLY for the GRE is the best way to beat test-taking jitters.

- Nothing calms unsteady nerves more than seeing problems you KNOW how to solve because the content is EASY for you.

- You should also **set up a test date that allows you enough time to schedule a retake**, if necessary. (Remember, you can take the GRE every 21 days and up to 5 times a year.) Knowing that you'll have a second shot at the GRE can take the pressure off your first exam.

  ➤ On test day, bring food and water with you to the exam center. You'll be there for nearly five hours.

- Doing anything for that length of time is fatiguing. Eating a few nuts and a piece of fruit before your exam (and during your break) will help keep you sharp.

- Just be sure to steer clear of drinking too much water or consuming too much sugar or caffeine. You don't want to take multiple bathroom breaks while your exam is running or to crash during the final hour of your test.

  ➤ If you can, **get to the test center early**. Taking the GRE is stressful enough. You don't want to exacerbate that stress by running late.

- Plan to get there a half hour in advance. If you're commuting to an unfamiliar area, research the commute carefully and allot an additional 15 minutes (in case you get lost).

- Once inside (don't forget your ID and admissions ticket!), use the extra time to warm up with a few practice problems or to review your notes. Doing so will help get your brain "in gear" before your exam.

  ➤ Finally, **brace yourself for broken air-conditioners, sniffling neighbors, and unfriendly staffers**.

- Although test centers are generally well run, it's important to remember that there can be problems.

- As long as you dress in layers, however, and make use of the headphones or earplugs that are supplied with your exam, these issues shouldn't pose you any problems.

Chapter 2

Statistics

Statistics

To be discussed:

Fundamental Concepts

Whether you're aiming for a perfect score or a score closer to average, mastery of the following concepts is essential.

1 Introduction
2 Averages
3 Weighted Averages
4 Medians & Modes
5 Equally Spaced Number Sets
6 Range, Quartiles, & Boxplots
7 Standard Deviation
8 Normal Distributions

Rare or Advanced Concepts

The following concepts are either advanced or are tested only on rare occasions. If you don't need an elite math score, don't waste your time!

9 Random Variables
10 Peaks & Tails
11 Maximization Problems
12 The Weighted Average Shortcut
13 Counting & Adding Equally Spaced Numbers

Practice Questions

There's no substitute for elbow grease. Practice your new skills to ensure that you internalize what you've studied.

14 Problem Sets
15 Solutions

Fundamental Concepts

(1) Introduction – For many students, the term Statistics conjures up visions of strange and complex mathematics.

• Fortunately, nothing can be further from the truth.

  ➢ Technically, Statistics refers to the mathematics of collecting, organizing, and interpreting data.

• For the GRE, however, Statistics largely focuses on a few basic concepts.

• In fact, if you can identify the **average, median,** and **range** of a set of numbers, you are already familiar with the most commonly tested Statistics topics.

  ➢ Of course, Statistics also involves concepts that may seem daunting, such as **standard deviation** and **normal distributions**.

• If these concepts are unfamiliar to you, we've got some good news: Not only are they relatively simple, but they're also tested far less frequently.

• And the exotic stuff such as **quartiles** and **random variables**? That stuff is pretty rare.

  ➢ No matter how familiar you may be with Statistics, we STRONGLY encourage you to work through this section carefully.

• No type of word problem is tested more frequently. Roughly 33% of GRE questions are word problems, and a third of these involve statistics.

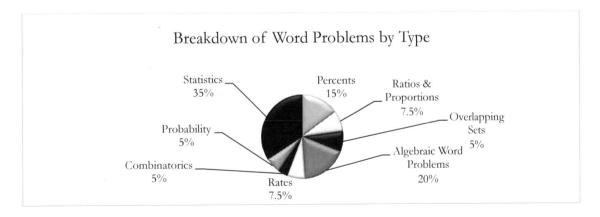

Breakdown of Word Problems by Type

Statistics 35% · Percents 15% · Ratios & Proportions 7.5% · Overlapping Sets 5% · Probability 5% · Algebraic Word Problems 20% · Combinatorics 5% · Rates 7.5%

• This may not seem like a lot, but it usually amounts **to 4-5 questions** on a typical exam.

(2) Averages – In Statistics, it's often useful to measure how "central" or typical a number is within a particular data set.

• Although there are several ways to gauge the "centrality" of a number set, the most common way is to take the AVERAGE, a term also known as the ARITHMETIC MEAN.

> ➤ The average of a number set is simply the SUM of its terms divided by the NUMBER of terms within the set.

• Formally, this relationship can be represented as follows:

$$\frac{S(\text{um of terms})}{N(\text{umber of terms})} = A(\text{verage})$$

• Thus, the average of the numbers 3, 6, 7, 8, and 11 is 7, since the sum of the 5 numbers is 35, and $35 \div 5 = 7$.

> ➤ To solve problems involving averages, simply PLUG the information that you've been provided into the AVERAGE FORMULA given above.

• The formula has 3 variables: S, N, and A. As long as you know two of these variables, the formula can always determine the third.

• To get a sense of what a basic Average problem looks like, consider the following:

If $x = -y$ and $z = 18$, then the average (arithmetic mean) of $x, y,$ and z is equal to

(A) 0   (B) 2   (C) 3   (D) 6   (E) 9

Answer: D. To determine the average of $x, y,$ and z, we must add them together and divide the sum by 3, since there are 3 terms in the set:

$$\frac{S}{N} = A \quad \rightarrow \quad \frac{x + y + z}{3} = A$$

• According to the problem, $x = -y$ and $z = 18$. If we plug this information into the equation above, we get $A = 6$, proving that the correct answer is (D):

Let $x = -y$ $\qquad$ $\dfrac{-y + y + 18}{3} = \dfrac{18}{3} = 6 = A$ $\qquad$ Let $z = 18$

➤ In more difficult Average Problems, you may encounter MORE than one average.

• For such problems, we encourage you to use the Average Formula for EACH example. Doing so will provide you with two equations that you should be able to combine. Consider the following:

The average (arithmetic mean) of 5, 9, k, and m is 12.

Quantity A	**Quantity B**
The average (arithmetic mean) of $k + 7$ and $m − 3$	20

Answer: B. According to the problem, the average of 5, 9, k, and m is 12. Since there are **four** terms, and the **sum** of the terms is $5 + 9 + k + m$, we can plug this information into the Average Formula as follows:

The **average** is 12

$$\frac{S}{N} = A \quad \rightarrow \quad \frac{5 + 9 + k + m}{4} = 12 \quad \longleftarrow$$

➤ From this, we can determine that $k + m = 34$, since:

$$\frac{5 + 9 + k + m}{4} = 12 \quad \rightarrow \quad 14 + k + m = 48 \quad \rightarrow \quad k + m = 34$$

• To determine the value of ☐ **Quantity A** ☐, let's plug the provided information into the Average Formula. Since there are **two** terms, and the **sum** of $k + 7$ and $m − 3$ equals $k + m + 4$, we get:

$$\frac{S}{N} = A \quad \rightarrow \quad \frac{k + m + 4}{2} = A$$

➤ We can reduce this information further by plugging in $k + m = 34$, which we determined from our earlier calculations:

$$\frac{k + m + 4}{2} = A \quad \rightarrow \quad \frac{34 + 4}{2} = 19 = A$$

• Thus, the correct answer is (B), since Quantity B is larger than Quantity A. (If you don't remember how the answer choices work for a Quantitative Comparison question, be sure to visit section ☐ 19 ☐ of the Introduction!).

➤ The most confusing average problems take an average and ALTER it by adding or removing items. We call such problems ALTERED AVERAGES.

• To solve them, simply set up BEFORE and AFTER equations using the Average Formula. Doing so will provide you with two equations that you can combine.

• Consider the following:

For the past N days, the average daily production at a certain company was 30 widgets. If today's production of 50 widgets raises the average production to 35 widgets per day, what is the value of N?

(A) 2   (B) 3   (C) 4   (D) 5   (E) 6

Answer. B. Before today, there was an average of 30 widgets produced daily. Today, **50 more widgets** were added to the production total, **1 more** day passed, and the **average** production of widgets increased to **35** per day. Thus, we can set up two equations:

BEFORE the increase   AFTER the increase

$$\frac{S}{N} = 30 \;\rightarrow\; S = 30N \qquad\qquad \frac{S+50}{N+1} = 35 \;\rightarrow\; S + 50 = 35N + 35$$

➤ According to the "before" equation, $S = 30N$. Substituting $S = 30N$ into the "after" equation, proves that $N = 3$, since:

The "after" equation

$$
\begin{aligned}
S + 50 &= 35N + 35 \\
30N + 50 &= 35N + 35 \\
15 &= 5N \;\rightarrow\; N = 3
\end{aligned}
$$

Let $S = 30N$

The average (arithmetic mean) of 8 numbers is 12.5. When one number is discarded, the average of the remaining numbers becomes 11.

Quantity A	**Quantity B**
The value of the discarded number	25

Answer. B. Before the number is discarded, the average of the 8 numbers is 12.5. After the number is discarded, the average of the 7 remaining numbers is 11:

BEFORE the discard   AFTER the discard

$$\frac{S}{8} = 12.5 \;\rightarrow\; S = 8(12.5) = 100 \qquad\qquad \frac{S}{7} = 11 \;\rightarrow\; S = 7(11) = 77$$

• Since the sum of the 8 numbers is 100, and the sum of 7 remaining numbers is 77, the value of the discarded number must be $100 - 77 = 23$. Thus, the correct answer is (B).

(3) Weighted Averages – A Weighted Average is simply an average in which some values count more than others.

• To illustrate the difference between an Average and a Weighted Average, imagine a class with 4 boys and 6 girls.

> ➢ If all 4 boys were to score an 80 on a certain quiz, and all 6 girls were to score a 90 on that same quiz, the average of the boys' score and the girls' would be 85.

• However, if we compute the average of all 10 quizzes, the girls' score of 90 has a larger impact on the overall tally since it is more heavily "weighted" than the boys' score of 80: there are simply more 90's than 80's.

<table>
<tr><td align="center">AVERAGE</td><td align="center">WEIGHTED Average</td></tr>
<tr><td align="center">$\dfrac{80 + 90}{2} = 85$</td><td align="center">$\dfrac{4(80) + 6(90)}{10} = 86$</td></tr>
</table>

• Thus, when we take a weighted average, we account for the FREQUENCY of each item within a set, as well as its VALUE.

> ➢ To solve problems involving weighted averages, always MULTIPLY each value by the weight that it holds. Then, divide the total by the SUM of the weights.

• Thus, if three shirts cost an average of $40 and two shirts cost an average of $80, the average price of all five shirts would be $56, since:

$$\frac{3(\$40) + 2(\$80)}{5} \;\rightarrow\; \frac{\$120 + \$160}{5} \;\rightarrow\; \frac{\$280}{5} = \frac{\$560}{10} = \$56$$

• To get a sense of what a basic weighted average problem looks like, consider the following:

In store T, the average (arithmetic mean) revenue over an 8-day period was $300 per day. During this period, if the average daily revenue was $240 for the first 5 days, what was the average daily revenue, in dollars, for the last 3 days?

(A) 400   (B) 425   (C) 450   (D) 475   (E) 500

Answer. A. According to the problem, the first 5 days had an average daily revenue of $240. Since the revenue of the 8-day period averaged $300 in total, the average daily revenue of the last 3 days must have been $400, since:

$$\frac{5(240) + 3(x)}{8} = 300 \;\rightarrow\; 1{,}200 + 3x = 2{,}400 \;\rightarrow\; 3x = 1{,}200 \;\rightarrow\; x = 400$$

> ➤ As Weighted Average problems grow more difficult, the NUMBERS involved sometimes become HARDER to work with.

• Consider the following:

On Monday, a retail shop paid an average price of $179 for 7 jackets. If the same shop paid an average price of $205 for another 6 jackets on Tuesday, what was the average price, in dollars, paid for all 13 jackets?

(A) 187   (B) 189   (C) 190   (D) 191   (E) 193

Answer: D. Setting up such a problem is not very difficult. If 7 of the jackets had an average price of $179 and 6 of the jackets had an average price of $205, then the average price for all 13 jackets can be determined as follows:

$$\frac{7(179) + 6(205)}{13} = x$$

• Solving for x, however, is quite difficult, since the numbers are large and awkward.

> ➤ Fortunately, weighted averages lend themselves to an effective shortcut that makes problems like this easy to solve. We call it the $\boxed{\textbf{"Big Average" Shortcut}}$.

• When solving averages with difficult numbers, first SUBTRACT the LARGEST amount in COMMON to each value. Then, take the average of what remains.

• Here, the largest amount in common to $179 and $205 is $179. If we subtract $179 from each, we're left with 7 jackets with an average difference of $0 and 6 jackets with an average difference of $26. Thus, the average of what remains is $12, since:

$$\frac{7(0) + 6(26)}{13} \quad \rightarrow \quad \frac{6(\cancel{26})}{\cancel{13}} = 6(2) = 12$$

> ➤ Once you've determined the average of what remains, ADD your solution to the amount that you SUBTRACTED.

• Since the amount you subtracted represents what the values have in COMMON, and your solution represents their average DIFFERENCE, their sum will equal the average value.

• Thus, the average price of all 13 jackets was $191, since each jacket cost at least $179 and the average difference among the 13 jackets was $12. The correct answer is therefore (D).

➢ Most Weighted Average problems, however, will test your understanding of something we call the ⌐Law of Weighted Averages⌐.

• In essence, a weighted average is a TUG-OF-WAR: the LARGER of two groups always drags the average CLOSER to itself.

• Imagine a class with MORE girls than boys. If the girls were to have an average grade of 90 and the boys an average grade of 80, the average grade for the entire class would be GREATER than 85, since the girls are the LARGER of the two groups.

➢ This observation, though simple, is the KEY to solving many Weighted Average problems on the GRE.

• Consider the following:

At company C, the average salary is $39,000. The male employees have an average salary of $34,000, and the female employees have an average salary of $42,000.

Quantity A	**Quantity B**
The number of male employees at company C.	**The number of female employees at company C.**

Answer. B. According to the Law of Weighted Averages, the larger of two groups always drags the closer to itself. Here, the average salary of $39,000 is closer to the women's salary of $42,000 than to the men's salary of $34,000, so the women are the larger group. Thus, company C has more female employees than male employees.

• A second example for you:

The average (arithmetic mean) weight of 40 men is 190 pounds, and the average weight of 20 additional men is 230 pounds.

Quantity A	**Quantity B**
The average of the 60 weights	**210**

Answer. B. According to the problem, more men have an average weight of 190 than 230, so the 190-pound men are the "larger" group. Thus, the average weight of all 60 men is closer to 190 than 230. Since 210 is equidistant between 190 and 230, Quantity A must be less than 210.

(4) Medians & Modes – An average is not the only way to gauge how "central" or typical a number is within a particular data set.

• Two other measurements can also be used. These measurements are commonly known as the median and the mode.

> ➢ The MEDIAN of a group of numbers is the number in the MIDDLE of the set, when the data is arranged in ASCENDING order.

• Thus, the number set {9, 3, 1, 7, 5} has a median of 5, since 5 is the middle term when the set is arranged from least to greatest: {1, 3, 5, 7, 9}.

• If a set of data has an EVEN number of terms, the median is the AVERAGE of the two MIDDLE terms. Thus, the number set {11, 1, 3, 9, 7, 5} has a median of 6, since 5 and 7 are the middle terms when the set is arranged in ascending order: {1, 3, 5, 7, 9, 11}.

> ➢ The MODE of a set of numbers is the value that occurs most FREQUENTLY.

• For example, the number set {1, 3, 3, 5, 7, 8, 9} has a mode of 3, since 3 is the term that occurs most frequently.

• Although a set of numbers can only have one median, it can have MULTIPLE MODES. For example, the number set {1, 2, 2, 3, 5, 7, 7} has modes of 2 and 7, since 2 and 7 are the most frequently occurring numbers within the set.

> ➢ Most questions that involve medians or modes are relatively straightforward and can be solved by locating the middle term or the term that occurs most frequently.

• Consider the following:

A group of children has the following ages: 6, 6, 8, 8, 8, 8, 5, 5, 4 and 9.

Quantity A	**Quantity B**
The median of the 10 ages	**The mode of the 10 ages**

Answer. B. Arranged in ascending order, the ages of the children are: 4, 5, 5, 6, 6, 8, 8, 8, 8, and 9. The median of the 10 ages is therefore 7, since the two middle numbers, 6 and 8, have an average of 7.

• The mode of the set must be 8, since the number 8 occurs four times, and no other number occurs more than twice. Thus, Quantity B is larger than Quantity A.

➤ As number sets grow larger, you may find it difficult to identify the middle terms of the set.

• Consider the following:

The frequency distribution for list X is presented below.

Number	1	2	3	4	5
Frequency	12	17	16	33	12

Quantity A

The median of the numbers in list X

Quantity B

The mode of the numbers in list X

• Determining the mode of list X is easy: the number 4 occurs 33 times, and thus occurs more frequently than 1, 2, 3, or 5. Determining the median, however, is trickier.

➤ According to the frequency distribution, list X has a TOTAL of 90 numbers, since $12 + 17 + 16 + 33 + 12 = 90$.

• A median SEPARATES the HIGHER HALF of a data sample from the LOWER HALF, so we can split this total into 45 numbers below the median and 45 numbers above the median.

• Since the median of an even list of numbers is the average of its two middle terms, the median of list X must be the average of its 45th and 46th terms.

➤ Listed in ascending order, list X begins with twelve "1"s. These "1"s are followed by seventeen "2"s, which are followed by sixteen "3"s.

• Since $12 + 17 + 16 = 45$, we therefore know that the 45th term in list X is a "3". Further, since the next thirty-three terms in the list are "4"s, the 46th term is a 4. Visually, we can depict this as follows:

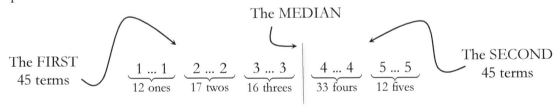

• Thus, the median of list X must be 3.5, since the average of 3 and 4 is 3.5. As discussed, the mode of the set is 4, so Quantity B must be larger than Quantity A.

➢ The trickiest median problems ask you to determine how the addition of a VARIABLE will affect the median of a number set.

• We call these problems FLUCTUATING MEDIAN problems, because the value of the median can change, depending on the value of the variable.

• Although Fluctuating Median problems often look daunting, there are a couple of simple things you can do to make them easy to solve.

➢ First, make a T-CHART to organize your information. On the left side place your VARIABLE (or variables) and on the right side place your MEDIAN.

• Then arrange the numbers in ascending order, leaving a SPACE between each number. These spaces will make it easier for you to test possible values for your variable, and to track how they affect the median.

• To get a sense of what we mean by all this, consider the following:

If $x + y = 8$, then the median of the set of positive integers $\{x, 6, y, 2, 5\}$ could equal which of the following?

Select all possible values.

$\boxed{A}$ 3 $\boxed{B}$ 3.5 $\boxed{C}$ 4 $\boxed{D}$ 4.5 $\boxed{E}$ 5 $\boxed{F}$ 5.5

Answer. C and E. According to the problem, x and y are positive integers and $x + y = 8$. Thus, potential **combinations** of $x + y$ include $1 + 7$, $2 + 6$, $3 + 5$, and $4 + 4$.

➢ Without x and y, the set $\{x, 6, y, 2, 5\}$ can be ordered from least to greatest as $\{2, 5, 6\}$.

• If we insert these combinations for x and y into the set $\{2, 5, 6\}$, we get:

If $x + y = 1 + 7$, the set becomes: $\{\mathbf{1}, 2, 5, 6, \mathbf{7}\}$

If $x + y = 2 + 6$, the set becomes: $\{\mathbf{2}, 2, 5, 6, \mathbf{6}\}$

If $x + y = 3 + 5$, the set becomes: $\{2, \mathbf{3}, 5, \mathbf{5}, 6\}$

If $x + y = 4 + 4$, the set becomes: $\{2, \mathbf{4}, \mathbf{4}, 5, 6\}$

x, y	median
1, 7	5
2, 6	5
3, 5	5
4, 4	4

• As our t-chart shows, the median of the set is 5, when $x, y = 1, 7$ or $2, 6$ or $3, 5$. And the median of the set $= 4$, when $x, y = 4, 4$. Thus, the correct answers are $\boxed{C}$ and $\boxed{E}$.

(5) Equally Spaced Number Sets – Any set of numbers in which the intervals between the terms are the same is commonly known as an equally spaced number set.

• Thus, the set on the left is equally spaced, since each term in the set is 3 greater than the term before it. The set on the right is not, since the gaps between the terms differ:

<table>
<tr><td align="center"><u>EQUALLY Spaced</u></td><td align="center"><u>NOT Equally Spaced</u></td></tr>
<tr><td align="center">{12, 15, 18, 21}</td><td align="center">{1, 3, 7, 11}</td></tr>
</table>

> ➢ Consecutive INTEGERS are spaced apart by intervals of 1, and consecutive MULTIPLES are divisible by the intervals between them.

• Below, the set on the left can be referred to as the set of consecutive integers from 9 to 12, since each term in the set is 1 greater than the term before it:

<table>
<tr><td align="center"><u>Consecutive INTEGERS</u></td><td align="center"><u>Consecutive MULTIPLES</u></td></tr>
<tr><td align="center">{9, 10, 11, 12}</td><td align="center">{10, 15, 20, 25}</td></tr>
</table>

• Likewise, the set on the right can be referred to as the set of consecutive multiples of 5 from 10 to 25, since each term in the set is 5 greater than the term before it, as well as divisible by 5.

> ➢ ALGEBRAICALLY, consecutive integers can be represented as x, $x + 1$, $x + 2$, $x + 3$, and so forth, where x is the smallest of the consecutive integers.

• Likewise, consecutive multiples of 5 can be represented as x, $x + 5$, $x + 10$, $x + 15$, and so forth, since every multiple of 5 is 5 bigger than the multiple before it. Thus, the consecutive multiples of 4 and 7 can be represented as:

<table>
<tr><td align="center"><u>MULTIPLES of 4</u></td><td align="center"><u>MULTIPLES of 7</u></td></tr>
<tr><td align="center">{x, $x + 4$, $x + 8$}</td><td align="center">{x, $x + 7$, $x + 14$}</td></tr>
</table>

> ➢ Consecutive EVEN integers (e.g. 4, 6, 8, …) can be represented as x, $x + 2$, $x + 4$, $x + 6$, and so forth, since every even integer is 2 bigger than the even before it.

• The SAME is true of consecutive ODDS integers (e.g. 3, 5, 7, …), since every odd integer is also 2 bigger than the odd integer before it:

<table>
<tr><td align="center"><u>Consecutive EVENS</u></td><td align="center"><u>Consecutive ODDS</u></td></tr>
<tr><td align="center">{x, $x + 2$, $x + 4$}</td><td align="center">{x, $x + 2$, $x + 4$}</td></tr>
</table>

➤ The KEY to solving many problems involving equally spaced number sets is to represent the terms ALGEBRAICALLY.

- Consider the following:

If the sum of 4 consecutive integers is 334, what is the sum of the 3 consecutive integers before them?

(A) 240   (B) 252   (C) 264   (D) 272   (E) 280

Answer. A. Algebraically, the sum of 4 consecutive integers equals $4x + 6$, since consecutive integers are spaced apart by intervals of 1:

$$x$$
$$x + 1$$
$$x + 2$$
$$\underline{x + 3}$$
$$4x + 6$$

If this sum equals 334, then the smallest of the 4 integers must be 82, since:

$$4x + 6 = 334 \quad \rightarrow \quad 4x = 328 \quad \rightarrow \quad x = \frac{328}{4} = 82$$

Thus, the correct answer is (A), since the 3 consecutive integers before 82 are 81, 80, and 79, and their sum is 240.

In an increasing sequence of 6 consecutive odd integers, how much greater is the sum of the last three integers than the sum of the first three?

(A) 6   (B) 9   (C) 12   (D) 15   (E) 18

Answer. E. Consecutive odd integers are spaced apart by intervals of 2. The sum of the first 3 terms is therefore $3x + 6$, and the sum of the last 3 terms is $3x + 24$:

First 3	Last 3
x	$x + 6$
$x + 2$	$x + 8$
$\underline{x + 4}$	$\underline{x + 10}$
$3x + 6$	$3x + 24$

Thus, the correct answer is (E), since the difference between the last 3 terms and the first 3 terms is 18:

$$\boxed{3x + 24} - \boxed{3x + 6} \quad \rightarrow \quad 3x + 24 - \mathbf{3x - 6} \quad \rightarrow \quad 24 - 6 = 18$$

➤ Equally spaced number sets also have two SPECIAL PROPERTIES that you may find tested from time to time.

• We strongly encourage you to memorize these properties. Certain Statistics questions cannot be solved without them. For any ⟨EQUALLY SPACED⟩ number set:

<u>Property #1</u>

The AVERAGE <u>always</u> EQUALS the MEDIAN.

<u>Property #2</u>

The AVERAGE of the FIRST and LAST terms equals the AVERAGE of the entire set.

• To get a sense of how the GRE might test your knowledge of these properties, consider the following:

If set S represents the multiples of 7 from 7 to 693, what is the median of the set?

(A) 336   (B) 343   (C) 350   (D) 357   (E) 364

Answer. C. Set S represents the multiples of 7 from 7 to 693, so it is an equally spaced number set. The average of the first and last terms of the set is 350, since:

$$\frac{7+693}{2} = \frac{700}{2} = 350$$

➤ For every equally spaced number set, the average of the first and last numbers equals the average of the entire set.

• Thus, the average of the set is 350. And since the average of every equally spaced number set always equals its median, the median of the set must also be 350.

The average of 12 equally spaced integers is 67. If the largest of the integers is 93, then which of the following equals the smallest?

(A) 39   (B) 41   (C) 43   (D) 45   (E) 47

Answer. B. According to the problem, the 12 integers are equally spaced. For every equally spaced number set, the average of the first and last numbers equals the average of the entire set. This set has an average of 67, so the average of its first and last numbers must be 67 too.

• The largest number in this set is 93. If the average of the first and last numbers is 67, then the smallest number must be 41, since:

$$\frac{x+93}{2} = 67 \quad \rightarrow \quad x+93 = 134 \quad \rightarrow \quad x = 41$$

(6) Range, Quartiles, & Boxplots – In Statistics, it can also be useful to measure the degree to which data is "dispersed" or spread out.

• As with "centrality", there are several ways to gauge the "dispersion" of a set of numbers. The most common way is to take the RANGE.

 ➢ The range of a data set is simply the DIFFERENCE between its GREATEST and LEAST terms.

• For example, the data set $\{-3, 4, 4, 5, 8, 8, 12\}$ has a range of 15, since the difference between its greatest value and least value is $12 - (-3) = 15$.

• Questions involving range are common on the GRE. To get a sense of what one might look like, consider the following:

In a recent game, the contestants earned the following scores: 7, 9, 3, −4, 8, and x. The range of the scores was 15. Which of the following could be the value of x?

Indicate all such values.

A −16   B −8   C −6   D 11   E 20   F 21

Answer: C and D. The range of a data set is the difference between its greatest and lest terms. According to the problem, the range of the scores was 15.

 ➢ If the highest score was x, the lowest would be −4. Thus, x could equal 11, since the **difference** between x and −4 would equal 15:

$$x - (-4) = 15$$
$$x + 4 = 15$$
$$x = 11$$

• If the lowest score was x, the highest would be 9. Thus, x could also equal −6, since the **difference** between 9 and x would equal 15:

$$9 - x = 15$$
$$-x = 6$$
$$x = -6$$

• Hence, the correct answers are C and D .

➤ A QUARTILE is one of three points that DIVIDE a data set into FOUR groups, each (more or less) with the same number of terms.

• Each group represents a fourth of the data set:

1. The FIRST QUARTILE (or lower quartile) cuts off the lowest 25% of the data and thus equals the 25th percentile.

2. The SECOND QUARTILE cuts the data set in half and thus equals the MEDIAN of the data set or the 50th percentile.

3. The THIRD QUARTILE (or upper quartile) cuts off the highest 25% of the data and thus equals the 75th percentile.

• Thus, the quartiles of the data set {1, 1, 3, 4, 4, 6, 6, 7, 8, 8, 9, 9} can be depicted as follows, where Q_1 = the first quartile, Q_2 = the second quartile, and Q_3 = the third quartile:

$$\left\{ \underbrace{1,1,3}_{\text{Bottom 25\%}} \vdots \underbrace{4,4,6}_{\text{Below 50\%}} \vdots \underbrace{6,7,8}_{\text{Above 50\%}} \vdots \underbrace{8,9,9}_{\text{Highest 25\%}} \right\}$$

$$Q_1 \qquad\qquad Q_2 \qquad\qquad Q_3$$

➤ As you can see, Q_2 cuts the data set in half, so it is the MEDIAN. Here, $Q_2 = 6$, since the average of the two middle numbers, 6 and 6, is 6.

• Likewise, Q_1 cuts the LOWER portion of the data in HALF and Q_3 cuts the UPPER portion of the data in HALF. Hence:

Q_1 is the MEDIAN of the FIRST HALF of the data

Q_3 is the MEDIAN of the SECOND HALF of the data

• As such, $Q_1 = 3.5$, since the median of the first six values is the average of 3 and 4, and $Q_3 = 8$, since the median of the last six values is the average of 8 and 8.

➤ In the list above, note that the number "3" is in the lowest 25 percent of the data. There are two ways to say this.

• You can say that the number 3 is "BELOW the first quartile" or that it's "IN the first quartile."

➤ The phrase "IN a quartile" refers to being in one of the FOUR groups determined by the quartiles.

• Consider the data set $\{1, 2, 2, 3, 3, 4, 5, 6, 6, 8, 8, 9\}$, where Q_1 = the first quartile, Q_2 = the second quartile, and Q_3 = the third quartile:

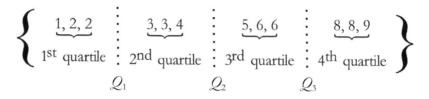

• In this set, the number 1 is "IN the FIRST quartile", while the number 9 is "IN the FOURTH QUARTILE".

➤ The difference between the THIRD and FIRST quartiles is known as the INTERQUARTILE RANGE or, informally, as the "middle 50".

• In the set above, the median of the first half of data is the average of 2 and 3, so Q_1 = 2.5. Likewise, the median of the second half of data is the average of 6 and 8, so Q_3 = 7.

• The set, therefore, has an interquartile range of 4.5, since difference between the third and first quartiles is $7 - 2.5 = 4.5$.

➤ One way to illustrate a group of data is with a BOXPLOT, a diagram that is also known as a "box-and-whisker plot".

• A boxplot organizes a data set along a number line. The interquartile range is indicated by a BOX. This box is divided by M, the median:

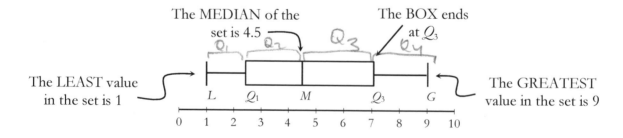

• Two "whiskers" extend out from the box to the LEAST and GREATEST values within the group, L and G, thereby showing the range of the data. In the figure above, Q_1 = 2.5 and Q_3 = 7, so the interquartile range is 4.5. The "whiskers" extend from a least value L of 1 to a greatest value G of 9. Thus, the range of the set is 8.

➢ Questions involving quartiles, interquartile range, or boxplots are somewhat UNCOMMON for the GRE.

• To get a sense of how the exam can test these topics, consider the following:

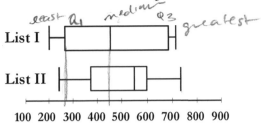

Quantity A ~ 170	Quantity B ~ 120
The range of data in the second quartile of list I	The range of data in the fourth quartile of list II

Answer. A. In any boxplot, the following is true:

The Data	The Quartile
From L to Q_1	Is in the 1st quartile
Between Q_1 and M	Is in the 2nd quartile
Between M and Q_3	Is in the 3rd quartile
From Q_3 to G	Is in the 4th quartile

• In List I, the approximate value of Q_1 is **275** and that of **the Median is 450**. Thus, Quantity A = 175, since the range of data **in the 2nd quartile** is roughly $450 - 275 = 175$.

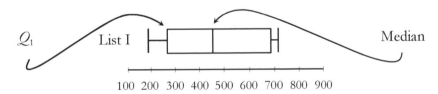

• In List II, the approximate value of Q_3 is **600** and that of **the Greatest Value is 730**. Thus, the correct answer is (B), since Quantity A = the range of data **in the fourth quartile**, which is roughly $730 - 600 = 130$.

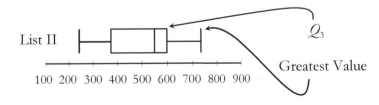

(7) Standard Deviation – Another way to measure the "dispersion" of a data set is to take its standard deviation.

• The standard deviation of a data set measures how far the numbers in the set typically fall from the average or "central" value.

> ➢ A LOW standard deviation indicates that the numbers tend to be very CLOSE to the MEAN (average).

• A HIGH standard deviation indicates that the numbers are SPREAD OUT over a wide range of values.

• Consider the following data sets. Both sets have a mean (average) of 5, but the set on the left shows a narrow range of variation, while the set on the right shows a much larger span of values:

<table>
<tr><td>Closely BUNCHED</td><td>SPREAD Out</td></tr>
<tr><td>{4, 4, 5, 6, 6}</td><td>{–7, –1, 5, 11, 17}</td></tr>
</table>

> ➢ The FIRST set has a relatively SMALL standard deviation, since its numbers are closely bunched around the mean.

• Conversely, the SECOND set has a relatively LARGE standard deviation. Although one of its numbers falls exactly on the mean, most fall far from it, particularly the numbers at the extreme ends of the set.

• Thus, the numbers are spread out over a wide range of values.

> ➢ Next, consider the number set {5, 5, 5, 5, 5), which also has a mean of 5. The numbers in this set have NO SPREAD at all.

• This set has a standard deviation of ZERO, since the distance between each term in the set and the mean is zero. Each term is essentially sitting right on top of the mean.

• It's worth noting that ZERO is the SMALLEST possible measurement for any standard deviation. This is so because standard deviation measures the typical distance of each number in a number set from the mean, and DISTANCES are inherently POSITIVE.

➤ It is HIGHLY UNLIKELY that you will ever need to calculate the standard deviation of a number set in order to solve a question on the GRE.

• On the contrary, GRE standard deviation problems test your understanding of the concept itself and its properties, as in the example below:

    1. 169, 170, 170, 174 ②
    2. 170, 170, 170, 170 ③
    3. 142, 159, 171, 173 ①

Rank data sets 1, 2, and 3, given above, in order from <u>greatest to least</u>, in terms of their standard deviation.

(A) 1, 2, 3 (B) 3, 1, 2 (C) 2, 1, 3 (D) 3, 2, 1 (E) 1, 3, 2

Answer: B. Any number set in which the terms are bunched around the mean has a relatively small standard deviation, and any number set in which the terms are spread out from the mean has a relatively large standard deviation.

➤ Thus, set 1 should have a **small** standard deviation, since its terms are **bunched together**, whereas set 3 should have a **large** standard deviation, since its terms are **spread out**.

Any number set in which the terms have **no spread** at all has a standard deviation of **zero**. Thus, the standard deviations of sets 1, 2, and 3, listed in order from greatest to least should be 3, 1, and 2, since 3 has a relatively large standard deviation and set 2 has a standard deviation of zero. The correct answer is therefore (B).

➤ The topic of standard deviation contains several TERMS and EXPRESSIONS that may NOT be self-evident.

• Just as we can speak of the standard deviation of a number set, so we can speak of MULTIPLE standard deviations of that same set.

• Phrases such as "1.5 standard deviations" and "2 standard deviations" represent 1.5×1 standard deviation and 2×1 standard deviation, respectively. Thus, if the standard deviation of a data set equals 7.0, then:

$$1.5 \text{ standard deviations of that set} = 1.5 \times 7.0 = 10.5$$
$$2 \text{ standard deviations of that set} = 2 \times 7.0 = 14.0$$

- Consider the following:

The arithmetic mean (average) and standard deviation of a distribution are 22.0 and 4.8, respectively. What value is exactly 1.5 standard deviations greater than the mean?

(A) 17.2   (B) 19.6   (C) 24.8   (D) 27.6   (E) 29.2

Answer. E. If the standard deviation of a distribution of numbers is 4.8, then 1.5 standard deviations of that distribution is 7.2, since:

$$1.5 \times 4.8 = 7.2$$

Thus, if the mean of the set is 22.0, then 29.2 is exactly 1.5 standard deviations greater than the mean, since 22.0 + 7.2 = 29.2.

> ➤ The expression "FALL (or LIE) WITHIN a standard deviation" can also be tricky if you've never encountered it.

- Imagine a number set with a standard deviation of 4.0 and a mean of 20.0.

- Since 1.5 standard deviations = 1.5 × 4.0 = 6.0, 1.5 standard deviations above the mean would be 20.0 + 6.0 = 26.0. Likewise, 1.5 standard deviations below the mean would be 20.0 – 6.0 = 14.0. Thus, every number from 14.0 to 26.0 can be said to "fall within 1.5 standard deviations of the mean".

> ➤ Finally, you should also be familiar with the term "VARIANCE", which is simply the SQUARE of the standard deviation.

- For example, if the standard deviation of a number set is 1.5, then its variance is 2.25, since $(1.5)^2 = 2.25$. Conversely, if the variance of a number set is 2.0, then its standard deviation is approximately 1.4, since $\sqrt{2.0} \approx 1.4$.

- Consider the following:

If the arithmetic mean (average) of a distribution is 10.3 and its variance is 9.0, then which of the following do <u>not</u> fall within 1.2 standard deviations of the mean?

Select <u>all</u> such values.

[A] 0.8   [B] 5.7   [C] 7.1   [D] 11.5   [E] 14.3

Answer. A, B, and E. If the variance of the set is 9.0, then its standard deviation is 3.0, since $\sqrt{9} = 3$. Thus, 1.2 standard deviations must equal 1.2 × 3.0 = 3.6.

A value 1.2 standard deviations above the mean, therefore, equals 10.3 + 3.6 = 13.9, and a value 1.2 standard deviations below the mean equals 10.3 – 3.6 = 6.7. Thus, every value from 6.7 to 13.9 falls within 1.2 standard deviations of the mean.

Therefore $\boxed{A}$, $\boxed{B}$, and $\boxed{E}$ do not fall within 1.2 standard deviations.

> ➤ On occasion, you may need to determine HOW MANY standard deviations a certain value is above (or below) the mean.

• To do so, first determine the DISTANCE from the value to the mean. Then DIVIDE that distance by the standard deviation:

$$\frac{\textbf{Distance}}{\textbf{Standard Deviation}} = \textbf{Number of Deviations}$$

• Thus, if set A has a mean of 8 and a standard deviation of 2, a value of 13 would be 2.5 standard deviations above the mean. Likewise, if set B has a mean of 9.6 and a standard deviation of 2.4, a value of 9.0 would be 0.25 standard deviations BELOW the mean, since:

Set A Set B

$$\frac{13-8}{2} = \frac{5}{2} = 2.5 \text{ standard deviations} \qquad \frac{9.6-9.0}{2.4} = \frac{0.6}{2.4} = 0.25 \text{ standard deviations}$$

> ➤ Most standard deviation questions, however, will test your understanding of how the standard deviation of a set is AFFECTED when its numbers CHANGE.

• To answer such questions, simply remember that there is a direct correlation between the SPREAD of the data and its standard deviation.

• Any change that bunches numbers CLOSER to the average DECREASES the standard deviation. Likewise, any change that SPREADS numbers further from the average INCREASES the standard deviation.

> ➤ Thus, MULTIPLYING a set by a factor greater than one INCREASES its standard deviation, since it SPREADS the data further from the average.

• Take the number set {1, 2, 3, 4}. If we triple each term in the set, we see that it causes the data to disperse: {3, 6, 9, 12}.

• Likewise, DIVIDING each number in a set by a factor greater than one DECREASES its standard deviation, since it BUNCHES the data towards the average. Thus, if we divide the set {6, 12, 18, 24} by 6, we see that it squeezes the data together: {1, 2, 3, 4}.

• Consider the following:

Set S contains the numbers 3, 5, 6, and 8. Which of the following values would most increase the standard deviation of set S, if the set were multiplied by the value?

(A) 0.5   (B) 1   (C) 2   (D) 2.5   (E) 4

Answer. E. Multiplying a data set by a factor greater than 1 spreads out the numbers, and larger factors do so more than smaller numbers.

For example, multiplying the set {3, 5, 6, 8} by a factor of 4 gives us {12, 20, 24, 32}, whereas multiplying the set by a factor of 2 gives us {6, 10, 12, 16}. Therefore, the answer must be (E), since 4 is the largest answer choice to choose from.

> ➤ Any change that NEITHER bunches numbers closer together NOR spreads them out does NOT affect their standard deviation.

• Thus, ADDING or SUBTRACTING the same amount from each number in a set does NOT affect its standard deviation, since addition and subtraction neither disperses numbers nor squeezes them together.

• Consider the following:

List L contains the measurements 4, 5, 6, 7, and 8, which have a standard deviation of approximately 1.4.

Quantity A	**Quantity B**
The standard deviation of List L if 5 is added to each term in the list	The standard deviation of List L if 2 is subtracted from each term in the list

Answer. C. List L contains the numbers 4, 5, 6, 7, and 8. If we add 5 to each term, we get 9, 10, 11, 12, and 13.

> ➤ Since the original values and the new values are both equally spaced, the values in the list have **neither spread out nor bunched together**.

• Thus, the standard deviation remains unchanged. Likewise, if we subtract 2 from each term in the list, we get 2, 3, 4, 5, and 6. Again, the original values and the new values are both equally spaced, so the values in list L have **neither spread out nor bunched together**. The standard deviation remains unchanged here, too.

• Since neither quantity changes the standard deviation of List L, the correct answer is (C).

(8) Normal Distributions – A set of data can be distributed in several ways.

• In some cases, the set of data can skew to the right. In other cases, it can skew to the left. And in some cases, it can be random:

Skewed to the RIGHT   Skewed to the LEFT   RANDOM

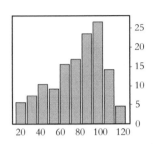 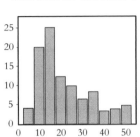 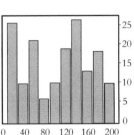

• There are many cases, however, when a data set clusters SYMMETRICALLY around a CENTRAL value.

➢ Such "bell-shaped" distributions are commonly known as NORMAL DISTRIBUTIONS.

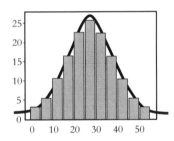

• Because normal distributions are symmetrical about the center, the MEAN, MEDIAN, and MODE are EQUAL.

• Further, the mean SPLITS the distribution in half, so 50% of the data is above the mean and 50% is below the mean.

➢ In every normal distribution, 68% of the data falls within 1 standard deviation of the mean.

• 95% falls within 2 standard deviations, and nearly 100% falls within 3 standard deviations.

• Thus, if you know the mean and standard deviation of a normal distribution, you also know that most values are likely to be within 1 standard deviation of that mean (68%) and very likely to be within 2 standard deviations of that mean (95%).

➢ To get a better sense of what this means, imagine a normal distribution with a MEAN of 12.4 and a STANDARD DEVIATION of 3.2.

• 68% of the data would have a value from 9.2 to 15.6, since:

1 standard deviation **below the mean** would be 12.4 – 3.2 = 9.2.	1 standard deviation **above the mean** would be 12.4 + 3.2 = 15.6.

• Likewise, less than 5% of the data would have a value less than 6.0 or greater than 18.8, since:

2 standard deviations **below the mean** would be 12.4 – 2(3.2) = 6.0.	2 standard deviations **above the mean** would be 12.4 + 2(3.2) = 18.8.

➢ Because a normal distribution is symmetrical about the center, its PERCENTILES ALWAYS correspond to the following CHART, which you should MEMORIZE:

The approximate PERCENTILES of a Normal Distribution

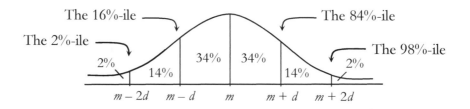

• In this chart, m = mean and d = standard deviation, so:

$m + d$ and $m + 2d$ represent 1 and 2 standard deviations **above the mean**.	$m - d$ and $m - 2d$ represent 1 and 2 standard deviations **below the mean**.

• Further, since the mean equals the 50th percentile, a data point that is:

1 standard deviation **above the mean**, $m + d$, equals the 84th percentile, as 50% + 34% = 84%.	2 standard deviations **below the mean**, $m - 2d$, equals the 2nd percentile, as 50% – 34% – 14% = 2%.

➢ When working with normal distributions, it's generally helpful to DRAW them or to VISUALIZE them.

- Thus, in EVERY normal distribution, notice that:

50% of the data falls below the MEAN

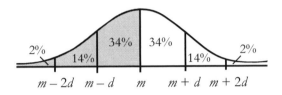

34% of the data is 1 standard deviation ABOVE the mean

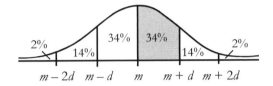

68% of the data falls WITHIN 1 standard deviation of the mean

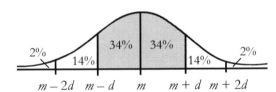

16% of the data is more than 1 standard deviation BELOW the mean

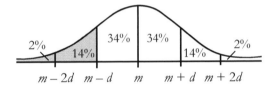

➢ EACH of the normal distributions below has a mean of 15.0 and a standard deviation of 3.

- Notice that:

48% of the data has a value BETWEEN 15.0 and 21.0

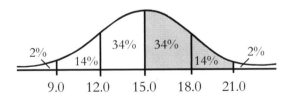

84% of the data has a value of 12.0 or GREATER

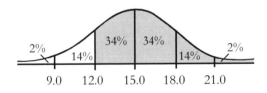

28% of the data has a value BETWEEN 9.0 and 12.0 or 18.0 and 21.0

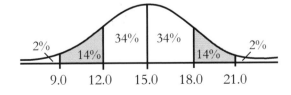

4% of the data is LESS than 9.0 or GREATER than 21.0

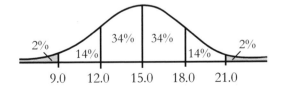

• To get a sense of how the GRE might test your knowledge of normal distributions, consider the following:

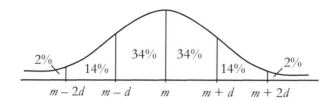

For a population of 6,000 cats, the number of mice consumed per cat last month was normally distributed with a mean of 24 mice and a standard deviation of 7 mice. Approximately how many of the cats ate between 31 and 38 mice last month?

(A) 400   (B) 850   (C) 1,250   (D) 1,650   (E) 2,000

Answer: B. According to the problem, the mean of the distribution was 24 and the standard deviation was 7. Since 31 is 1 standard deviation above the mean and 38 is 2 standard deviations above the mean, the cats who ate "between 31 and 38 mice" are more than 1 standard deviation above the mean but less than 2.

➢ In any normal distribution, 14% of the data lies is more than 1 standard deviation above the mean but less than 2.

• In the graph above, this section of the data falls between the lines labeled *m* + *d* and *m* + 2*d*. Since 14% of 6,000 is 840, the correct answer must be (B).

At school *S*, all of the students weigh between 62 kg and 98 kg, inclusive. If this data is normally distributed, what is the approximate standard deviation of the weights?

(A) 4.5   (B) 5   (C) 5.5   (D) 6   (E) 6.5

Answer: D. Since the student weights are normally distributed, we know that the data is symmetrical about the mean. Thus, the mean of the set should be 80 kg, since 80 is half way between 62 and 98.

➢ In any normal distribution, nearly 100% (99.7%) of the data falls within 3 standard deviations of the mean.

• If the students weigh between 62 kg and 98 kg, inclusive, then 62 kg is 3 standard deviations below the mean and 98 kg is 3 standard deviations above it. Because the distance between the mean (80) and 3 standard deviations below (62) or above (98) the mean is 18, the standard deviation of the student weights must be 6, since:

$$\frac{\text{Distance}}{\text{Number of Deviations}} = \frac{18}{3} = 6$$

➤ Every now and then, you may run across a distribution that is APPROXIMATELY or NEARLY normal.

• The data of such distributions clusters around the mean in a manner that is ALMOST, but perhaps not exactly, symmetrical.

• Thus, the mean, median, and mode may be identical or ALMOST identical. Likewise, NEARLY 68% of the data should fall within 1 standard deviation and 95% within 2 standard deviations.

➤ Finally, it can be helpful to remember that a FLAT, LONG distribution indicates a relatively LARGE standard deviation, since the data is spread out from the mean.

• Conversely, a STEEP, NARROW distribution indicates a relatively SMALL standard deviation, since the data is bunched around the mean.

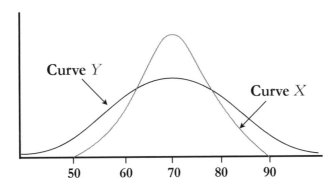

In the diagram above, distribution curves X are Y are approximately normal. Curve X represents the scores of a group of girls on a recent quiz. Curve Y represents the scores of a group of boys on that same quiz.

Quantity A	**Quantity B**
The standard deviation of the girls' scores	The standard deviation of the boys' scores

• In the distributions above, curve X is narrow and steep and curve Y is flat and long.

➤ The data in distribution X, therefore, is relatively bunched about the mean and that in distribution Y is relatively spread out.

• Since the standard deviation of a number set increases as the data disperses, curve Y must have a larger standard deviation than curve X. Thus, the correct answer is (B), since curve Y represents the distribution of the boys' scores.

Rare or Advanced Concepts

(9) Random Variables – From time to time, GRE questions involve random variables.

• A random variable is a variable whose value depends on chance.

  ➤ Because the area under a normal distribution curve is divided into PREDICTABLE percentiles, normal distributions lend themselves to questions about such variables.

• Imagine a set of data, normally distributed, with a mean of 8.0 and a standard deviation of 1.5. In such as a distribution, there is a 34% chance that a data point CHOSEN AT RANDOM has a value between 6.5 and 8.0, since:

  34% of the data set has a value between the mean and 1 standard deviation below the mean:

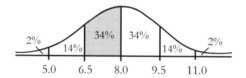

• Thus, we can say that there is a 34% chance that a RANDOM VARIABLE, such as X, has a value between 6.5 and 8.0.

  ➤ Now imagine a set of data, normally distributed, with a mean of 12.0 and a standard deviation of 4.0.

• In this distribution, there is a 32% chance that a data point chosen AT RANDOM has a value less than 8.0 or greater than 16.0, since:

  16% of the data set has a value less than 8.0, and 16% of the data set has a value greater than 16.0:

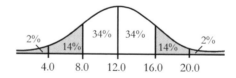

• Thus, we can say that there is a 32% chance that a RANDOM VARIABLE, such as Y, has a value less than 8.0 or greater than 16.0.

➢ To get a sense of how the GRE might test your knowledge of random variables, consider the following:

A random variable V is normally distributed with a mean of 80 and a standard deviation of 10.

Quantity A	Quantity B
The probability of the event that the value of V is between 70 and 80	$\frac{1}{4}$

Answer. A. If the mean of a normal distribution is 80 and its standard deviation is 10, a value between 70 and 80 falls somewhere between the mean and 1 standard deviation below the mean.

• Since 34% of the data in a normal distribution falls between the mean and 1 standard deviation below the mean, the probability that V has a value between 70 and 80 is 34%:

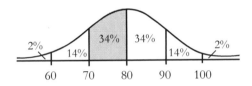

• Thus, Quantity A must be larger than Quantity B, since $\frac{1}{4} = 25\%$. The correct answer is therefore (A).

➢ In more difficult questions, you may need to consider the PERCENTILE of a value BETWEEN two points.

• Consider the following:

The random variable X is normally distributed. The values 150 and 350 are at the 10th and 40th percentiles of the distribution of X, respectively.

Quantity A	Quantity B
The value at the 25th percentile of the distribution of X	250

• *Answer.* A. Because the 25th percentile is halfway between the 10th and 40th percentiles, and 250 is halfway between the values 150 and 350, you may be tempted to assume that the two quantities are equal.

> Unfortunately, this is INCORRECT. To understand why, take a look at the following diagram:

The normal distribution of random variable X

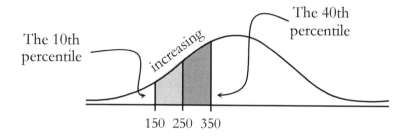

- 150 is the value at the <u>10th</u> percentile of the distribution and 350 is the value at the <u>40th</u> percentile of the distribution. Thus, | **30% of the AREA under the curve** | lies between these two values.

> Because this area INCREASES as the curve rises from 150 to 350, **the area between 150 and 250 is SMALLER than the area between 250 and 350**.

- In other words, since 15% is half of 30%, the area between 150 and 250 represents LESS than 15% of the area under the curve.

- Thus, **a value of 250 represents LESS than 25% of the distribution**, because 150 is the value at the 10th percentile of the distribution and less than 15% of the distribution lies between the values 150 and 250:

$$10\% + \text{LESS than } 15\% = \text{LESS than } 25\%$$

> Graphically, we can depict this relationship like so:

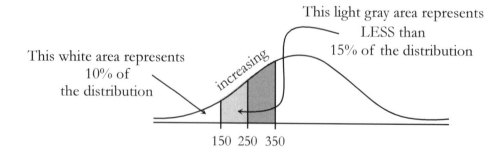

- If less than 25% of the distribution lies to the left of the 250, the value at the 25% of the distribution must be greater than 250. Therefore, the correct answer is (A).

(10) Peaks & Tails – Every now and then, the GRE will test your understanding of skewed distributions.

• In a normal distribution, the data "peaks" symmetrically about the center of the distribution, so the mean equals the median.

➤ In a skewed distribution, the data tends to produce a "peak" on one side of the distribution and a (relatively) long, thin "tail" on the other.

Here, the PEAK is on the LEFT   Here, the PEAK is on the RIGHT

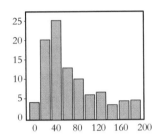   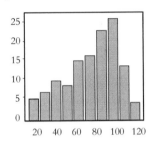

So the TAIL is on the RIGHT   So the TAIL is on the LEFT

• In such distributions the MEDIAN generally does NOT equal the MEAN.

➤ While there is no set relationship between the median and the mean in a skewed distribution, in almost all cases **"the MEAN follows the TAIL"**.

• Likewise, "the MEDIAN follows the PEAK". Thus, in the distribution below, notice how the mean is closer to the tail, and the median is closer to the peak:

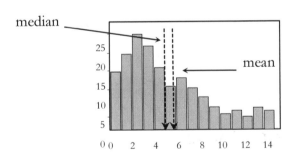

Median = 5, Mean = 5.83

• Is this always the case? No, but unless a data set involves an EXTREMELY odd distribution, which in our <u>experience</u> is never the case on the GRE, it's a very safe bet.

• To understand why the mean follows the tail, consider the following:

Chapter 2: Statistics

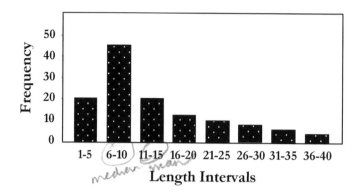

In a recent study, the lengths, in centimeters, of 130 worms were recorded and grouped into 7 intervals. The graph above shows the frequency distribution of the 130 lengths by interval.

Quantity A	Quantity B
The average (arithmetic mean) of the 130 lengths, in centimeters	The median of the 130 lengths, in centimeters

Answer: A. Because the 130 lengths have been grouped into intervals, we do not know their exact values. Thus, we cannot calculate the exact value of either the mean or the median.

➤ We do know, however, that the MEDIAN of the 130 lengths is the 65th measurement, when the data is grouped in order from least to greatest.

• From the diagram, you can see that the interval from 1 to 5 centimeters contains 20 worms and that the interval from 6 to 10 centimeters contains 45 worms. Thus, the median could equal anything from 6 to 10 centimeters, since the 65th measurement lies within this interval.

• The MEAN is a bit trickier to gauge. Imagine for a moment that the median is 10, its maximum possible value.

➤ The 64 measurements to the left of the median would range in value from 1 to 10, but the 64 measurements to the right of the median would range from 11 to 40.

• Like any weighted average, the LARGER of two groups always drags the average closer to itself. Because a group of 64 values ranging from 11 to 40 is CONSIDERABLY larger than a group of 64 values ranging from 1 to 10, the average of the distribution must be a LOT closer to a value from 11 to 40 than it is to a value from 1 to 10.

• Since the median only has a value from 6 to 10, the mean is therefore the greater value. The correct answer must be (A).

Sherpa
Prep

(11) Maximization Problems – Some of the trickiest statistics questions involve scenarios in which some value must be maximized (or minimized).

- Here's an example:

In a company of 20 employees, 3 employees have no sick days, 6 employees have 1 sick day, 7 employees have 2 sick days, and the rest have 3 or more sick days. If the average (arithmetic mean) number of sick days per employee is 2, what is the greatest number of sick days that any single employee could have?

(A) 3   (B) 4   (C) 7   (D) 11   (E) 13

- For the most part, maximization problems are easy to spot, since they almost always contain phrases such as **greatest**, **maximum**, **smallest**, or **least**.

  ➤ To solve them, simply consider the OPPOSITE possibility. For example, to MAXIMIZE one possibility, MINIMIZE another.

- Likewise, to minimize one possibility, maximize another.

- In the problem above, we need to determine the **greatest** number of sick days that a single employee could have. To do so, we'll need to **minimize** the sick days of the other employees.

  ➤ According to the problem, the company has 20 employees and the average number of sick days that each employee has is 2. Thus, the company has 40 total sick days.

- If 3 employees have no sick days, 6 employees have 1 sick day, and 7 employees have 2 sick days, then **16 employees account for 20 of the 40 sick days**, since:

$$3(0) + 6(1) + 7(2) = 6 + 14 = 20$$

- The other 20 sick days, therefore, must be split among the 4 employees that have "3 or more sick days".

  ➤ **To maximize** the number of sick days that any one of these 4 employees could have, **we need to minimize** the sick days of the other 3.

- If 3 of the 4 employees each have 3 sick days (the smallest number possible), they would account for 9 of the 20 sick days. The correct answer is therefore (D), since the fourth employee would then be responsible for all 11 of the remaining sick days.

➢ To give you a bit more practice, here's a second example:

**A certain distribution consists of 13 different integers, of which the
median and range are both 20.**

	Quantity A		Quantity B
The greatest possible integer in
the distribution	34		35

Answer: B. According to the problem, the distribution contains 13 distinct integers and has
a MEDIAN of 20.

➢ Thus, 6 of the integers must be SMALLER than 20 and 6 of the integers must be
LARGER than 20.

• Furthermore, if the RANGE of the distribution is 20, then the difference between the
smallest and the largest of these integers must be 20.

• To determine the distribution's largest possible integer, **we need to make its smallest
integer as large as possible**. After all, the largest integer in the set will be 20 more than the
smallest integer.

➢ In other words, to make the largest integer as large as possible, we need the smallest
integer to be as large as possible, too.

• If 20 is the median of the set, and 6 integers must be smaller than 20, then the 6 *different*
integers that will make **the smallest integer as large as possible** must be 14, 15, 16, 17, 18,
and 19.

• Other options – such as 13, 14, 15, 16, 17, and 18, or 13, 14, 15, 16, 17, and 19 – contain 6
integers smaller than 20, but have **smaller minimums** than required by the problem.
Remember, the integers must have a range of 20.

➢ Thus, if 14 is the largest minimum possible and the distribution's range is 20, then its
largest possible integer must be 34, since 14 + 20 = 34.

• Because Quantity A equals 34, the correct answer is therefore (B).

(12) The Weighted Average Shortcut – Imagine a quiz on which the girls had an average score of 90, the boys an average score of 81, and the class an average score of 84.

• Now imagine that you needed to determine what percentage of the class was girls or what percentage of the class was boys.

➢ Although there are several ways to answer such questions, the EASIEST way is with a three-step technique that we call the ⟨ **Weighted Average Shortcut** ⟩.

• To start, draw a NUMBER LINE between the INDIVIDUAL averages.

• Here, the GIRLS have an average score of 90 and the BOYS have an average score of 81, so a number line between those averages would look as follows:

➢ Next, SPLIT the number line into two sections by plotting the COMBINED average of the two groups.

• The number line above has a total of 9 spaces, so plotting the class average of 84 splits it into sections of 3 and 6 spaces, like so:

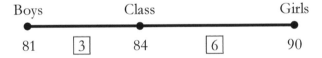

➢ Once split, the LONGER section of the number line will tell you what percentage of the weighted average comes from the "LARGER" group.

• Likewise, the SHORTER section will tell you what percentage comes from the "SMALLER" group.

• Here, for example, we know that the LARGER group of students represents 67% of the class, since the LONGER section spans 6/9 of the number line. Similarly, we know that the SMALLER group of students represents 33% of the class, since the SHORTER section spans 3/9 of the number line.

- <u>As a LAST step</u>, look back at the number line to see which end of the number line is "pulling" the COMBINED average more.

  ➤ **Since a weighted average is essentially a "TUG-OF-WAR", the LARGER of <u>two</u> groups will always drag the average CLOSER to itself.**

- In this example, the boys are the larger group of students, since the boys are winning the tug-of-war. As we can see, the class average, at 84, is closer to the boys' average than to the girls' average:

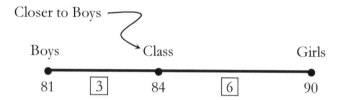

- Thus, we know that 67% of the class is boys, since boys are the larger group. Likewise, we know that 33% of the class is girls, since girls are the smaller group.

  ➤ To ensure that you've got the hang of it, let's work through a practice problem together.

- Consider the following:

When John bowls during the day, he has an average score of 195. When he bowls at night, he has an average score of 220. If John's average bowling score is 210, what percent of John's games are bowled at night?

(A) 25% (B) 33% (C) 40% (D) 60% (E) 67%

Answer: D. According to the problem, John's average score during the **day** is 195, his average score at **night** is 220, and his **combined** average is 210. This information can be represented on a number line as follows:

```
    Day              Combined        Night
    ●─────────────────●──────────────●
    195      15      210      10     220
```

  ➤ As we can see, the number line has 25 spaces, so John's combined average splits it into sections of 15 spaces and 10 spaces.

- Because, the LONGER section spans 15/25 of the number line, the LARGER group of games represents 60% of all of John's games.

• Likewise, the SHORTER section spans 10/25 of the number line, so the SMALLER group of games represents 40% of all of John's games.

➢ We can also see that "night" is WINNING the tug-of-war, since John's combined average, at 210, is closer to "night" than to "day".

• Thus, **John's night games are the larger group of games**:

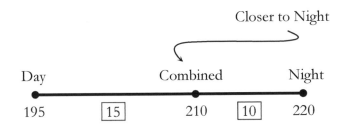

➢ Because the longer section of the number line represents the larger of the two groups, we therefore know that 60% of all John's games are bowled at night.

• Thus, the correct answer is (D).

• If the question had asked us what percentage of the John's games are bowled during the day, the answer would have been 40%, since "day" is losing the tug-of-war, and the shorter section, which equals 40% of this number line, always refers to the smaller of the two groups.

(13) Counting & Adding Equally Spaced Numbers – Imagine that you needed to COUNT every multiple of 7 from 14 to 294, or to ADD every odd number from 61 to 99.

• Could you do so in less than a minute? If not, the most difficult questions involving equally spaced number sets will be hard for you to solve.

> ➤ Although counting every multiple of 7 from 14 to 294 in under 60 seconds might seem like an impossible task, it's actually fairly easy to do.

• To start, get the difference between the FIRST and LAST terms. Then, DIVIDE the difference by the INTERVAL between the terms.

• Since the difference between 294 and 14 is 280, and the interval between multiples of 7 is 7 (every multiple of 7 is 7 bigger than the multiple before it), we get $280 \div 7 = 40$.

> ➤ Finally, ADD 1 to the result. We add 1 because both 14 and 294 are INCLUDED in the numbers we're counting.

• If we just get the difference of 294 and 14, we're forgetting to count 14, since we're subtracting it out (along with the numbers from 1 to 13).

• Thus, there are 41 multiples of 7 from 14 to 294, since $40 + 1 = 41$.

> ➤ If this seemed easy, then there's good news: We can do the same thing to count other equally spaced numbers sets, too.

• In fact, we can summarize the process as follows:

$$\frac{\textbf{Difference of the First and Last Terms}}{\textbf{Interval}} + 1$$

• To be sure that you've got the hang of it, let's count the number of even integers from 32 to 118. Since the difference of the first and last terms is $118 - 32 = 86$, and the interval between even integers is 2 (every even number is 2 bigger than the even number before it), there are 44 even integers from 32 to 118, as:

$$\frac{118 - 32}{2} + 1 \quad \rightarrow \quad \frac{86}{2} + 1 = 43 + 1 = 44$$

➢ Finding the SUM of an equally spaced number set is almost as easy. To prove it, let's ADD every odd integer from 61 to 99.

• To start, COUNT the number of terms in the set. Because the difference of 99 and 61 is 38, and the interval between odd integers is 2, there are 20 odd numbers from 61 to 99, as:

$$\frac{99-61}{2}+1 \quad \rightarrow \quad \frac{38}{2}+1=20$$

• Then get the AVERAGE of the set. The average of an equally spaced number set equals the average of its first and last terms, so the average of this set must be 80, since:

$$\frac{61+99}{2}=80$$

➢ Finally, multiply the NUMBER of terms by their AVERAGE to get the SUM of the set. Why? Think back to the average formula:

$$\frac{S}{N}=A \quad \rightarrow \quad S=N \times A$$

• The sum of a set of numbers equals the number of terms times their average. Thus, the SUM of EVERY equally spaced number set equals:

The Number of Terms × The Average of Set

• The sum of every odd integer from 61 to 99 is therefore 1,600, since there are 20 terms within the set and their average value is 80:

$$20 \times 80 = 1,600$$

➢ To be sure that you've got the hang of it, let's get the sum of every multiple of 3 from 30 to 90.

• Because the difference of 90 and 30 is 60, and the interval between multiples of 3 is 3, there are 21 odd numbers from 61 to 99, since:

$$\frac{90-30}{3}+1 \quad \rightarrow \quad \frac{60}{3}+1=21$$

• The average of the first and last terms is $(30 + 90) \div 2 = 60$, so the average of the entire set is also 60. Thus, the sum of the set is 1,260, as:

$$21 \times 60 = 1,260$$

➤ On occasion, you may notice that the END numbers of a number set are NOT examples of the multiple in question.

• To count such sets, simply find the SMALLEST and LARGEST multiples <u>within</u> the set. Then use them as the first and last terms.

• Consider the following:

What is the sum of every multiple of 9 between 30 and 208?

(A) 2,421 (B) 2,430 (C) 2,439 (D) 2,448 (E) 2,457

Answer. B. To start, notice that the question specifies the integers **between** 30 and 208. The word "between" indicates that 30 and 208 are NOT included among the numbers. Thus, the integers in question start at 31 and end at 207.

➤ To count the multiples of 9 from 31 to 207, we need to find the smallest and largest examples within the set.

• The **smallest** is 36, since 31, 32, 33, 34, and 35 are not multiples of 9. The **largest** is 207, since the sum of its digits is divisible by 9.

• In this set, the **first** multiple of 9 is 36 and the **last** multiple of 9 is 207. Thus, there are 20 multiples of 9 between 30 and 208, since:

$$\frac{207 - 36}{9} + 1 \quad \rightarrow \quad \frac{171}{9} + 1 = 20$$

➤ Because the **average** of these multiples is $(36 + 207) \div 2$, their **sum** must be 2,430, since:

$$20 \times \frac{36 + 207}{2} \quad \rightarrow \quad 10 \times (36 + 207) = 2,430$$

• The correct answer is therefore (B).

(14) Problem Sets – The following questions have been arranged into three groups: fundamental, intermediate, and rare or advanced.

• Whether you're aiming for a perfect score or a score closer to average, mastery of the concepts in the FUNDAMENTAL questions is absolutely essential.

➢ As you might expect, the INTERMEDIATE questions are more difficult but are essential for test-takers who need an above-average score or higher.

• Finally, the RARE or ADVANCED questions test concepts that are very sophisticated or seldom encountered on the GRE. Mastery of such questions is required only if you need a math score above the 90th percentile.

• As always, if you find yourself confused, bogged down with busy work, or stuck, don't be afraid to fall back on your "Plan B" strategies!

> Fundamental

The average (arithmetic mean) of n, p, and 8 is 6.

Quantity A	ⓒ	Quantity B

1. $\dfrac{n+p}{2}$ 5

Hours Studied per Day	0	1	2	3	4+
Number of Days	17	31	23	12	7

2. Last fall, Kyle had 90 days to study. For each of the amounts shown in the top row of the table above, the bottom row gives the number of days that Kyle studied that amount. What is the median number of hours that Kyle studied per day last fall?

(A) 1   (B) 1.5   (C) 2   (D) 2.5   (E) 3

Three consecutive integers have a sum of –42.

Quantity A	Quantity B

3. The least of the three integers   –13

4. This month, Celine purchased 12 books weighing an average (arithmetic mean) of $2\frac{7}{12}$ pounds. Last month, she purchased 6 books weighing an average of $1\frac{5}{6}$ pounds. What was the average weight, in pounds, of all the books that Celine purchased during both months?

   (A) $1\frac{3}{4}$ (B) $2\frac{1}{6}$ (C) $2\frac{1}{3}$ (D) $2\frac{4}{5}$ (E) $3\frac{3}{8}$

   A student has test scores of 75, a, and b, respectively, and an average (arithmetic mean) score of 85 on the three tests.

Quantity A		Quantity B
	c	

5. The average (arithmetic mean) of a and b 90

6. A list of numbers has a mean of 12 and a standard deviation of 3. If n is a number in the list that is 1.5 standard deviations above the mean, what is the value of n?

   16.5

   In a set of 18 positive integers, 9 of the integers are less than 30. The rest are greater than 30.

Quantity A		Quantity B
	D	

7. The median of the 18 integers   30

8. The average of two numbers is $2r$. If one of the numbers is s, the other number must be

   (A) $r + s$ (B) $2r + s$ (C) $4r + s$ (D) $2r - s$ (E) $4r - s$

Quantity A		Quantity B
	c	

9. The standard deviation of a set of 8 different integers, each of which is between 10 and 30   The standard deviation of a set of 8 different integers, each of which is between 20 and 40

   20   20

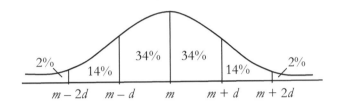

Classes A and B, which have no common students, will merge to form class C. The average (arithmetic mean) age of the students of class A is 16.2 years and the average age of the students of class B is 17.1 years. The average age of the students of class C will be 16.7 years.

Quantity A	Quantity B
The number of students in class A	The number of students in class B

10.

11. The normal distribution above has a mean of 11.2 and a standard deviation of 1.6. What percentage of the data has a value greater than 9.6?

(A) 14%   (B) 16%   (C) 34%   (D) 68%   (E) 84%

12. A certain distribution has 80 measurements of weight, whose range is 14 ounces. If one of the measurements is 57.5 ounces, which of the following could be another of the 80 measurements, in ounces?

Indicate all such measurements.

A 43.0   B 51.0   C 63.0   D 71.0   E 78.0

13. The average (arithmetic mean) of five numbers is 13. After one of the numbers is removed, the average (arithmetic mean) of the remaining numbers is 16. What number has been removed?

(A) 1   (B) 6   (C) 11   (D) 24   (E) 31

Set S contains all the integers from 36 to 64.

Quantity A	Quantity B
The average (arithmetic mean) of set S	50

14.

Go back to 9

Intermediate

15. A certain company has 8 employees. It pays annual salaries of $16,000 to each of 3 employees, $18,000 to each of 2 employees, $22,000 to 1 employee, and $23,000 to each of the remaining 2 employees. The average (arithmetic mean) annual salary to these employees equals which of the following?

(A) $18,500   (B) $18,800   (C) $19,000   (D) $19,300   (E) $19,500

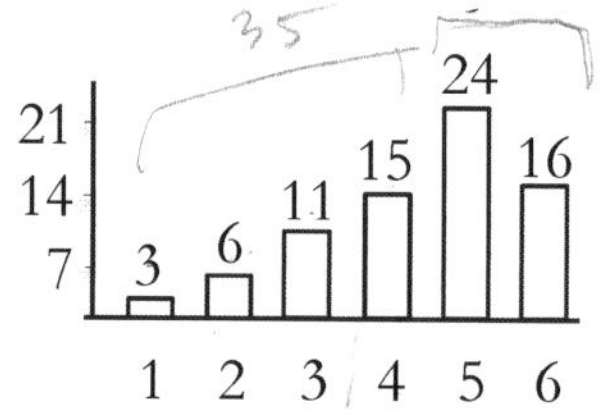

The graph above shows the frequency distribution of 75 measurements ranging from 1 to 6

	Quantity A	Quantity B
16.	The average (arithmetic mean) of the 75 values	The median of the 75 values

17. Which of the following numbers is NOT the sum of three consecutive even integers?

(A) 18   (B) 72   (C) 126   (D) 294   (E) 314

mislead problem

G is the median of the first 12 positive multiples of 7, and g is the arithmetic mean (average) of the first 12 positive multiples of 7.

	Quantity A		Quantity B
18.	G		g

19. Three-hundred adult cats were weighed for a recent study. Their weights had a mean of 12.4 pounds and a standard deviation of 4.8 pounds. How many standard deviations below the mean is a weight of 11.2 pounds?

(A) 0.25   (B) 0.40   (C) 0.55   (D) 0.80   (E) 1.25

20. For a population of 40,000 pedestrians, the number of taxi rides taken per pedestrian last year are approximately normally distributed with a mean of 28 trips and a standard deviation of 6 trips. Approximately how many of the pedestrians took between 16 and 22 trips last year?

(A) 2,500 (B) 5,500 (C) 7,500 (D) 10,000 (E) 13,500

21. A certain company has 40 employees, each of whom has a different salary. Phil's salary of $38,500 is the third-highest salary in the second quartile of the 40 salaries. If the company were to hire 8 new employees at salaries that are less than the lowest of the 40 salaries, what would Phil's salary be with respect to the quartiles of the 48 salaries at the company, assuming no other changes in the salaries?

(A) The fifth-highest salary in the first quartile
(B) The third-highest salary in the second quartile
(C) The second-lowest salary in the third quartile
(D) The fourth-highest salary in the third quartile
(E) The lowest salary in the fourth quartile

Frequency Distribution for List R

Number	1	2	3	5
Frequency	8	12	11	9

Frequency Distribution for List S

Number	6	7	8	9
Frequency	14	11	8	7

List R and list S each contain 40 numbers. Frequency distributions for each list are given above. The average (arithmetic mean) of the numbers in list R is 2.55, and the average of the numbers in list S is 7.2. List T contains 80 numbers: the 40 numbers in list R and the 40 numbers in list S.

Quantity A	Quantity B
The average of the 80 numbers in list T	The median of the 80 numbers in list T

22.

23. A list of measurements contains 8 values. If 4 were to be added to each value in the list, which of the following statistics would change?

Select all such measurements.

[A] The mean [B] The median [C] The mode [D] The range
[E] The interquartile range [F] The standard deviation

24. Data set S contains the values 5, 10, 15, 20, and 25. Which of the following, if inserted into set S would most decrease the standard deviation of set S?

(A) 0 (B) 5 (C) 15 (D) 20 (E) 25

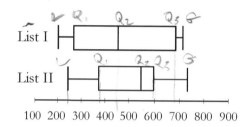

	Quantity A	Quantity B
25.	The range of data from the median to the third quartile of list I	The interquartile range of list II

26. A report consisting of S words has an average of 100 words per N paragraphs. If 2 new paragraphs add 150 words to the report, and the average number of words per paragraph decreases to 90, how many paragraphs does the altered version of the report consist of?

(A) 2 (B) 3 (C) 4 (D) 5 (E) 6

27. The average (arithmetic mean) of the set {10, 3, x, 12, and 7} is equal to its median. If x is the median of the set, what is the value of x?

Rare or Advanced

A random variable P is normally distributed with a mean of 120 and
a standard deviation of 30.

        Quantity A   Quantity B

28.   The probability of the event that the $\frac{6}{7}$

        value of P is between 60 and 150

29.   In a recent study, the average height of the male subjects was 70 inches and the
average height of the female subjects was 62 inches. If the average height of all the
subjects was 65 inches, what percent of the subjects was female?

62.5%

        Quantity A   Ⓒ   Quantity B   *distance* *+1*
                                                      interval

30.   The number of integers from 180   81   ↑
        through 900 that are multiples of 9   *forgot*

15 items of clothing were purchased from store S. The average (arithmetic mean)
sale price of the items was $140 and the median sale price was $120.

        Quantity A   Quantity B

31.   The minimum price at which the most $155
        expensive item could be purchased

x is a positive integer, and the average of the set of integers from
1 to x is 11.

Consecutive integers   *average = median*

        Quantity A   Quantity B

32.   The median of the set of integers =11   11
        from 1 to x

Ⓒ

33. A certain stock portfolio has 36 shares of stocks S and stock T, combined. Stock S is worth $40 per share and stock T is worth $80 per share. The average value per share in the portfolio is $70. How many shares of stock T does the portfolio hold?

27

A certain data set contains the values n_1, n_2, n_3, n_4, ..., n_{20}. For each value, the difference between the mean and that value is 3.

Quantity A	Quantity B
9	

34. The variance of the data set   6

35. The average (arithmetic mean) salary is $35,000 for the residents in tax bracket A and $60,000 for the residents in tax bracket B. If there are at least three times as many residents in tax bracket A as tax bracket B, which of the following amounts could be the average salary for all of the residents in tax brackets A and B?

Indicate all such amounts.

A $39,000 B $40,000 C $41,000 D $43,000 E $44,000

Got the average of 41,250 but realize as A becomes more numerous, makes average smaller

Set S contains the positive integers w, x, y, and z.
$w < x < y < z$, and $x + y = 2(w + z)$.

Quantity A		Quantity B
	C	

36. The median of set S The arithmetic mean of set S

cross-multiply

37. The sum of every odd multiple of 5 between 5 and 200 equals

not including

15 — 195 | 410
gap of 10 (every other multiple)

The random variable x is normally distributed. The values of x at the 55th, the 85th, and the kth percentiles of the distribution are 650, 850, and 750, respectively.

Quantity A	Quantity B

38. The value of k 70

(15) Solutions – Video solutions for each of the previous questions can be found on our website at **www.sherpaprep.com/videos**.

- BOOKMARK this address for future visits!

  ➤ To view the videos, you'll need the LOGIN and PASSWORD that you created upon registering your copy of Statistics & Data Interpretation.

- If you have yet to register your book yet, please go to **www.sherpaprep.com/activate** and enter your email address, last name, and shipping address.

- Be sure to provide the SAME last name and shipping address that you used to purchase your copy of Master Key to the GRE or to enroll in your GRE course with Sherpa Prep!

  ➤ When checking your answers, we encourage you to watch the solution for any problem that you answered INCORRECTLY

- The same goes for any problem that took you MORE than TWO MINUTES to solve.

- After digesting the explanation, REVISIT your mistake a couple of days later to ensure that the problem no longer poses issues to you.

  ➤ If you struggle to solve the problem a SECOND time, add it to your "LOG of ERRORS" and redo it every few weeks.

- Solving tricky questions MORE THAN ONCE is the best way to learn from your mistakes and to avoid similar difficulties on your actual exam.

Fundamental		Intermediate		Rare or Advanced	
1. C	11. E	15. C	25. A	28. B	38. A
2. A	12. B, C, D	16. B	26. D	29. 62.5	
3. B	13. A	17. E	27. 8	30. C	
4. C	14. C	18. C		31. A	
5. C		19. A		32. C	
6. 16.5		20. B		33. 27	
7. D		21. C		34. A	
8. E		22. B		35. A, B, C	
9. D		23. A, B, C		36. A	
10. B		24. C		37. 1,995	

Chapter 3

Combinatorics

Combinatorics

To be discussed:

Fundamental Concepts

Whether you're aiming for a perfect score or a score closer to average, mastery of the following concepts is essential.

1. Introduction
2. Counting
3. Factorials
4. Permutations
5. Duplicate Arrangements
6. Combinations
7. Separate Pools
8. Summary

Rare or Advanced Concepts

The following concepts are either advanced or are tested only on rare occasions. If you don't need an elite math score, don't waste your time!

9. "Must Be Together" Problems
10. Reverse Combinations
11. Circular Arrangements
12. "Fake Combinatorics" Questions
13. Special Notation
14. Slot Diagrams for Combinations

Practice Questions

There's no substitute for elbow grease. Practice your new skills to ensure that you internalize what you've studied.

15. Problem Sets
16. Solutions

Fundamental Concepts

(1) Introduction – Combinatorics, like Statistics, is a branch of mathematics that you may know little about.

- If you've never heard of it before, you're not alone. Combinatorics is rarely taught in high school, so most people who take the GRE haven't heard of it either.

  ➤ In essence, the term Combinatorics refers to the mathematics of counting, arranging, and grouping.

- To get a sense of what such math looks like, consider the following:

> **A class has 6 boys and 4 girls. How many ways can 4 students be selected if exactly 2 of the students must be girls?**

> **How many ways can the letters in the word "racecar" be arranged if every arrangement must be unique?**

- If these sorts of questions are unfamiliar to you, we've got some good news: Not only are they easy to solve, but they're also quite UNCOMMON for the GRE.

  ➤ In fact, no type of word problem is tested LESS frequently. As pointed out earlier, roughly $\frac{1}{3}$ of GRE questions are word problems.

- Of these, approximately 1 in 25 tend to involve Combinatorics. This means that your exam is UNLIKELY to have more than one example, if it has any at all.

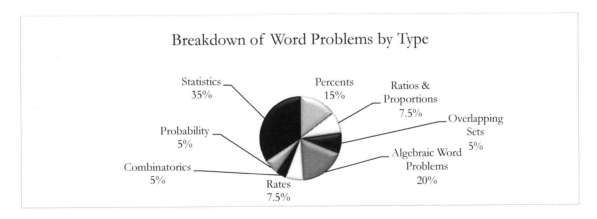

Breakdown of Word Problems by Type

- So unless you need a perfect score, your time may be better served studying more frequently tested topics. You can always circle back to this material once you've covered the critical stuff, should you want to.

(2) Counting – Imagine that you're planning a day out.

• You'd like to start with lunch, then do something fun, and finish with an evening activity.

> ➢ For lunch, you want sushi or empanadas. Afterwards, you'd like to kayak, golf, or go to the beach. In the evening, you want to go out with friends or watch a movie.

• Now imagine that you need to count how many possible outings you could have, given these options.

• One way you could do so is with a tree diagram, like this:

First pick a LUNCH: Then pick an ACTIVITY:

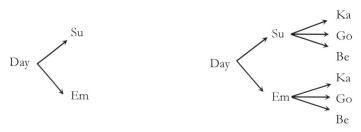

Then pick an EVENING activity:

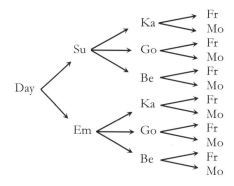

> ➢ Since the "tree" ends with a total of 12 "leaves", there are 12 ways to plan the day out.

• The drawback to such an approach, however, is that it's extremely tedious.

• Imagine that you had 5 ideas for lunch, 8 for entertainment, and 9 for the evening. Not only would your tree take several minutes to draw, it would require more than one sheet of paper!

➢ Fortunately, there is a very EASY way to count options. It's called the FUNDAMENTAL COUNTING PRINCIPLE.

• In short, this principle states:

If there are *m* ways to do one thing and *n* ways to do another, then there are *m* × *n* ways to do both.

• For example, a t-shirt company that makes shirts that come in 4 sizes and 5 colors can make a total of $4 \times 5 = 20$ different shirts, since every one of the 5 colors comes in 4 sizes. Likewise, a day out that consists of 5 options for lunch, 8 for entertainment, and 9 for the evening has 360 possible variations, since $5 \times 8 \times 9 = 40 \times 9 = 360$.

➢ If this seems easy to you, then there's GOOD news: this counting principle is ALL you need to solve plenty of Combinatorics questions on the GRE.

• Consider the following:

At a certain bank, every depositor has an ATM password that consists of two letters and four digits, in that order. How many different passwords are possible if the repetition of letters and digits is allowed?

(A) 234,000   (B) 608,400   (C) 676,000   (D) 6,084,000   (E) 6,760,000

Answer. E. The alphabet consists of 26 letters, so there are 26 ways to choose the first letter of a password at this bank.

➢ The same is true of the second letter, since the bank allows letters to be repeated. Thus, there are 676 ways to select the two letters of a password, since:

$$26 \times 26 = 676$$

• Similarly, the numeric system contains 10 digits (0 through 9), so there are 10 ways to select the first digit of a password at this bank. The same is true for each of the remaining digits, since the bank allows digits to be repeated. Thus, there are 10,000 ways to select the four digits of a password, as:

$$10 \times 10 \times 10 \times 10 = 10,000$$

➢ Since there are 676 ways to select the letters and 10,000 ways to select the digits, there are $676 \times 10,000 = 6,760,000$ ways to select a password at this bank.

• Note, by the way, **that this question can be solved just by counting the digits**. Since the 4 digits can be selected $10 \times 10 \times 10 \times 10$ ways, the answer had to end with 4 zeroes.

- A second example for you:

**A positive three-digit integer has a tens digit greater than 7
and a units digit less than 4.**

Quantity A	Quantity B
The number of possible three-digit integers that meet these criteria	**80**

Answer. B. Our numeric system has 10 digits (0 through 9). If the units digit must be less than 4, then there are 4 options for that digit: 3, 2, 1, and 0. Likewise, if the tens digit must be greater than 7, then there are 2 options for that digit: 8 and 9.

The problem gives no restrictions for the hundreds digit. However, **a three-digit integer cannot begin with a 0**: a number such as 087 is properly written as 87. Thus, there are only 9 options for the hundreds digit: 1 through 9.

Since there are 9 options for the hundreds digit, 2 for the tens digit, and 4 for the units digit, the correct answer must be (B), as there are only 72 three-digit integers that meet the restrictions given above: $9 \times 2 \times 4 = 9 \times 8 = 72$

 ➤ Every now and then, you may run across a problem with HIDDEN OPTIONS. In particular, watch out for problems in which NOTHING must be selected.

- Consider the following:

A menu contains four salad options, five entrée options, and three dessert options. How many different meals can a customer order if he or she selects no more than one item from each category?

(A) 12   (B) 60   (C) 72   (D) 90   (E) 120

Answer. E. Although the menu contains 4 salads, 5 entrées, and 3 desserts, the phrase "if he or she selects no more than one from each category" indicates that a customer does not have to choose something from each category.

For example, a customer could order ice cream, pie, or cake, or NO dessert at all.

As such, there are really 5 salad options, 6 entrée options, and 4 dessert options, since **in each category a customer has the additional option of selecting nothing at all**. Thus, the correct answer is (E), since 120 different meals can be ordered, as $5 \times 6 \times 4 = 120$.

(3) Factorials – Expressions such as 5! and *n*! are known as FACTORIALS.

- The exclamation mark doesn't mean that the number is screaming at you.

  ➤ It's a SYMBOL we use to indicate the PRODUCT of every integer from that number down to 1.

- For example, $5! = 5 \times 4 \times 3 \times 2 \times 1$. Likewise, $3! = 3 \times 2 \times 1$. Variables are a bit trickier to express, but the notation *n*! equals:

$$n! = n \times (n-1) \times (n-2) \times (n-3) \ldots \times 1$$

- (For you math nerds out there, this particular notation of course assumes that *n* is greater than 4. If *n* were, say, to equal 4, then $n! = n \times (n-1) \times (n-2) \times 1$.)

  ➤ We encourage you to memorize the first six factorials. When doing so, learn the relationships in BOTH directions.

- It's useful to know that $4! = 24$ and $5! = 120$, but it can be just as useful to know that $24 = 4!$ or that $120 = 5!$:

$1! = 1$	$4! = 4 \times 3 \times 2 \times 1 = 24$
$2! = 2 \times 1 = 2$	$5! = 5 \times 4 \times 3 \times 2 \times 1 = 120$
$3! = 3 \times 2 \times 1 = 6$	$6! = 6 \times 5 \times 4 \times 3 \times 2 \times 1 = 720$

- You should also memorize $\boxed{0! = 1}$. The arithmetic behind this equation is abstract. Just know that if it didn't equal 1, some of the concepts and calculations to follow wouldn't work.

  ➤ When working with factorials, it's usually best to WRITE them OUT, especially if math isn't your forte.

- Imagine that you needed to determine $\frac{6!}{3!}$.

- A lot of test-takers assume this equals 2!, since $6 \div 3 = 2$. But this is WRONG. It actually equals 120, since:

$$\frac{6!}{3!} = \frac{6 \cdot 5 \cdot 4 \cdot \cancel{3} \cdot \cancel{2} \cdot \cancel{1}}{\cancel{3} \cdot \cancel{2} \cdot \cancel{1}} = 6 \cdot 5 \cdot 4 = 120$$

- ➤ To save time, try to IDENTIFY any terms that your factorials may SHARE with one another.

- For example, imagine that you needed to reduce $\frac{8!}{5!}$ or $\frac{11!}{9!}$.

- Rather than writing out such expressions in full, you could save time by writing them as follows:

$$\frac{8!}{5!} = \frac{8 \cdot 7 \cdot 6 \cdot \cancel{5!}}{\cancel{5!}} = 8 \cdot 7 \cdot 6 = 336 \qquad \frac{11!}{9!} = \frac{11 \cdot 10 \cdot \cancel{9!}}{\cancel{9!}} = 11 \cdot 10 = 110$$

- ➤ If the factorials get more COMPLICATED, you can always fall back on writing them out.

- Thus, $\frac{5!}{2!3!} = 15$, since:

$$\frac{5!}{2!3!} = \frac{5 \cdot 4 \cdot \cancel{3} \cdot \cancel{2} \cdot \cancel{1}}{2 \cdot 1 \cdot \cancel{3} \cdot \cancel{2} \cdot \cancel{1}} = \frac{20}{2} = 10$$

- If possible, though, look to save time by identifying common factorials, as we did above. Thus, $\frac{10!}{2!8!} = 45$ and $\frac{7!}{3!4!} = 35$, since:

$$\frac{10!}{2!8!} = \frac{10 \cdot 9 \cdot \cancel{8!}}{2 \cdot 1 \cdot \cancel{8!}} = \frac{90}{2} = 45 \qquad \frac{7!}{3!4!} = \frac{7 \cdot 6 \cdot 5 \cdot \cancel{4!}}{3 \cdot 2 \cdot 1 \cdot \cancel{4!}} = \frac{7 \cdot \cancel{6} \cdot 5}{\cancel{6}} = 35$$

(4) Permutations – A permutation is an arrangement in which the ORDER matters.

• Imagine that you wanted to arrange 3 books on a shelf. How many different ways could you do so? One way would be:

• But, you could also arrange them as follows:

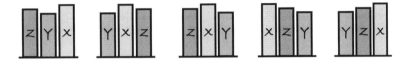

  ➤ Thus, there are 6 ways to arrange 3 books on a shelf. But what if you wanted to arrange 4 books, *W, X, Y,* and *Z*?

• Diagramming the options would be time consuming and a real pain. Fortunately, there's a SIMPLE way to count arrangements. To start, set up a SLOT DIAGRAM, like this:

— — — —

• In this case, our diagram has 4 slots, since we need to arrange 4 books.

  ➤ Next, fill each slot, ONE by ONE, with the number of POSSIBLE options for that slot.

• Here, we have **4** books to choose from, so there are 4 ways to select the first book:

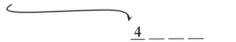

• Imagine that we put book *X* there. We would then only have **3** books that could go beside it:

➤ After choosing the first 2 books, we would then have 2 books left to pick from, so there are only **2** ways to select the third book:

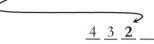

$$\underline{4}\ \ \underline{3}\ \ \underline{\textbf{2}}\ \ \underline{}$$

• Finally, just a single book would remain. Since there is only **1** way to select a single book, our diagram ends with a 1:

$$\underline{4}\ \ \underline{3}\ \ \underline{2}\ \ \underline{\textbf{1}}$$

• Because EACH slot in a slot diagram represents a set of OPTIONS, the Fundamental Counting Principle applies. Thus, there are exactly 24 ways to arrange 4 books, since $4 \times 3 \times 2 \times 1 = 24$.

➤ As you just saw, 4 objects can be arranged 4! ways. This is not accidental. As long as there are no restrictions, | ***n* objects can always be arranged *n*! ways** |.

• While you can ALWAYS use a slot diagram to arrange objects, it's quicker to arrange *n* objects *n*! ways if their arrangements are UNRESTRICTED.

• Consider the following:

At a certain assembly, an elementary school teacher has 6 students that she must arrange in a straight line. In how many different orders can she do so?

(A) 120   (B) 240   (C) 360   (D) 720   (E) 960

Answer: D. There are two ways to solve this problem. Let's start with a slot diagram. Because there are 6 students, we'll need 6 slots. There are 6 ways to choose the first student, 5 ways to choose the second, 4 ways to choose the third, and so forth. Thus, there are 720 different ways to arrange all 6 students, since:

$$\underline{6} \times \underline{5} \times \underline{4} \times \underline{3} \times \underline{2} \times \underline{1} = 720$$

Alternatively, because there are *n*! ways to arrange *n* objects without restriction, there must be 6! ways to arrange these 6 students, since the order of the students is not constrained in any way. $6! = 6 \times 5 \times 4 \times 3 \times 2 \times 1 = 720$, so there are 720 unique ways to arrange the students.

➢ Let's make things a little harder. Imagine that 5 friends want to sit on a bench, but that there is only space for 3 of them. How many arrangements would be possible?

• Whenever you work with arrangements, a slot diagram is ALWAYS a SAFE way to start. Here, the park bench only has space for 3, so our diagram should have 3 slots.

• Initially, 5 people can take the first seat. Once that seat is taken, 4 people can take the second. And once those seats are taken, 3 people can take the third. Therefore, there are 60 possible arrangements, since:

$$\underline{5} \times \underline{4} \times \underline{3} = 60$$

➢ Notice that the "Friends on the bench" problem is very similar to the "Books on the shelf" problem we saw earlier.

• The only difference is that "Friends on the bench" involves the arrangement of a SUBSET, whereas "Books on the shelf" involves the arrangement of the ENTIRE group.

• From a mathematical standpoint, however, the problems are identical. No matter how messy (or simple) an arrangement may seem, you can ALWAYS use a slot diagram to count out the possibilities. Consider the following:

A certain class has 4 boys and 5 girls. If 2 boys and 2 girls are arranged in a line ordered boy-girl-boy-girl, how many arrangements are possible?

(A) 36   (B) 80   (C) 240   (D) 360   (E) 400

Answer: C. To start, let's set up 4 slots: 2 for the boys and 2 for the girls. To keep track of which slots require boys and which slots require girls, let's label the slots as follows:

$$\overline{b} \quad \overline{g} \quad \overline{b} \quad \overline{g}$$

➢ Next, let's fill in the boys, one at a time. If there are 4 boys in the class, there are 4 ways to choose the first boy and 3 ways to choose the second:

$$\frac{4}{b} \quad \frac{}{g} \quad \frac{3}{b} \quad \frac{}{g}$$

• Then, let's fill in the girls. If there are 5 girls in the class, there are 5 ways to choose the first girl and 4 ways to choose the second:

$$\frac{4}{b} \times \frac{5}{g} \times \frac{3}{b} \times \frac{4}{g}$$

• Thus, the answer is (C), since there are $4 \times 5 \times 3 \times 4 = 20 \times 12 = 240$ possible arrangements.

> ➢ Let's make things harder one more time. What happens if an arrangement has RESTRICTIONS?

• The good news is that not a lot changes. The only wrinkle is that the RESTRICTED slots of a slot diagram MUST be filled FIRST!

• Imagine that 5 cars, each with its own color, are stopped in a line at a red light. How many ways could those cars be arranged, if the blue car is never last in line?

> ➢ To start, let's set up 5 slots and LABEL the restricted slots. Here, only the final slot is restricted, since the blue car can never be last in line:

$$\underline{\quad}\ \underline{\quad}\ \underline{\quad}\ \underline{\quad}\ \underset{\cancel{B}}{\underline{\quad}}$$

• Next, let's fill the restricted slot. Since there are 5 cars, and every car but the blue car can be last in line, there are 4 ways to choose the last car.

$$\underline{\quad}\ \underline{\quad}\ \underline{\quad}\ \underline{\quad}\ \underset{\cancel{B}}{\underline{4}}$$

• Finally, let's fill in the UNRESTRICTED slots.

> ➢ Once a car has been chosen for the final slot, 4 cars remain. So 4 cars can be selected for the first slot.

• Once that car has been chosen, then 3 cars remain for the next slot, and so on and so forth. Thus, the final 4 cars can be selected in 4, then 3, then 2, then 1 ways:

$$\underline{4} \times \underline{3} \times \underline{2} \times \underline{1} \times \underset{\cancel{B}}{\underline{4}}$$

• Thus, there are 96 possible arrangements, since $4! \times 4 = 24 \times 4 = 96$.

> ➢ To help you get a better feel for working with restrictions, let's work through a second example.

• Consider the following:

4 of the letters A, B, C, D, E, and F are to be selected at random.

Quantity A	Quantity B
The number of ways the selections can be arranged if neither the letter A nor the letter D begin or end the arrangement	144

• Since we are looking to arrange 4 letters, we'll need 4 slots. The first and the last slots cannot contain the letters A or D, so let's label the restrictions as follows:

➤ Next, let's fill the RESTRICTED slots. If neither the A nor the D can appear in the first position, the first slot has 4 options: B, C, E, and F.

• Likewise, if neither the A nor the D can appear in the last position either, the last slot must have 3 options: B, C, E, and F, minus whichever letter was assigned to the first slot.

$$\underset{\cancel{AD}}{\underline{4}} \quad \underline{} \quad \underline{} \quad \underset{\cancel{AD}}{\underline{3}}$$

• Finally, let's fill the UNRESTRICTED slots.

➤ Now that 2 letters have already been selected, the second slot must have **4** options: A through F, minus whichever letters were assigned to slots 1 and 4.

• Similarly, the third slot must have **3** options: A through F, minus whichever letters were assigned to slots 1, 2, and 4:

$$\underset{\cancel{AD}}{\underline{4}} \times \underline{4} \times \underline{3} \times \underset{\cancel{AD}}{\underline{3}}$$

• Thus, there are 144 ways that the letters A through F can be arranged given the stated restrictions, since $4 \times 4 \times 3 \times 3 = 12 \times 12 = 144$. Since the two quantities are equal, the correct answer is therefore (C).

(5) Duplicate Arrangements – As you now know, there are 6! ways to arrange the letters in the word CARPET, since it contains 6 letters.

- But how many unique ways are there to arrange the letters in the word PILLOW?

  ➤ Although PILLOW also has 6 letters, two of its letters are identical, so some of its arrangements will be duplicates.

- For example, the "lipowls" below may seem unique, since each starts with a different "L":

- In practice, however, the arrangements are the same because we can't tell which "L" is which simply by reading "lipowl".

  ➤ Fortunately, there's an EASY way to eliminate duplicate arrangements. You just have to DIVIDE them OUT.

- In the case of PILLOW, there are 6! ways to arrange the 6 letters. And there are 2! ways to arrange the two L's. Thus, there are 360 ways to arrange the letters in PILLOW, since:

$$\text{Total letters} \searrow$$
$$\frac{6!}{2!} = \frac{6 \cdot 5 \cdot 4 \cdot 3 \cdot \cancel{2}}{\cancel{2}} = (6 \cdot 5) \cdot (4 \cdot 3) = 30 \cdot 12 = 360$$
$$\text{Duplicate L's} \nearrow$$

- Dividing away the duplicate "L"s allows us to find the number of unique arrangements.

  ➤ Now imagine that you needed to determine the number of unique arrangements for the letters in PEPPERS.

- PEPPERS has 7 letters, so there are 7! ways to arrange them.

- However, it also has three P's and two E's. Since there are 3! ways to arrange the three P's and 2! ways to arrange the two E's, there are 420 ways to arrange the letters in PEPPERS, as:

$$\text{Total letters} \searrow$$
$$\text{Duplicate P's} \longrightarrow \frac{7!}{3!2!} = \frac{7 \cdot 6 \cdot 5 \cdot 4 \cdot \cancel{3}}{\cancel{3} \cdot 2 \cdot 1} = (7 \cdot 6) \cdot (5 \cdot 2) = 42 \cdot 10 = 420$$
$$\text{Duplicate E's}$$

(6) Combinations – In English, the word COMBINATION is used in two ways.

• When we say "my lunch was a combination of crackers, grapes, and pizza," it's not clear in which ORDER we ate the items.

➤ Such a statement could mean that we ate crackers, then grapes, and then pizza, or that we ate the three foods in an interchangeable order.

• However, when we say "the combination to my locker is 3-4-7," we indicate that the ORDER of the numbers MATTERS.

• We have to enter the numbers in that specific order, or the locker won't open.

➤ In Mathematics, the word COMBINATION has a technical meaning. It means that ORDER does <u>NOT</u> matter.

• If the order MATTERS, we use the word PERMUTATION.

• To get a better sense of the distinction, consider the letters *ABC*. There is only 1 **combination** of these letters, but there are 6 different **permutations**: *ABC, ACB, BAC, BCA, CAB,* and *CBA*.

➤ Like permutations, combinations are easy to solve. However, DISTINGUISHING the two can sometimes be DIFFICULT.

• Compare the problems below. See if you can figure out which one is a combination and which one is a permutation:

P   *C*

How many ways can 4 books be arranged from a collection of 7?   **How many ways can any 4 books be selected from a collection of 7?**

➤ If you thought the first was a permutation and the second a combination: you were right. How do we know?

• Although the questions are nearly identical, the first asks us to ARRANGE books and the second to SELECT them.

• The word "arrange" means "place in order", so the order of the books matters. The word "select" just means "choose" or "pick". Since the question doesn't specify that the order of the books is relevant, the order doesn't matter.

> Once you've identified a question as a combination, the hard part is over. Solving it will be EASY.

• Simply DIVIDE the factorial of the TOTAL group by the factorials of the group that IS selected and that ISN'T selected:

$$\frac{\text{Factorial of the } \textbf{TOTAL} \text{ group}}{\text{Factorial of the } \textbf{SELECTED} \text{ group} \times \text{Factorial of the } \textbf{UNSELECTED} \text{ group}}$$

• This sounds a lot worse than it is. Imagine that you want to select 2 of 6 friends to go with you to the movies. How many combinations can you select?

> Since 2 friends WILL be selected and 4 will NOT, there are 15 combinations of any 2 friends that you can choose, as:

Total friends

Selected

$$\frac{6!}{2!4!} = \frac{6 \cdot 5 \cdot \cancel{4!}}{2 \cdot 1 \cdot \cancel{4!}} = \frac{30}{2} = 15$$

Not Selected

• Likewise, imagine that you want to select 5 kittens from a litter of 7. Since 5 of the kittens will be selected and 2 will not, there are 21 ways you can do so, as:

Total kittens

Selected

$$\frac{7!}{5!2!} = \frac{7 \cdot 6 \cdot \cancel{5!}}{\cancel{5!} \cdot 2 \cdot 1} = \frac{42}{2} = 21$$

Not Selected

> To ensure that you've got the hang of it, let's work through a couple of sample questions together.

• Consider the following:

Set P consists of 6 objects.

Quantity A   **Quantity B**

The number of subsets of set   The number of subsets of set
P that consist of 1 object P that consist of 5 objects

• If 1 object is selected from a set of 6, then 5 of the objects in the set will not be selected. Thus, there are 6 ways to form a subset of 1 from set P, since:

$$\frac{6!}{1!5!} = \frac{6 \cdot \cancel{5!}}{1 \cdot \cancel{5!}} = 6$$

➤ Likewise, if 5 objects are selected from a set of 6, then 1 of the objects in the set will not be selected.

• Thus, there are 6 ways to form a subset of 5 objects from set P, since:

$$\frac{6!}{5!1!} = \frac{6 \cdot \cancel{5!}}{\cancel{5!} \cdot 1} = 6$$

• Because both quantities equal 6, the correct answer is (C). Note, however, **that this question can be solved without reducing the factorials**, since:

$$\frac{6!}{1!5!} \text{ is the same thing as } \frac{6!}{5!1!}$$

➤ A trickier example for you:

Oge is one of 6 employees, 3 of whom will be selected to form a committee. If Oge must be on the committee, how many committees are possible?

(A) 9   (B) 10   (C) 12   (D) 20   (E) 24

• If Oge must be on the committee, only 2 of the remaining 5 employees can be selected to join her. If 2 of these 5 are selected, then 3 of the 5 will not be selected. Thus, there are 10 possible committees, since:

$$\frac{5!}{2!3!} = \frac{5 \cdot 4 \cdot \cancel{3!}}{2 \cdot 1 \cdot \cancel{3!}} = \frac{20}{2} = 10$$

• The correct answer is therefore (B).

➢ On occasion, combination questions can be somewhat DIFFICULT to RECOGNIZE.

• Although there's no easy tip we can give you to help you "unmask" such problems, we can provide you with a couple of examples to give you a sense of what they can look like.

• Consider the following:

There are ten teams in a certain tournament. If each team in the tournament is to play each of the other teams in the tournament exactly once, and every match only features two teams, what is the total number of matches that will be played?

(A) 45 (B) 50 (C) 81 (D) 90 (E) 100

Answer. A. There are 10 teams in the tournament, and the order in which the teams play does not matter. Since every match will involve 2 of these teams and NOT involve 8 of them, there are 45 possible matches between any two teams:

$$\frac{10!}{2!8!} = \frac{10 \cdot 9 \cdot \cancel{8!}}{2 \cdot 1 \cdot \cancel{8!}} = 45$$

Since every team plays one another once, only 45 matches will be played. If every team were to play one another twice, 90 matches would be played.

Quantity A	**Quantity B**
The number of triangles that can be drawn using any 3 vertices of a pentagon	The number of hexagons that can be drawn using any 6 vertices of an octagon

Answer. B. A pentagon has 5 vertices (points). If a triangle is to be drawn from 3 of them, then 3 of the 5 points will be selected and 2 will not. Thus, there are 10 ways to draw a triangle from the points of a pentagon, since:

$$\frac{5!}{3!2!} = \frac{5 \cdot 4 \cdot \cancel{3!}}{\cancel{3!} \cdot 2 \cdot 1} = 10$$

An octagon has 8 vertices (points). If a hexagon is to be drawn from 6 of them, then 6 of the 8 points will be selected and 2 will not. Thus, there are 28 ways to draw a hexagon from the points of an octagon, since:

$$\frac{8!}{6!2!} = \frac{8 \cdot 7 \cdot \cancel{6!}}{\cancel{6!} \cdot 2 \cdot 1} = 28$$

The correct answer is therefore (B).

(7) Separate Pools – From time to time, combinatorics questions will include more than one pool of candidates to choose from.

• Imagine a pet store with 6 cats and 5 dogs. If 2 cats and 3 dogs are chosen at random, how many ways could the 5 animals be selected?

➢ Since the store has a total of 11 cats and dogs, you might be tempted to select the 5 animals like this: $\frac{11!}{5!6!}$.

• However, the cats and dogs each have SEPARATE pools, so you have to select each party SEPARATELY.

• In general, **the words "CHOOSE" and "SELECT" indicate that you have a combinations question**, so there are 15 ways to choose 2 of 6 cats and 10 ways to choose 3 of 5 dogs, since:

$$\text{CATS} \qquad\qquad \text{DOGS}$$
$$\frac{6!}{2!4!} = \frac{6 \cdot 5 \cdot \cancel{4!}}{2 \cdot 1 \cdot \cancel{4!}} = 15 \qquad\qquad \frac{5!}{3!2!} = \frac{5 \cdot 4 \cdot \cancel{3!}}{\cancel{3!} \cdot 2 \cdot 1} = 10$$

➢ Finally, to COMBINE the combinations, you need to MULTIPLY them together.

• Remember, the Fundamental Counting Principle: if there are m ways to do one thing and n ways to do another, then there are $m \times n$ ways to do both.

• Thus, there are 150 ways to choose 2 of 6 cats and 3 of 5 dogs, since $15 \times 10 = 150$.

➢ Likewise, imagine that you wanted to select 3 boys and 5 girls from a class with 4 boys and 7 girls.

• Because there are SEPARATE pools of boys and girls, you need to select each group separately.

• There are 4 ways to choose 3 of 4 boys and 21 ways to choose 5 of 7 girls, since:

$$\text{BOYS} \qquad\qquad \text{GIRLS}$$
$$\frac{4!}{3!1!} = \frac{4 \cdot \cancel{3!}}{\cancel{3!} \cdot 1} = 4 \qquad\qquad \frac{7!}{5!2!} = \frac{7 \cdot 6 \cdot \cancel{5!}}{\cancel{5!} \cdot 2 \cdot 1} = 21$$

• Thus, there are 84 ways to choose 3 of 4 boys and 5 of 7 girls, since $4 \times 21 = 84$.

> ➤ To ensure that you've got the hang of it, let's work through a couple of sample questions together.

- Consider the following:

Congress wishes to form a committee composed of three Democrats and two Republicans. The selection panel is considering six candidates for the three Democratic positions, and five candidates for the two Republican positions.

Quantity A	**Quantity B**
The number of distinct committees that the panel can select	**200**

Answer. C. According to the problem, there are TWO pools of candidates: 6 Democrats and 5 Republicans. Thus, we need to select each group SEPARATELY. There are 20 ways to select 3 of 6 Democrats and 10 ways to select 3 of 5 Republicans, as:

DEMOCRATS

$$\frac{6!}{3!3!} = \frac{6 \cdot 5 \cdot 4 \cdot \cancel{3!}}{3 \cdot 2 \cdot 1 \cdot \cancel{3!}} = 20$$

REPUBLICANS

$$\frac{5!}{3!2!} = \frac{5 \cdot 4 \cdot \cancel{3!}}{\cancel{3!} \cdot 2 \cdot 1} = 10$$

Therefore, there are 200 possible committees that the panel can select, since $20 \times 10 = 200$. Because the two quantities are equal, the correct answer is (C).

A certain company has 10 employees, of whom 6 are men and 4 are women. A 4-person committee is to be selected from these employees. If this committee is to have exactly 2 women on it, how many committees are possible?

(A) 24 (B) 90 (C) 100 (D) 150 (E) 210

Answer. B. If the 4-person committee is to have exactly 2 women on it, then the other 2 members must be men. Thus, to fill out the committee, the company must select 2 of the 6 men and 2 of the 4 women.

There are 15 ways to select 2 of 6 men and 6 ways to select 2 of 4 women, as:

MEN

$$\frac{6!}{2!4!} = \frac{6 \cdot 5 \cdot \cancel{4!}}{2 \cdot 1 \cdot \cancel{4!}} = 15$$

WOMEN

$$\frac{4!}{2!2!} = \frac{4 \cdot 3 \cdot \cancel{2!}}{2 \cdot 1 \cdot \cancel{2!}} = 6$$

Therefore, there are 90 possible committees that the company can select, since $15 \times 6 = 90$.

(8) Summary – As you've seen, Combinatorics math is not particularly difficult.

• If you can work with factorials and fill in a slot diagram, you can do the work. The real challenge is knowing "when to do what".

➤ When solving a Combinatorics problem, the first question you should ask yourself is "does the ORDER matter?"

• If the order DOES matter, you'll probably want to set up a SLOT DIAGRAM.

• Are there RESTRICTIONS? If so, fill out the most restricted slots first. Is there REPETITION? If so, divide it out.

➤ If the order DOESN'T matter, you're working with COMBINATIONS.

• Divide the TOTAL factorials by the factorials of the group that IS selected and that ISN'T selected.

• Is there MORE THAN ONE pool of candidates to choose from? If so, you have more than one combination. Solve each one separately and multiply the results together.

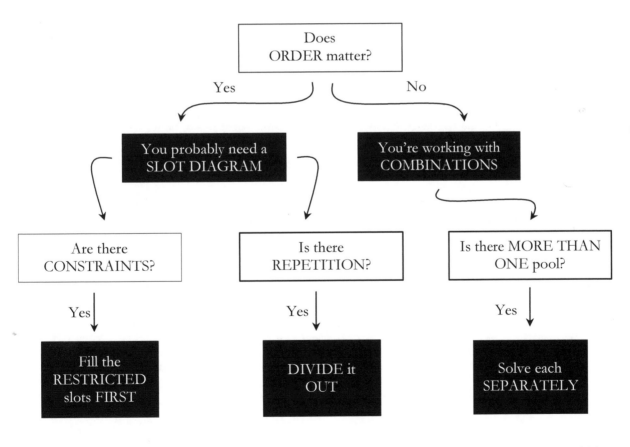

Rare or Advanced Concepts

(9) "Must Be Together" Problems – Imagine five friends, each with a unique name, standing in a straight line.

• How many ways can the friends be arranged, if two of the friends, Alice and Betty, must stand next to one another?

➤ "Must Be Together" problems are easily solved with a technique we like to call the **Monster Shortcut**.

• To start, FUSE the people who must be together into a monster with a SINGLE body but MULTIPLE heads.

• Then ARRANGE their BODIES. Here, there are 5 friends. If Alice and Betty were to share a single body, there would only be 4 bodies, which we can arrange 4! ways.

➤ Once you've arranged the bodies, ARRANGE the HEADS of the monster. The "Alice-Betty" monster has 2 heads, so we can arrange those heads 2! ways:

• As a last step, **multiply the arrangements for the bodies × the arrangements for the heads**. (Remember, if there are m ways to do one thing and n ways to do another, there are $m \times n$ ways to do both.)

• Because the bodies can be arranged 4! ways and the heads can be arranged 2! ways, there are 48 ways to arrange the friends if Alice and Betty must be together, since:

$$4! \times 2! = 24 \times 2 = 48$$

➤ Likewise, now imagine that there are seven friends in line, each with a unique name, but that Alice, Betty, and Carol must stand next to one another.

• If we fuse Alice, Betty, and Carol into a monster with a single body but 3 heads, there would only be 5 bodies (the other 4 friends + the monster), which we could arrange 5! ways.

• The "Alice-Betty-Carol" monster would have 3 heads, which we could arrange 3! ways. Thus, there are 720 ways to arrange the friends, since **the bodies × the heads** give us:

$$5! \times 3! = 120 \times 6 = 720$$

> ➤ If you need to determine the number of ways that people <u>CAN'T BE TOGETHER</u>, simply determine the number of ways that they MUST be together.

- Then SUBTRACT this total from the number of UNRESTRICTED arrangements, like this:

$$\underset{\text{Arrangements}}{\text{UNRESTRICTED}} - \text{MUST be Together} = \text{CAN'T be Together}$$

- To get a sense of what we mean by this, consider the following:

Alexis, Bart, Cara, Dave, Eric, and Faye form a conga line. If Cara, Dave, and Eric refuse to dance three-in-a-row, and no other dancers join in, how many different conga lines could be formed?

(A) 21^2 (B) 22^2 (C) 23^2 (D) 24^2 (E) 25^2

- To start, let's imagine that Cara, Dave, and Eric "must be together".

  > ➤ If we fuse them into a monster with a single body but 3 heads, the conga line would have 4 bodies, which we would could arrange 4! ways.

- The "Cara-Dave-Eric" monster would have 3 heads, which we could arrange 3! ways. Thus, there are 144 ways that Cara, Dave, and Eric must be together, since **the bodies × the heads**:

$$4! \times 3! = 24 \times 6 = 144$$

  > ➤ Next, let's imagine that the conga line had no restrictions. The line has 6 people, so it has 6! possible arrangements.

- The number of arrangements in which Cara, Dave, and Eric can't be together equals the number of unrestricted arrangements minus the arrangements in which they must be together. Thus, a total of 576 conga lines could be formed, since:

$$6! - 144 = 720 - 144 = 576$$

- Because $24^2 = 576$, the correct answer must therefore be (D).

(10) Reverse Combinations – On rare occasion, you may come across a combination problem in which you need to work "in reverse".

- Imagine that there are 28 ways to select any 2 students from a certain class. How many students are in the class?

  ➢ In a typical combination question, you know the size of the pool from which to select candidates, but not the number of combinations.

- In a reverse combination question like this, you know the number of combinations, but not the size of the pool.

- To solve such questions, first WRITE OUT what you're given. Here, if n = size of the pool and $n - 2$ = the number of candidates NOT selected, we have:

$$\frac{n!}{2!(n-2)!} = 28$$

  ➢ Next, REWRITE $n!$. As you may recall, $n! = n(n-1)(n-2) \ldots \times 1$. Another way of writing this is $n \times (n-1) \times (n-2)!$.

- If this seems strange to you, think about it with numbers rather than variables. $5! = 5 \times 4 \times 3!$. Thus, $n \times (n-1) \times (n-2)!$.

- Finally, SIMPLIFY the resulting equation. Since, $2! = 2 \times 1 = 2$, first we can multiply both sides of this equation by 2. Then we can CANCEL the $(n-2)$'s:

$$\frac{n!}{2!(n-2)!} = 28 \quad \rightarrow \quad \frac{n!}{(n-2)!} = 56 \quad \rightarrow \quad \frac{n(n-1)\cancel{(n-2)!}}{\cancel{(n-2)!}} = 56$$

  ➢ If $n(n-1) = 56$, there are two ways we can solve for n. The FASTEST way is to recognize that n and $n-1$ represent CONSECUTIVE numbers.

- Thus, $n = 8$, since $8 \times 7 = 56$. Alternatively, you can solve $n(n-1) = 56$ as a QUADRATIC equation:

$$n^2 - n = 56$$
$$n^2 - n - 56 = 0$$
$$(n-8)(n+7) = 0 \quad \rightarrow \quad n = 8, -7$$

- Because n represents STUDENTS, it cannot be negative. Therefore, the class has 8 students.

> ➤ Since the Algebra at the end can get difficult and time consuming, it's highly UNLIKELY that the GRE would select a subset greater than 2.

- To understand why, imagine that the previous previous question had stipulated that there are 20 ways to select any 3 students from the class. The math would have been:

$$\frac{n!}{3!(n-3)!} = 20 \quad \rightarrow \quad \frac{n!}{(n-3)!} = 120 \quad \rightarrow \quad \frac{n(n-1)(n-2)\cancel{(n-3)!}}{\cancel{(n-3)!}} = 120$$

- However, guessing which 3 consecutive integers multiply to 120 is pretty difficult (hint: 4, 5, 6), as is solving the equation $n(n-1)(n-2) = 120$. Remember, the GRE is testing your "quantitative reasoning", not your ability to solve complex, time-consuming equations.

> ➤ As such, there is a simple FORMULA that you can use to solve reverse combinations, since the subset in such questions is almost ALWAYS two:

$$C = \frac{n(n-1)}{2}$$

- Let's go back to the initial question. If there are 28 ways to select any 2 students from a certain class, then that class has 8 students, since:

$$28 = \frac{n(n-1)}{2} \quad \rightarrow \quad 56 = n(n-1) \quad \rightarrow \quad 56 = 8 \times 7, \text{ so } n = 8$$

- Likewise, if there are 45 ways to select any 2 letters from a certain word, then that word has 10 letters, since:

$$45 = \frac{n(n-1)}{2} \quad \rightarrow \quad 90 = n(n-1) \quad \rightarrow \quad 90 = 10 \times 9, \text{ so } n = 10$$

> ➤ This formula is worth remembering for another reason: a LARGE number of REGULAR combinations have subsets of 2, too.

- Thus, if you have to choose 2 of 5 items, or 2 of 7 items, you could do the math as follows, rather than reduce the factorials:

<u>Choose 2 of 5 items</u>

$$\frac{n(n-1)}{2} = \frac{5(4)}{2} = 10 \text{ ways}$$

<u>Choose 2 of 7 items</u>

$$\frac{n(n-1)}{2} = \frac{7(6)}{2} = 21 \text{ ways}$$

(11) Circular Arrangements – Imagine a family of four sitting around a circular dinner table.

• How many ways can the family be arranged? You might be tempted to say 4! ways, since the family has 4 members.

> ➢ While this is true of arrangements in a LINE, it is NOT true of arrangements in a CIRCLE.

• To understand why, consider the arrangement of the letters *A*, *B*, *C*, and *D*. In a linear arrangement, the following orders would be considered unique:

$$A \ B \ C \ D \qquad B \ C \ D \ A \qquad C \ D \ A \ B \qquad D \ A \ B \ C$$

> ➢ In a circular arrangement, however, such orders would be considered DUPLICATES, since the order $\underline{A} \ \underline{B} \ \underline{C} \ \underline{D}$ can be rotated to form any of the other three:

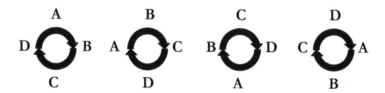

• As with any repetitive arrangement, we can eliminate the duplicate arrangements by DIVIDING them OUT. To do so, simply place the number of linear arrangements over the number of objects in the circle:

$$\frac{\text{Number of LINEAR Arrangements}}{\text{Objects in the CIRCLE}}$$

> ➢ Thus, there are 6 ways a family of 4 can be arranged around a circular dinner table, since:

$$\frac{4!}{4} = \frac{24}{4} = 6$$

• Likewise, there are 24 ways a family of 5 can be arranged around a circular dinner table, since:

$$\frac{5!}{5} = \frac{120}{5} = \frac{240}{10} = 24$$

> ➢ To ensure that you've got the hang of it, let's work through a sample question together.

• Consider the following:

A designer has 7 beads, each of a different color, from which to make a bracelet. If that bracelet is to have exactly 4 beads, how many different bracelets can the designer arrange?

(A) 180 (B) 210 (C) 420 (D) 630 (E) 840

• Since a bracelet is a circular arrangement, we first need to determine the number of ways the designer can arrange 4 of 7 beads in a line.

> ➢ To do so, let's use a slot diagram. Because the arrangement will have 4 beads, we'll need 4 slots.

• There are 7 beads to choose from, so there are 7 ways to choose the first bead, 6 ways to choose the second, and so forth.

• Thus, there are $7 \times 6 \times 5 \times 4$ ways to arrange 4 of 7 beads in a line, since:

$$\underline{7} \times \underline{6} \times \underline{5} \times \underline{4}$$

> ➢ Next, we need to divide the number of linear arrangements by the number of objects in the circle.

• Because the bracelet will have 4 beads, the circle will have 4 objects. Therefore, the designer can arrange 210 different bracelets, as:

$$\frac{7 \times 6 \times 5 \times \cancel{4}}{\cancel{4}} = 7 \times 30 = 210$$

• Thus, the correct answer is (B).

(12) "Fake Combinatorics" Questions – Every now and then, the GRE will design questions that seem to involve Combinatorics, but don't.

• Like Combinatorics questions, such questions often ask how many ways a group of objects can be counted, grouped, or distributed.

➢ Unlike Combinatorics questions, however, these "imposters" essentially ask "WHO GETS WHAT?"

• In some cases, you may need to distribute a stack of dollar bills among several friends. In others, you may need to distribute passengers among a group of cars.

• Whatever the specifics may be, such problems boil down to a matter of "who gets what."

➢ To solve them, you have to consider OPPOSITE scenarios.

• For example, you might try to distribute things EVENLY, then make the distribution as LOPSIDED as possible. Or you might try to maximize one group and minimize another, and then try the reverse.

• To get a sense of what we mean by this, consider the following:

Seven red coins are to be distributed among three friends so that each person receives at least one red coin.

Quantity A	**Quantity B**
The number of ways to distribute the coins so that at least one friend receives at least 3 coins	The total number of ways to distribute the coins

• To understand how the coins can be distributed, let's consider two scenarios: the most uneven distribution possible, and the most even distribution possible.

➢ According to the problem, all 3 friends get at least 1 coin. Thus, the most UNEVEN distribution would give 1 coin to 2 of the friends, and the other 5 coins to the third.

• Conversely, the most EVEN distribution would give 2 coins to all 3 friends, and the remaining coin to 1 of the 3 friends.

• In each scenario, 1 person ALWAYS ends up with 3 or more coins. Hence, the correct answer is (C), since EVERY possible distribution (Quantity B) involves AT LEAST ONE person receiving 3 or more coins (Quantity A).

➢ To ensure that you've got the hang of it, let's work through a second sample question together.

• Consider the following:

6 cars were used to transport the members of a baseball team to their game. Some of the members were transported in a group of 4 and others were transported in a group of 3. Which of the following could represent the number of members on the team?

Select all such numbers.

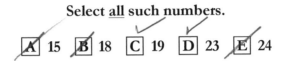

⬛A 15 ⬛B 18 ⬛C 19 ⬛D 23 ⬛E 24

• To get a sense of how many people could be on the team, let's consider two scenarios: one in which as many cars as possible carried 4 team members, and one in which as few cars as possible carried 4 team members.

➢ According to the problem, there are 6 cars, some of which contained 4 team members and others that contained 3 team members.

• This information IMPLIES that at least one car contained 4 team members and that at least one car contained 3 team members.

• Since there are 6 cars, the GREATEST number of cars that could carry 4 team members would be 5. If 5 cars carried 4 team members and the remaining car carried 3 team members, the team would have 23 members, since $5(4) + 1(3) = 23$.

➢ Conversely, the LEAST number of cars that could carry 4 team members would be 1.

• If 1 car carried 4 team members and the remaining 5 cars carried 3 team members, the team would have 19 members, since $1(4) + 5(3) = 19$.

• Because the team can have as few as 19 members and as many as 23 members, the only correct answers are ⬛C and ⬛D .

Chapter 3: Combinatorics

(13) Special Notation – On very rare occasions, Combinatorics questions feature a special sort of notation.

- Given n objects, the notation $\binom{n}{r}$ represents the number of ways that r of those objects can be selected or arranged.

  ➤ For example, if a classroom has 6 students, there are $\binom{6}{2}$ ways to select a combination of any 2 of those students.

- Likewise, if a competition has 9 athletes, there are $\binom{9}{3}$ ways to arrange a permutation of any 3 of those athletes.

- To get a sense of how the GRE might test your knowledge of this notation, let's work through a practice problem together. Consider the following:

An organization has 8 volunteers, of whom 5 are part-time and 3 are full-time. If a team of 3 is to be selected from these volunteers, how many teams with exactly 2 part-time volunteers are possible?

(A) $\binom{8}{5}\binom{3}{2}$ (B) $\binom{8}{3}\binom{3}{3}$ (C) $\binom{5}{3}\binom{3}{2}$ (D) $\binom{5}{3}\binom{2}{1}$ (E) $\binom{5}{2}\binom{3}{1}$

Answer: E. If the 3-person team is to have exactly 2 part-time volunteers, then 1 person on the team must be a full-time volunteer. Therefore, to select the team, the organization must choose 2 of 5 part-time volunteers and 1 of 3 full-time volunteers.

  ➤ The number of ways to select a combination of 2 of 5 part-time volunteers and a combination of 1 of 3 full-time volunteers can be depicted as follows:

PART-TIME	FULL-TIME
$\binom{5}{2}$	$\binom{3}{1}$

- Thus, the correct answer is (E), since the number of ways to select a combination of any two part-time volunteers and one full-time volunteer equals:

$$\binom{5}{2} \times \binom{3}{1} = \binom{5}{2}\binom{3}{1}$$

(14) Slot Diagrams for Combinations – If you're like many test takers, you may wonder whether combination problems can be solved with slot diagrams.

- They can. Imagine that we needed to select 2 of the following 6 students, in no particular order: Alice, Bill, Cal, Deb, Ed, and Fatma.

  ➤ If we were to set up a slot diagram, how many ways could we select the first student? 6 ways. How many ways could we select the second student? 5 ways.

- In other words, our slot diagram would look like this:

$$\underline{6}\ \ \underline{5}$$

- Of course, the answer to the question isn't as simple as $6 \times 5 = 30$. We need to account for DUPLICATE combinations. After all, selecting Alice and then Deb would yield the same combination as selecting Deb then Alice.

  ➤ Since there are 2! ways that we can arrange the two people we select, we need to DIVIDE the slot diagram by 2! to determine the number of UNIQUE combinations.

- Now imagine that we wanted to select 3 of 6 people. Our slot diagram would look like this:

$$\underline{6}\ \ \underline{5}\ \ \underline{4}$$

- In this case, however, we'd need to divide $6 \times 5 \times 4$ by 3!, since there are 3! ways to arrange the 3 people that we choose.

  ➤ Remember, slot diagrams give us the number of ways we can ORDER what we select.

- Since order doesn't matter in combination problems, we need to RID our slot diagram of duplicate combinations (think ABC vs. BCA vs. CAB). That's why we divide them out.

- (If this strategy seems familiar to you, you're not imagining things. This is the same approach we discussed in our section on duplicate arrangements!)

  ➤ To understand why we can solve combination problems with FACTORIALS, imagine again that we need to choose 2 of 6 friends.

- Now compare the answer we get using a slot diagram to the answer we get using factorials:

Slot Diagram	Factorials

$$\frac{6 \times 5}{2!} \qquad\qquad \frac{6!}{2!4!} = \frac{6 \times 5 \times \cancel{4}!}{2!\cancel{4}!}$$

- The arithmetic may look different, but the answers are the same. In other words, we can use factorials to solve combination problems because they yield the same result as dividing a slot diagram by the number of duplicate combinations.

➢ If using slot diagrams to solve combination problems seems confusing, don't worry: you DON'T need to learn this strategy.

- You can always use factorials instead. If this strategy makes sense, however, we encourage you to make use of it. It's FASTER than the factorial strategy and great for solving some of the most DIFFICULT combination problems. Consider the following:

A group of students consists of 4 sets of twins and no one else. How many ways can 3 students be selected from this group, if every student selected is unrelated?

(A) 24 (B) 32 (C) 40 (D) 48 (E) 56

- To start, there are 4 sets of twins to choose from, so there are 8 ways that we can select the first student.

➢ Next, 7 students remain, 1 of whom is the twin of the student we've selected. Since we don't want to select a twin, there are only 6 ways to choose the second student.

- Finally, 6 students remain, 2 of whom are twins of the 2 students we've selected. Thus, there are 4 ways to select the final student, giving us the following slot diagram:

$$\underline{8} \;\; \underline{6} \;\; \underline{4}$$

- Since there are 3! ways that we can ORDER the 3 students we've selected, we simply need to divide our slot diagram by 3! to determine the number of unique combinations. Doing so proves that (B) is the correct answer, since:

$$\frac{8 \times 6 \times 4}{3!} = \frac{8 \times \cancel{6} \times 4}{\cancel{3} \times \cancel{2} \times 1} = 32$$

(15) Problem Sets – The following questions have been arranged into three groups: fundamental, intermediate, and rare or advanced.

• Whether you're aiming for a perfect score or a score closer to average, mastery of the concepts in the FUNDAMENTAL questions is absolutely essential.

➤ As you might expect, the INTERMEDIATE questions are more difficult but are essential for test-takers who need an above-average score or higher.

• Finally, the RARE or ADVANCED questions test concepts that are very sophisticated or seldom encountered on the GRE. Mastery of such questions is required only if you need a math score above the 90th percentile.

• As always, if you find yourself confused, bogged down with busy work, or stuck, don't be afraid to fall back on your "Plan B" strategies!

Fundamental

1. In how many different ways can the letters in the word FLORA be ordered? *permutation*

$$120$$

Box *B* has 8 lightbulbs.

Quantity A   Ⓒ   Quantity B

2. The number of different sets of any 2 lightbulbs that <u>can be removed</u> from box *B*. *combination*   28

3. To register for a certain website, each visitor must choose a login ID and a password. Each password must contain 2 letters and 3 digits, in that order. The site does not <u>differentiate</u> between upper- and lower-case letters. If the <u>repetition</u> of letters and digits is allowed, how many different passwords are possible?

(A) 23,400   (B) 60,840   (C) 67,600   (D) 608,400   (E) 676,000

4. In a certain game of musical chairs, five contestants are down to two chairs. How many different ways can the contestants seat themselves in those two chairs?

(A) 6   (B) 10   (C) 12   (D) 16   (E) 20

A spelling bee has 8 contestants. Judges must award prizes for first, second, and third places, with no ties.

Quantity A	Quantity B
5. The number of different ways the judges award the 3 prizes	The number of different groups of 3 people that can get the prizes

6. In how many different ways can the letters in the word FAUNA be ordered?

60

Hazel is planning her morning schedule, which will be comprised of five meetings. Three of these meetings are to be interviews, and none of these interviews are to be consecutive.

Quantity A	Quantity B
7. The number of different schedules that Hazel can put together	12

8. How many 3-digit positive integers are odd and do not contain the digit 8?

(A) 215   (B) 270   (C) 312   (D) 360   (E) 405

9. Company X has seven female employees and four male employees. How many different teams can the company put together that consist of four female employees and one male employee?

(A) 120   (B) 140   (C) 160   (D) 180   (E) 200

Intermediate

10. A certain flower shop sells five different flowers: roses, tulips, irises, carnations and daisies. How many arrangements of four different flowers are possible if a daisy must be the second flower in the arrangement and a tulip the fourth?

$$\boxed{6}$$

A fast-food restaurant is handing out party-packs with its low-priced value meal. Each party-pack consists of three different action figures, and the restaurant has an infinite supply of nine different action figures.

Quantity A	Quantity B

11. The number of different party-packs that can come with the value meal | 81

12. Tabitha invited 4 classmates to go with her to a concert. There are 120 different ways in which they can sit together in a row of 5 seats, one person per seat. In how many of those ways is Tabitha sitting in the middle seat?

(A) 12 (B) 24 (C) 48 (D) 60 (E) 72

Class *C* has 6 boys and 4 girls. The teacher of class *C* selects 4 of its students to work on a special project.

Quantity A	Quantity B

two combination pools + multiply

13. The number of different groups containing exactly two girls that can be selected | 80

14. How many ways can the letters in the word BASIC be ordered if the arrangement can neither begin nor end with the letter *B*?

(A) 48 (B) 72 (C) 96 (D) 108 (E) 120

A certain car has 6 seats, each of which can hold no more than one passenger.

Quantity A	Quantity B
15. The number of ways that 4 passengers can be arranged in the 6 seats	24

16. Talia has five shirts and six skirts. If she refuses to wear either of her two pink shirts with any of her three plaid skirts, how many outfits consisting of one shirt and one skirt is Talia willing to wear?

(A) 16 (B) 18 (C) 21 (D) 24 (E) 30

Quantity A	Quantity B
17. The arrangements of any length that can be formed from five or fewer objects	150

18. A first-grade class is on a fieldtrip. For safety purposes, each student must hold the hand of another student, and no student is allowed to hold the hand of two students. If there are 12 students in the class, how many ways can the students hold hands? (Assume that the order in which the students hold hands does not matter.)

(A) 66 (B) 96 (C) 121 (D) 132 (E) 144

From the set of letters K, L, M, N, O and P, there are 15 different 4-letter subsets that could be selected.

Quantity A	Quantity B
19. The number of 4-letter subsets that include the letter L	10

20. John has 3 hats, 3 shirts, and 3 pairs of pants, each of which comes in 3 colors: red, white, and blue. If John wants to wear a red, white, and blue outfit consisting of one hat, one shirt, and one pair of pants, how many different outfits are possible?

(A) 3 (B) 6 (C) 9 (D) 12 (E) 27

Rare or Advanced

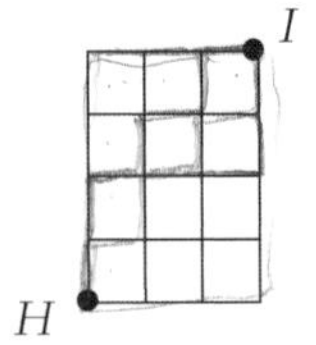

[Handwritten: → total blocks]

[Handwritten: 7!]

[Handwritten: 3! 4!]

[Handwritten: east   → north]

[Diagram: grid with point I at top right, point H at bottom left]

(21.) In the diagram above, each square represents a city block. How many ways can one travel from point *I* to point *H* if the route is to consist of exactly seven blocks?

(A) 12   (B) 24   (C) 35   (D) 48   (E) 70

22. Two kittens are to be selected at random from a recent litter. If there are 21 ways to select any two of them, how many kittens are in the litter?

(A) 5   (B) 6   (C) 7   (D) 8   (E) 9

30 oranges are divided into *X* mutually exclusive groups in such a way that the number of oranges in any group does not exceed the number in any other group by more than 1.

Quantity A	Quantity B

[Handwritten: D]

23. The value of *X* if at least one of the groups consists of 4 oranges

8

24. A bag contains 10 marbles, of which 4 are red and the rest are blue. 4 marbles are to be drawn from the bag simultaneously and at random. Of all the possible combinations, how many can contain 2 or more red marbles?

[Handwritten: 3 scenarios in which 2+ Red chosen]

[Handwritten: ① multiply option sets for red + blue]

[Handwritten: ② add totals for each scenario]

Quantity A	Quantity B

25. The number of ways that 2 apples, 3 bananas, and 1 carrot can be distributed among 8 students if no student receives more than 1 item

[Handwritten: 2 bags w/ nothing]

1,500

[Handwritten: 8! total / 3! 2! 2! / duplicates]

circular

26. A certain merry-go-round has 4 seats, each of which can contain no more than 1 rider. How many ways can 8 students arrange themselves among the 4 seats if every seat must have a rider?

# of linear arrangements / # of objects

(A) 70   (B) 210   (C) 420   (D) 630   (E) 840

In a certain experiment, 6 subjects are arranged in a straight line. Each subject has a unique color, and the red and blue subjects cannot be positioned next to one another.

monster shortcut
5! · 2!
6! − 5!2!
total   *red + blue together*

Quantity A	Quantity B
27. The number of ways that the 6 subjects be arranged.	480

28. A 4-person committee is to be selected from a pool of 7 candidates, 2 of whom are Lindsay and Elise. If Lindsay and Elise cannot work together, how many different committees can be formed?

why not monster?

(A) 15   (B) 25   (C) 35   (D) 45   (E) 55

A group of 3 people is to be selected from among 4 pairs of siblings so that the team does not include two people who are siblings.

Quantity A		Quantity B
29. The number of possible teams	C	32

(16) Solutions – Video solutions for each of the previous questions can be found on our website at **www.sherpaprep.com/videos**.

• BOOKMARK this address for future visits!

> ➤ To view the videos, you'll need the LOGIN and PASSWORD that you created upon registering your copy of <u>Statistics & Data Interpretation</u>.

• If you have yet to register your book yet, please go to **www.sherpaprep.com/activate** and enter your email address, last name, and shipping address.

• Be sure to provide the SAME last name and shipping address that you used to purchase your copy of <u>Master Key to the GRE</u> or to enroll in your GRE course with Sherpa Prep!

> ➤ When checking your answers, we encourage you to watch the solution for any problem that you answered INCORRECTLY

• The same goes for any problem that took you MORE than TWO MINUTES to solve.

• After digesting the explanation, REVISIT your mistake a couple of days later to ensure that the problem no longer poses issues to you.

> ➤ If you struggle to solve the problem a SECOND time, add it to your "LOG of ERRORS" and redo it every few weeks.

• Solving tricky questions MORE THAN ONCE is the best way to learn from your mistakes and to avoid similar difficulties on your actual exam.

Fundamental	Intermediate	Rare or Advanced
1. 120	10. 6	21. C
2. C	11. A	22. C
3. E	12. B	23. D
4. E	13. A	24. 115
5. A	14. B	25. A
6. 60	15. A	26. C
7. C	16. D	27. C
8. D	17. A	28. B
9. B	18. A	29. C
	19. C	
	20. B	

Probability

Probability

To be discussed:

Fundamental Concepts

Whether you're aiming for a perfect score or a score closer to average, mastery of the following concepts is essential.

Rare or Advanced Concepts

The following concepts are either advanced or are tested only on rare occasions. If you don't need an elite math score, don't waste your time!

Practice Questions

There's no substitute for elbow grease. Practice your new skills to ensure that you internalize what you've studied.

Fundamental Concepts

(1) Introduction – Of all the concepts tested by the GRE, perhaps none is more feared than Probability.

• We understand the fear. If you're like most people who take the GRE, you've never studied Probability before, so even the most basic questions can seem like witchcraft.

> ➤ However, we think the fear is misplaced. For starters, probability questions are pretty RARE.

• Most exams contain no more than 1 or 2 examples, if they have any at all. So even if you know nothing about Probability, it's unlikely to affect your score by more than a point or two.

• More importantly, the majority of probability questions are pretty EASY. In fact, all but the trickiest examples boil down to a FEW simple concepts.

> ➤ Before proving this to you, let's first make sure that you are comfortable with some basic BACKGROUND information.

• As you probably know, Probability measures the likelihood that something will occur. Formally, the chance something may happen can be stated as:

$$\frac{\text{The Number of Ways it } \textbf{CAN} \text{ Happen}}{\text{The } \textbf{TOTAL} \text{ Number of Outcomes}}$$

• For example, the probability of rolling a "2" with a fair six-sided die is 1/6, since a six-sided die has 6 total outcomes, and only 1 of those outcomes is a "2".

> ➤ Of course, for a probability to be accurate, the likelihood of its outcomes must be EQUALLY WEIGHTED.

• For instance, one might think there's a 1/2 chance of selecting the ace of spades from a full deck of cards, since picking a card can result in 1 of 2 things: selecting the ace of spades, or not selecting it.

• However, the actual probability is 1/52, since a full deck of cards has 52 cards, each of which has an EQUAL chance of being selected, if chosen at random.

Chapter 4: Probability

> In Probability Theory, some terms have special meanings. The most important of these terms are EXPERIMENT, OUTCOME, and EVENT.

• An EXPERIMENT is simply an action whose OUTCOME is uncertain. Rolling a die, flipping a coin, and picking a card are all considered experiments, since their outcomes depend on chance.

• A particular outcome (or set of outcomes) is known as an EVENT.

• Imagine picking a number from 1 to 10. Two sample EVENTS would include picking the number "2", which is a single outcome (just the number 2), and picking an even number, which is a set of five outcomes (the numbers 2, 4, 6, 8, and 10).

> Considerably less important is the term SAMPLE SPACE, which is rarely used on the GRE.

• The SAMPLE SPACE for an experiment is the set of all possible outcomes.

• For example, rolling a six-sided die has 6 possible outcomes. Thus, its sample space would include the numbers from 1 to 6. Likewise, flipping a coin has 2 outcomes, so its sample space would include Heads and Tails.

> On a final note, be aware that Probability Theory has a special type of NOTATION. For any event E, the probability that E occurs is denoted $P(E)$.

• Likewise, the probability that events E and F both occur is denoted $P(E$ and $F)$.

• Thus, if there is a 60% chance that a random experiment results in event A, we would say that $P(A) = 0.6$. Similarly, if there is 75% chance that the same experiment results in event A or event B, we would say that $P(A$ or $B) = 0.75$.

• Although this notation is uncommon for the GRE, we encourage you to familiarize yourself with it, since exam-makers do use it from time to time.

Sherpa
Prep

(2) The Probabilities Add to One – For any experiment, the probabilities of ALL possible outcomes ADD to ONE.

• To understand why, imagine a jar with 6 marbles, of which 3 are red, 2 are white, and 1 is blue.

 ➢ If we choose one marble at random, the probability that it's RED is 3/6, the probability that it's WHITE is 2/6, and the probability that it's BLUE is 1/6.

• The sum of these probabilities is 1, since:

Red + White + Blue = Total Outcomes

$$\frac{3}{6}+\frac{2}{6}+\frac{1}{6}=1$$

 ➢ Likewise, imagine picking a number from 1 to 10. The probability of picking a PRIME number is 4/10, since 4 of the numbers are prime (2, 3, 5, and 7).

• The probability of NOT picking a prime number is 6/10, since 6 of the numbers are not prime (1, 4, 6, 8, 9, and 10). Remember, 1 is NOT prime, because a prime number has exactly two distinct factors.

• Again, the sum of these probabilities is 1, since:

Prime + NOT Prime = Total Outcomes

$$\frac{4}{10}+\frac{6}{10}=1$$

 ➢ If this seems simple to you, then there's GOOD news: this principle is ALL you need to solve some Probability questions.

• We told you that probability can be easy, right?

• To get a sense of how the GRE might test your knowledge of this concept, consider the problem at the top of the next page:

Experiment E has three possible outcomes. The probabilities of these mutually exclusive outcomes are:

$$P, \frac{P}{2}, \text{ and } \frac{P}{3}$$

Quantity A	**Quantity B**
P	$\frac{5}{9}$

Answer. B. For any experiment, the probabilities of ALL possible outcomes ADD to ONE. Because the outcomes P, $\frac{P}{2}$, and $\frac{P}{3}$ are mutually exclusive and the only ones possible for experiment E, their probabilities must add to 1:

$$P + \frac{P}{2} + \frac{P}{3} = 1$$

➢ To solve for P, let's first use the "Denominator Trick" to get rid of the denominators. 2 and 3 both go into 6, so let's multiply the entire equation by 6:

$$6(P + \frac{P}{2} + \frac{P}{3} = 1) \;\rightarrow\; 6(P) + \cancel{6}(\frac{P}{\cancel{2}}) + \cancel{6}(\frac{P}{\cancel{3}}) = 6(1) \;\rightarrow\; 6P + 3P + 2P = 6$$

• Thus, $P = \frac{6}{11}$, since:

$$11P = 6 \;\rightarrow\; P = \frac{6}{11}$$

• According to the "Comparison Trick", $\frac{5}{9}$ must be a larger fraction that $\frac{6}{11}$, since 55 is greater than 54. Thus, the correct answer is (B):

$$\begin{array}{ccc} 54 & & 55 \\ \frac{6}{11} & \diagup\!\!\!\!\diagdown & \frac{5}{9} \end{array}$$

(3) From Zero to One – The probability that an event will occur ranges from impossible to certain.

• Numerically, an impossible event has a PROBABILITY of ZERO and a certain event has a PROBABILITY of ONE.

    ➤ To understand why, imagine rolling a six-sided die. There are zero ways to roll a "10", so the probability of doing so is 0, since:

$$P(\text{rolling } 10) = \frac{\text{The Number of Ways it } \textbf{CAN} \text{ Happen}}{\text{The } \textbf{TOTAL} \text{ Number of Outcomes}} = \frac{0}{6} = 0$$

• Likewise, there are six ways to roll a number less than 7. Thus, the probability of doing so is 1, since:

$$P(\text{rolling} < 7) = \frac{\text{The Number of Ways it } \textbf{CAN} \text{ Happen}}{\text{The } \textbf{TOTAL} \text{ Number of Outcomes}} = \frac{6}{6} = 1$$

    ➤ Because one is the greatest value that a probability can have, and zero is the smallest, NO EVENT can have a probability greater than 1 or less than 0.

• Consequently, any event that is neither certain nor impossible must have a probability BETWEEN 0 and 1.

• Although such statements may seem obvious or trivial, they're actually fairly IMPORTANT.

    ➤ As you may recall from our book on <u>Arithmetic & "Plan B" Strategies</u>, any number between 0 and 1 behaves in the OPPOSITE manner of positive numbers greater than 1.

• For example, MULTIPLYING a positive value (such as 10) by a number greater than 1 makes that value bigger. Multiplying a positive value by a number between 0 and 1, however, makes it SMALLER.

Larger than 1: $10 \times \boxed{5} = 50$ Between 0 and 1: $10 \times \boxed{0.5} = 5$

• Conversely, DIVIDING a positive value (such as 10) by a number greater than 1 makes that value smaller. Dividing a positive value by a number between 0 and 1, however, makes it BIGGER.

Larger than 1: $10 \div \boxed{2} = 5$ Between 0 and 1: $10 \div \boxed{0.5} = 20$

> To give you a sense of why this is important, let's look at a sample probability question for the GRE.

• Consider the following:

For a certain experiment, x is the probability that event A will occur, and y is the probability that event A will <u>not</u> occur.

<u>Quantity A</u>	**<u>Quantity B</u>**
$x + y$	xy

Answer. A. As we saw earlier, for any event, the probabilities of ALL possible outcomes ADD to ONE. Since x and y are the only possible outcomes for event A, we know that $x + y = 1$.

> We also know that NO PROBABILITY can be greater than 1 or less than 0.

• Thus, if $x + y = 1$, then either x and y are BOTH values BETWEEN 0 and 1, or one of the two equals 1 and the other is 0.

• If both x and y are values between 0 and 1, their product will be less than 1, since numbers between 0 and 1 get SMALLER when they're multiplied. For example, $0.6 \times 0.4 = 0.24$.

> Likewise, if one variable equals 1 and the other 0, their product will be 0, since $1 \times 0 = 0$.

• Since Quantity A must equal 1, and Quantity B must either equal 0 or a value greater than 0 but less than 1, the correct answer is (A).

(4) Multiple Events – For many test-takers, Probability questions really start to get "scary" when there is more than one event.

• We get it. If you're not a math nerd, or have never studied Probability, questions involving one event look bad enough. Questions with two events? They must seem cruel.

> ➢ Fortunately, nothing could be further from the truth. Although questions with MULTIPLE events may look evil, they're pretty easy to solve.

• As you'll see, the KEY is knowing whether you have an "AND probability" or an "OR probability".

> **"AND Probabilities" involve SEPARATE events, in which two (or more) outcomes BOTH occur.**

• For example, the probability that a fair coin lands heads up and then tails up on consecutive tosses would be an "AND probability", since TWO outcomes are required: first the coin must land heads up AND then it must land tails up.

> **"OR Probabilities" involve ONE or more events, in which ONE outcome OR ANOTHER may occur.**

• For example, the probability of selecting a red marble or a blue marble from a jar of marbles would be an "OR probability", since we're only interested in the probability of drawing ONE outcome OR the OTHER.

> ➢ While there's no simple rule of thumb that will always help you distinguish an "AND probability" from an "OR probability", the following guidelines generally help:

"AND Probabilities"	"OR Probabilities"
Use the words AND or BOTH	Use the word OR
Happen IN A ROW	Use the phrase AT LEAST
Happen AT THE SAME TIME	

• It can also be helpful to remember that most "OR Probabilities" use the word "or". So if your probability question DOESN'T contain the word "or", there's a pretty good chance it's an "AND probability".

> ➤ Below, you'll find six questions. Your job is to determine whether each question is an "AND probability" or an "OR probability".

• Don't worry about solving them. Our immediate goal is to help you distinguish the two types of probabilities. Let's start with a couple of easy examples:

A jar has 5 marbles. 3 are red and 2 are blue. If two marbles are chosen, what is the probability that the first marble is red and the second is blue?

Each face of a six-sided die is equally weighted. If rolled, what is the probability that the die lands on "2" or "5"?

• The marble question asks for the probability of getting a red <u>and</u> then a blue, so it's an "AND probability". The die question asks for the probability of rolling a "2" <u>or</u> a "5", so it's an "OR probability".

> ➤ The next two examples are a little harder. When in doubt, remember that "OR probabilities" typically use the word "or".

• Consider the following:

A box has 10 shirts, 4 of which are white. If two shirts are selected at random, what is the probability that both shirts are white?

A fair coin is flipped 3 times. What is the probability that the coin will turn up tails each time?

• The shirt question asks for the probability that <u>both</u> shirts are white, so it's an "AND probability". The coin question is also an "AND probability", since the coin must be flipped 3 times IN A ROW for it to turn up tails each time.

> ➤ The last examples are a bit trickier still. If you can get these, you've got the basic distinction.

• The second example is particularly tough:

John drops 3 slices of toast. If each slice is buttered on one side only, what is the probability that all three slices land buttered side down?

A penny is flipped 4 times. What is the probability that the penny turns up heads at least twice?

• The toast question is an "AND probability", since all 3 slices fall <u>at the same time</u>. The penny question, however, is an "OR probability". For the penny to turn up heads <u>at least</u> twice, it can do so 2 times <u>or</u> 3 times <u>or</u> 4 times.

(5) "AND Probabilities" – If you can now distinguish "AND probabilities" from "OR probabilities", you're almost ready to solve them.

- In fact, you've already mastered the hardest part. The rest is easy.

  ➢ To determine the probability that Events *A* <u>and</u> *B* both happen, simply MULTIPLY their individual probabilities together.

- For example, if the probability of Event *A* is 0.4 and the probability of Event *B* is 0.6, the probability that Events *A* and *B* both occur is 0.24, since $0.4 \times 0.6 = 0.24$.

- To help you get comfortable with "AND probabilities", let's work through a few sample questions together. Consider the following:

In a certain board game, every player must roll a six-sided die and then flip a quarter. If both the die and the coin are fair, what is the probability that a player rolls a "3" and flips the quarter so that it lands tails up?

$$\text{(A) } \frac{1}{16} \quad \text{(B) } \frac{1}{12} \quad \text{(C) } \frac{1}{8} \quad \text{(D) } \frac{1}{4} \quad \text{(E) } \frac{1}{2}$$

Answer: B. The probability of rolling a "3" with six-sided die is 1/6. The probability that a fair coin lands tails up is 1/2. Thus, the probability that BOTH events happen is 1/12, since:

$$\frac{1}{6} \times \frac{1}{2} = \frac{1}{12}$$

A fair six-sided die is thrown twice.

Quantity A	**Quantity B**
The probability that both throws result in prime numbers	$\frac{1}{4}$

Answer: C. A six-sided die has 6 outcomes: 1, 2, 3, 4, 5, and 6. Of these, 2, 3, and 5 are prime numbers. Thus, the probability that each throw results in a prime number is 3/6, or 1/2. The probability that the first AND second throws BOTH result in prime numbers is therefore 1/4, since:

$$\frac{1}{2} \times \frac{1}{2} = \frac{1}{4}$$

Hence, the two quantities are equal.

➢ To understand why we can MULTIPLY to solve "AND Probability" questions, let's go back to our discussion of Combinatorics.

• Imagine a menu that offers 8 entrées and 7 desserts. Further, imagine that 3 of those entrées are served cold and that 4 of those desserts contain chocolate.

• If we were to choose 1 entrée and 1 dessert from this menu, there would be $8 \times 7 = 56$ ways to do so, since the fundamental counting principle states: **if there m ways to do one thing and n ways to do another, there are $m \times n$ ways to both.**

➢ Likewise, if we were to choose 1 cold entrée and 1 chocolate dessert, there would be $3 \times 4 = 12$ ways to do so, since the menu has 3 cold entrées and 4 chocolate desserts.

• Thus, the odds of selecting 1 cold entrée and 1 chocolate dessert, at random, from the menu would be 12/56, or 3/14, since 12 of the 56 possible options consist of 1 cold entrée and 1 chocolate dessert.

• Now, let's leave Combinatorics aside and look at this menu through the lens of probability theory.

➢ Note that the odds of selecting a cold entrée are 3/8 and the odds of selecting a chocolate dessert are 4/7.

• If we multiply these probabilities together, we see that our odds of selecting a cold entrée AND a chocolate dessert, at random, are $3/8 \times 4/7 = 12/56$, or 3/14.

• This is the same answer what we get using Combinatorics! The two methods are equivalent because placing 3×4 over 8×7 is the SAME THING as multiplying $3/8 \times 4/7$. In other words:

$$\frac{3 \times 4}{8 \times 7} = \frac{3}{8} \times \frac{4}{7}$$

➤ When solving "AND Probabilities", just BE CAREFUL if you have to select items from a COLLECTION.

• Unless items are REPLACED upon selection, subsequent selections will have FEWER choices. Imagine, for example, a jar with 5 marbles, 2 of which are blue.

• If you had to select 2 marbles at random, what is the probability that both marbles would be blue? If you're like many test-takers, you might be tempted to answer 4/25 (or 0.16). After all, this is an "AND probability", and the odds of selecting a blue marble on any given pick would seem to be 2/5, so we should get:

$$\frac{2}{5} \times \frac{2}{5} = \frac{4}{25}$$

➤ Unfortunately, this solution contains a MISTAKE. It fails to account for the effect that the first selection has upon the second.

• With the initial selection, there are 5 marbles to choose from, and 2 of these are blue, so the odds of selecting a blue marble is 2/5. However, with the second selection, there are only 4 marbles left to choose from, and only 1 of these blue, since the first selection was NOT REPLACED. Thus, the odds that the second marble is blue are 1/4.

• The actual probability of selecting 2 blue marbles is therefore 1/10 (or 0.1), since:

$$\frac{2}{5} \times \frac{1}{4} = \frac{1}{10}$$

➤ In general, the GRE will TELL you if you are supposed to REPLACE an item after selection.

• In such cases, the first selection will not affect the second.

• However, the GRE will NOT remind you that an item has been removed. It is up to you to recognize that an initial selection has diminished the options that remain. So consider your events carefully when working with "AND probabilities". Flipping coins and rolling dice are independent events: a prior flip or roll has no effect on the one that follows. Drawing items from a collection is different. Each choice reduces the pool.

➤ To ensure that you feel comfortable working with problems without replacement, let's work through several examples together.

• Consider the following:

There are 12 applicants for a job, of which are 8 men and 4 are women. If two of the applicants are to be hired at random, what is the probability that the first applicant hired is a woman and the second is a man?

(A) $\frac{1}{48}$ (B) $\frac{2}{9}$ (C) $\frac{8}{33}$ (D) $\frac{3}{8}$ (E) $\frac{1}{2}$

Answer. C. The odds that the first person hired is a woman are 4/12, as 4 of the 12 applicants are women. The odds that the second person hired is a man are 8/11, as 8 of the remaining 11 applicants are men. Thus, the odds that the first applicant hired is a woman <u>and</u> the second a man are 8/33, as:

$$\frac{4}{12} \times \frac{8}{11} = \frac{1}{3} \times \frac{8}{11} = \frac{8}{33}$$

**A coin purse contains 3 quarters, 4 dimes, 1 nickel, and nothing else.
Elena is to select 3 coins from the purse.**

Quantity A		**Quantity B**
The probability that she picks 3 dimes		$\frac{1}{14}$

Answer. C. The odds that the first coin is a dime are 4/8, since 4 of the 8 coins are dimes. The odds that the second coin is a dime are 3/7, since 3 of the 7 remaining coins are dimes. Finally, the odds that the third coin is a dime are 2/6, since 2 of the 6 remaining coins are dimes. Thus, the probability that Elena picks 3 dimes is 1/14, since:

$$\frac{4}{8} \times \frac{3}{7} \times \frac{2}{6} = \frac{1}{2} \times \frac{\cancel{3}}{7} \times \frac{1}{\cancel{6}} = \frac{1}{14}$$

**A large bowl contains 9 balls, of which 4 are black, 3 are orange, and 2 are green.
Three friends close their eyes and <u>simultaneously</u> pick one ball apiece from the bowl.
What is the probability that all three pick orange balls?**

(A) $\frac{1}{84}$ (B) $\frac{1}{54}$ (C) $\frac{1}{27}$ (D) $\frac{1}{16}$ (E) $\frac{1}{9}$

Answer. A. While the odds that each friend picks an orange ball are 3/9, the odds that all 3 do so are <u>not</u> $3/9 \times 3/9 \times 3/9$. After all, the moment that 1 of the 3 friends picks an orange ball, the other 2 only have 8 balls left to pick from, 2 of which are orange. Likewise, the moment that 2 of the 3 friends have picked orange balls, the last friend only has 7 balls left to pick from, 1 of which is orange. Thus, the odds that all 3 pick orange balls are 1/84, as:

$$\frac{3}{9} \times \frac{2}{8} \times \frac{1}{7} = \frac{1}{3} \times \frac{1}{4} \times \frac{1}{7} = \frac{1}{84}$$

(6) "OR Probabilities" – As we just saw, "AND probabilities" come with a wrinkle.

• In some cases, prior events affect those that follow (e.g. drawing items from a pool), and in other cases they don't (e.g. flipping coins).

➢ "OR probabilities" come with a similar wrinkle. Sometimes the events are MUTUALLY EXCLUSIVE and sometimes they're INDEPENDENT.

• To get a sense of the distinction, compare the following questions:

> **A jar has 10 marbles, of which 5 are red, 3 are blue, and 2 are white. If one marble is chosen at random, what is the probability that the marble is red or blue?**

$\frac{5}{10} + \frac{3}{10} = \frac{8}{10}$

> **When flipped, a penny has a 50% chance of landing "heads". The same is true for a dime. If both are flipped, what is the probability that the penny or the dime lands "heads"?**

• In the marble question, if we select a red marble, we CANNOT select a blue marble. The events are mutually exclusive, since a red marble cannot be blue.

➢ In the coin question, however, the events are NOT mutually exclusive. It's possible that both the penny and the dime land "heads".

• In cases like this, the events are called independent, since **they have no bearing on one another**. The penny's outcome CANNOT affect the dime's outcome, and vice versa.

• (No, one coin can't magnetically control the other.)

➢ To solve "OR probabilities", you MUST be able to DISTINGUISH events that are mutually exclusive from events that are independent.

• To help you do so, we want you to ASK yourself ONE question at the start of every "OR probability": CAN BOTH EVENTS OCCUR?

• If the answer is NO, the events are MUTUALLY EXCLUSIVE.

➢ **To solve "OR probabilities" in which the events are mutually exclusive, simply ADD the probabilities together.**

• For example, in the "red or blue marble" question, the probability that the marble is red is 5/10 and the probability that it is blue is 3/10.

- The probability that the marble is red or blue is therefore 4/5 (or 0.8), since the marble CANNOT be red and blue at the same time:

$$\frac{5}{10} + \frac{3}{10} = \frac{8}{10} = \frac{4}{5}$$

- (Note, by the way, that we ADD the probabilities because a statement such as 5/10 + 3/10 = 8/10 is another way of saying that 8 of the 10 marbles are either red or blue!)

> ➤ If the is answer is <u>YES</u>, the events will be INDEPENDENT.

- **To solve "OR probabilities" in which the events are independent, first <u>ADD</u> the probabilities. Then <u>SUBTRACT the probability that BOTH events OCCUR</u>.**

- For example, in the coin question, the probability that penny lands "heads" is 50%, or 1/2, and the same is true for the dime. Thus, the probability that BOTH coins land "heads" is 1/4, since 1/2 × 1/2 = 1/4. The probability that the penny <u>OR</u> the dime lands "heads" is therefore 3/4, since:

Odds that the PENNY lands "heads"

Odds that the DIME lands "heads"

$$\left(\frac{1}{2} + \frac{1}{2}\right) - \left(\frac{1}{2} \times \frac{1}{2}\right) = \frac{3}{4}$$

Odds that BOTH coins land "heads"

> ➤ To understand WHY we subtract the probability that both events occur, imagine that we were to flip the penny and the dime 100 times each.

- On average, the penny would land "heads" 50 times, as would the dime. In some of the 50 instances where the penny lands "heads", however, the dime would too.

- If we don't subtract those instance from our tally — the instances where both coins land "heads" — we in effect count them TWICE. Recall the phrasing of the question. **We're looking for the probability that either the penny OR the dime land "heads".** We must subtract the instances where BOTH land "heads" to REMOVE the DOUBLE COUNT.

> ➤ To ensure that you've got the hang of "OR probabilities", let's work through a couple of examples together.

- At the start of each question, remember to ask yourself whether BOTH events are possible!

A certain basket has 2 white onions, 5 red onions, 3 yellow onions, and nothing else. If one onion is selected at random, what is the probability that it is white or yellow?

(A) 0.2   (B) 0.3   (C) 0.44   (D) 0.5   (E) 0.8

Answer. D. Since the onion cannot be both white and yellow, these events are <u>mutually exclusive</u>. Therefore, we only have to add the probabilities.

> ➤ The odds that the onion is white are 2/10, since 2 of the onions are white. The odds that the onion is yellow are 3/10, since 3 of the onions are yellow.

- Thus, the odds that the onion is white or yellow are 0.5, since:

$$\frac{2}{10} + \frac{3}{10} = \frac{5}{10} = 0.5$$

- The correct answer is therefore (D).

The probability that Sam passes a certain exam is 0.4, and the probability that Will passes the same exam is 0.7. If Sam and Will's exam results have no bearing on one another, what is the probability that either Sam or Will pass the exam?

(A) 0.58   (B) 0.65   (C) 0.72   (D) 0.75   (E) 0.82

Answer. E. The probability that Sam passes the exam is 0.4, and the probability that Will passes the exam is 0.7.

> ➤ Because Sam's results have no bearing on Will's exam results, and vice versa, the events are <u>independent</u>.

- Thus, to determine the probabilities that either Sam <u>or</u> Will pass the exam, we need to add the 0.4 + 0.7, but subtract the probability that Sam <u>and</u> Will both pass the exam, like so:

$$0.4 + 0.7 - (0.4 \times 0.7) = 1.1 - 0.28$$

- The correct answer is therefore (E), since $1.1 - 0.28 = 0.82$.

> ➤ On a final note, is it worth pointing out that **there are some "OR probabilities" in which the relationship between the events is UNKNOWN**.

- Such probabilities are RARE for the GRE. They can also be tricky. If you're interested in learning about them, be sure to check out section **11** titled "<u>Unknown Relationships</u>".

(7) Complements – Imagine that you needed to select one student, at random, from a class of 4 girls and 6 boys.

• You likely know that the probability of selecting a girl would be 4/10. You may not know, however, that the probability of selecting its complement would be 6/10.

> ➤ The term COMPLEMENT simply refers to the OTHER outcomes: the ones that you DON'T WANT (or didn't get).

• Because the probability of an outcome (4/10) and the probability of its complement (6/10) ADD to 1, it's sometimes EASIER to determine the probability of something by getting the probability of its complement and subtracting that value from 1.

• To understand why this is so, consider the following:

In a random experiment, two 6-sided dice, each with faces numbered 1 to 6, are to be rolled once, and for both dice each of the 6 outcomes is equally likely to occur. What is the probability that the two dice have different outcomes?

$$\text{(A) } \frac{1}{6} \quad \text{(B) } \frac{11}{36} \quad \text{(C) } \frac{25}{36} \quad \text{(D) } \frac{7}{9} \quad \text{(E) } \frac{5}{6}$$

• According to the problem, both dice have 6 outcomes and are to be rolled once each. Determining how many ways these dice can be rolled is pretty easy.

> ➤ Remember the Fundamental Counting Principle: if there are m ways to do one thing and n ways to do another, then there are $m \times n$ ways to do both.

• Thus, there are 36 possible ways to roll the two dice, since $6 \times 6 = 36$. Determining how many of these ways involve DIFFERENT outcomes, however, is a bit trickier.

• We could try to count them out – (1, 6), (1, 5), (1, 4), and so forth – but doing so would be time-consuming. We might also miscount the total, because there are so many possibilities.

> ➤ Since the COMPLEMENT to rolling DIFFERENT numbers is rolling the SAME numbers, an easy approach would be to identify the outcomes that we DON'T want.

• There only 6 ways to roll the same numbers: (1, 1), (2, 2), (3, 3), (4, 4), (5, 5), (6, 6)

• If 6 of the 36 possible outcomes do NOT involve different outcomes, then 30 of the 36 outcomes must. Thus, the probability that the two dice have different outcomes is 5/6, since $1 - 6/36 = 30/36 = 5/6$. The correct answer is therefore (E).

• Let's work through a more challenging example:

In a certain box, there are 5 white balls, 3 green balls, 2 black balls, and nothing else. If two balls are drawn at random from the box, what is the probability that the two balls will have different colors?

$$\text{(A) } \frac{19}{50} \quad \text{(B) } \frac{14}{45} \quad \text{(C) } \frac{31}{50} \quad \text{(D) } \frac{27}{42} \quad \text{(E) } \frac{31}{45}$$

Answer. E. According to the problem, the box has 10 balls and 2 are to be selected. Because each selection reduces the remaining pool by 1, there are 10 ways to draw the first ball and 9 ways to draw the second.

> ➢ Remember, if there are m ways to do one thing and n ways to do another, then there are $m \times n$ ways to do both. Thus, there are 90 ways to draw 2 balls, since $10 \times 9 = 90$.

• The complement to getting DIFFERENT colors is getting the SAME color. Although we can solve this problem by counting out the scenarios in which each of the colors are different, it's far easier to identify the outcomes that we DON'T want.

• There are three scenarios in which the colors are the same:

1. We select two white balls
2. We select two green balls
3. We select two black balls

• The odds of selecting two ‖white balls‖ are 20/90, since the odds of picking a white ball with the first selection is 5/10 and the odds of selecting another with the second selection are 4/9. The odds of selecting two ‖green balls‖ are 6/90, since $3/10 \times 2/9 = 6/90$. The odds of selecting two ‖black balls‖ are 2/90, since $2/10 \times 1/9 = 2/90$.

> ➢ Thus, 28 of the 90 scenarios involve balls with the same color, since:

$$\frac{20}{90} + \frac{6}{90} + \frac{2}{90} = \frac{28}{90}$$

• If 28 of the 90 possible outcomes involve the SAME colors, then 62 of the 90 outcomes don't. Hence, the probability of selecting two balls with different colors is 31/45, since $1 - 28/90 = 62/90 = 31/45$. The correct answer is therefore (E).

(8) The "At Least Once" Shortcut – Complements are also helpful for determining the probability that an event occurs AT LEAST ONCE.

- Imagine that a fair coin is flipped 4 times. What is the probability that it lands tails up at least once?

  ➤ If you try to determine the odds without a shortcut, you have to determine ALL the scenarios in which the coin lands tails up one or more times.

- This means you have to identify the probability that it lands tails ONCE, or TWICE, or THREE times, or FOUR times, and then ADD those probabilities together.

- Could you do this is 2 minutes? Perhaps, but remember: any question that contains a LOT of busy work can likely be solved quite quickly in some other way.

  ➤ As you may recall, for any experiment, the probabilities of ALL possible outcomes ADD to ONE.

- In the case of an event and its complement, this can be stated as:

$$\text{Odds of an EVENT} + \text{Odds of its COMPLEMENT} = 1$$

  ➤ Since the complement of getting something at least once is NEVER getting it, the odds of getting something at least once must therefore equal:

$$\text{At Least ONCE} = 1 - \text{NEVER}$$

- Thus, to determine the odds that a coin, when flipped 4 times, lands tails up at least once, we simply need to determine the probability that it never lands tails up and to subtract that probability from 1.

- If a coin never lands tails up, it lands heads up each time. The probability of flipping a coin 4 times and getting heads on every toss is 1/16, since:

$$\frac{1}{2} \times \frac{1}{2} \times \frac{1}{2} \times \frac{1}{2} = \frac{1}{16}$$

- Therefore, the probability of getting tails at least once on 4 flips is 15/16, since:

$$1 - \frac{1}{16} = \frac{15}{16}$$

➢ Problems involving events that happen AT LEAST TWICE are a lot trickier, and quite rare, so we'll discuss them in the ADVANCED section of our material.

• In the meantime, let's work through one more practice question to ensure that you've got the hang of "At Least Once" problems:

In a certain bowl, there are 6 tangerines, 5 plums, and nothing else. Two pieces of fruit are to be drawn from the bowl at random.

Quantity A	**Quantity B**
The probability that at least one selection is a plum	$\dfrac{7}{9}$

Answer: B. To determine the probability of selecting a plum at least once, let's first determine the probability of never selecting one.

➢ If a plum is **never** drawn, then every selection **must** be a tangerine.

• The probability of drawing a tangerine with the first selection is 6/11, since 6 of the 11 pieces of fruit are tangerines. The probability of drawing a tangerine with the second selection is 5/10, since only 5 of the remaining 10 pieces of fruit are tangerines.

• The probability that these two events **both** occur is 3/11, since:

$$\frac{6}{11} \times \frac{5}{10} = \frac{6}{11} \times \frac{1}{2} = \frac{3}{11}$$

➢ Thus, the probability of selecting **at least one** plum is 8/11, since 1 − 3/11 equals 11/11 − 8/11 = 3/11.

• According to the "Comparison Trick", 7/9 must be a larger fraction that 8/11, since 77 is greater than 72. Thus, the correct answer is (B):

$$\overset{72}{\underset{}{\frac{8}{11}}} \quad \overset{77}{\underset{}{\frac{7}{9}}}$$

(9) Brute Force – You're now familiar with the concepts behind most GRE probability questions.

• There's just one last thing you should know: some questions are easier to solve with brute force.

➤ For us, the term BRUTE FORCE simply means COUNTING out the WINNING scenarios.

• For example, if you need to determine the odds that the outcomes of two 6-sided dice add to "11 or above", you're better off counting the outcomes that add to "11" or "12" – (5, 6), (6, 5), (6, 6) – than using the "AND or "OR" formulas.

• Is brute force a strategy that you'll need often to solve probability questions? No, but it comes in handy when ALL ELSE FAILS.

➤ To give you a sense of what a typical "Brute Force" question looks like, consider the following:

Set A: 1, 2, 3, 4   Set B: 3, 4, 5, 6, 7

Two integers will be randomly selected from the sets above, one from set A and one from set B. What is the probability that the sum of the two integers will equal 9?

(A) 0.15   (B) 0.20   (C) 0.25   (D) 0.30   (E) 0.33

• There are 4 ways to select an integer from set A and 5 ways to select one from set B.

➤ Remember, if there are m ways to do one thing and n ways to do another, then there are $m \times n$ ways to do both.

• Thus, there are 20 ways to draw one integer from both sets, since $4 \times 5 = 20$. Of these ways, exactly 3 add to 9:

Set A	2	3	4
Set B	7	6	5

• Because there are 20 ways to select an integer from each set, and precisely 3 of these ways add to 9, the correct answer must be (A):

$$\frac{3}{20} = \frac{3(5)}{20(5)} = \frac{15}{100} = 0.15$$

(10) Summary – As you've seen, Probability questions involve very little math.

• If you can multiply and add fractions, you can do the work. The real challenge is knowing when to do what.

> ➢ When solving a Probability problem, the first question you should ask yourself is "Are there MULTIPLE events?"

• If you have a SINGLE event, the chance that something may happen equals:

$$\frac{\text{The Number of Ways it } \textbf{CAN} \text{ Happen}}{\text{The } \textbf{TOTAL} \text{ Number of Outcomes}}$$

> ➢ If you have MULTIPLE events, you need to determine whether you have an "AND probability" or an "OR probability".

• "AND probabilities" involve events that happen in succession or at the same time. To solve them, simply MULTIPLY the individual probabilities together.

• Remember, selecting items from a COLLECTION will DIMINISH the options that remain. So, subtract from the numerator and/or the denominator as needed.

> ➢ "OR probabilities" involve events in which ONE or the OTHER may happen. In some cases, the events are mutually exclusive. In others, they overlap.

• To distinguish the two scenarios, ASK yourself "Are BOTH events POSSIBLE?"

• If the answer is NO, just ADD the probabilities. If the answer is YES, add the probabilities and SUBTRACT the OVERLAP. If you can't identify the overlap, you should subtract the possibility that BOTH events occur.

> ➢ If you need to determine the probability that DIFFERENT events may happen, you may find it easier to determine the odds that the events are the SAME.

• Likewise, if you need to determine the probability that something happens AT LEAST ONCE, it's generally easier to determine the odds that it NEVER happens.

• Finally, it's always worthwhile to bear in mind that:

1. For any event, the probabilities of all possible outcomes ADD to ONE.
2. The probability of any event lies between ZERO and ONE, inclusive.

> ➤ The most IMPORTANT decisions in this summary can be depicted with the following FLOW CHART.

• The white boxes represent questions, and the black box represent the proper responses to those questions:

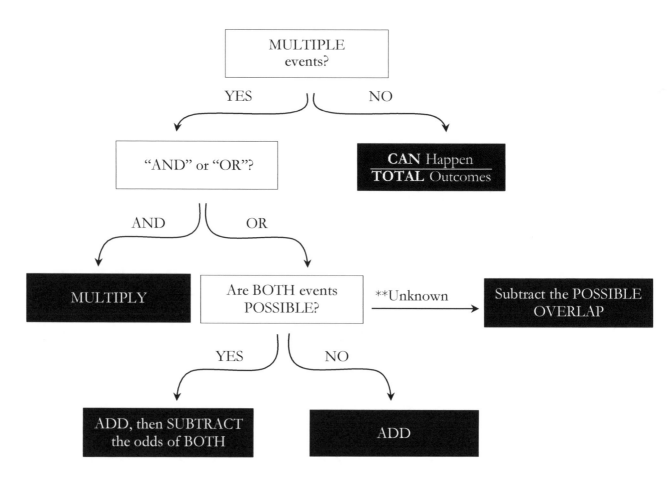

Note: ** = Advanced. (See section 11 for details).

(11) Unknown Relationships – Earlier, in our discussion of "OR probabilities", we pointed out that some events are mutually exclusive and that others are independent.

• In some cases, however, the relationship between two events may be UNSTATED or UNKNOWN.

➢ Imagine drawing one item, at random, from a hamper with 10 articles of clothing, of which 4 are shirts and 6 are blue.

• Because we don't know whether any of the shirts are blue, we don't know whether BOTH events CAN occur.

• After all, it could be that none of the shirts are blue, in which case it would be impossible for both events to occur. Alternatively, it could be that all the shirts are blue, in which case there would be significant overlap between the two events.

➢ In situations where the relationship between two events is UNKNOWN, **we must consider the EXTENT to which the events can OVERLAP**.

• Here, for example, the overlap can range from zero shirts to four shirts, so the probability of selecting a blue shirt can range from 0/10 to 4/10.

• Thus, the probability of selecting an item that is either a shirt <u>OR</u> something blue would range from 6/10 to 1, since in a "MAXIUMUM OVERLAP" scenario, the probability that both events occur would be 4/10, and in a "MINIMUM OVERLAP" scenario, the probability that both events occur would be 0/10:

EVERY SHIRT IS BLUE

$$\frac{4}{10} + \frac{6}{10} - \frac{4}{10} = \frac{6}{10}$$

P(Shirt) + P(Blue) – P(Overlap)

NO SHIRTS ARE BLUE

$$\frac{4}{10} + \frac{6}{10} - \frac{0}{10} = 1$$

P(Shirt) + P(Blue) – P(Overlap)

➢ Probability questions with UNKNOWN RELATIONSHIPS are rare for the GRE, but they do exist. They can also be quite tricky.

• To give you a sense of what one might look like, let's work through the following example together:

In a certain experiment, the probability that event X will occur is 1/3 and the probability that event Y will occur is 1/4. Which of the following values could be the probability that the event $X \cup Y$ will occur?

Indicate <u>all</u> such values.

$\boxed{A}\ \frac{1}{4}$ $\boxed{B}\ \frac{1}{3}$ $\boxed{C}\ \frac{2}{5}$ $\boxed{D}\ \frac{3}{5}$

Answer. B and C. As you may recall from the Overlapping Sets chapter of our book on Word Problems (see "Intersections & Unions"), the symbol $\cup$ denotes the UNION of two sets: the set of elements that are ONLY in ONE of the two sets <u>or</u> in BOTH sets.

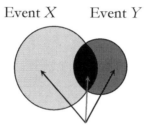

Event X Event Y

The UNION of events X and Y equals the <u>SUM</u> of these three regions.

➢ One way to answer this question, therefore, is to determine the probability that X <u>and</u> Y both occur and to subtract it from the probability that X <u>or</u> Y occurs.

• (Why? If we add events X and Y, we count the overlap TWICE. By subtracting the overlap ONCE, we remove the double-count!)

• Unfortunately, we DON'T KNOW the RELATIONSHIP between events X and Y, so we don't know whether the events are mutually exclusive (or whether they're independent, either). Thus, **we need to consider the extent to which the events can OVERLAP.**

➢ The OVERLAP would be <u>smallest</u> if the two events were to have NO INTERSECTION. Visually, you can imagine this relationship like so:

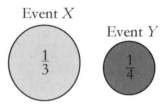

Event X

Event Y

$\frac{1}{3}$ $\frac{1}{4}$

• In such a case, the probability that X and Y <u>both</u> occur would be zero. Thus, the probability of the <u>union</u> of X and Y would equal 7/12, since the sum of the two regions minus their overlap equals $1/3 + 1/4 - 0 = 7/12$.

➤ Conversely, the OVERLAP would be <u>greatest</u> if event *Y* were a SUBSET of event *X*. Visually, this relationship can be depicted as follows:

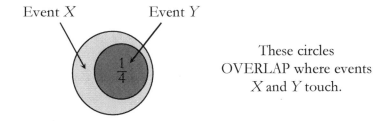

These circles OVERLAP where events *X* and *Y* touch.

• In this case, the probability that *X* and *Y* both occur would equal 1/4, since **the overlap between the two regions equals the probability of event *Y*.**

• The probability of the <u>union</u> of *X* and *Y* would therefore equal 1/3, since the sum of the two regions minus their overlap equals 1/3 + 1/4 – 1/4 = 1/3. Thus, the correct answers are (B) and (C), as the probability that *X* or *Y*, or both, will occur can be any value from 1/3 to 7/12, and only 1/3 and 2/5 fall within this range.

➤ If you prefer, questions like this can also be solved with an **Overlapping Sets table**.

• For example, in this question, we've been told that the probability of event *X* is 1/3 and the probability of event *Y* is 1/4.

• If we were to treat this problem as a FUQ (notice that there are no concrete values here!), we could first imagine a TOTAL of 12 events, since the product of the denominators equals 3 × 4 = 12.

➤ Next, we could set up two tables. In the first, we could let the "BOTH slot" equal ZERO, in order to **minimize the overlap**:

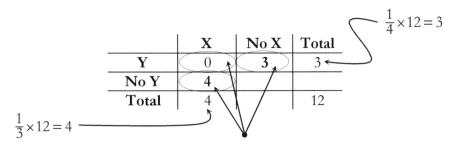

In an overlapping sets table, these 3 slots represent the <u>union</u> of two sets.

➢ In the second, we could let the "BOTH slot" equal THREE, in order to **maximize the overlap**:

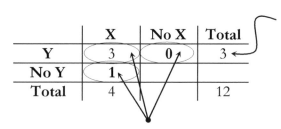

The BOTH slot cannot exceed this value.

Remember, these 3 slots represent the **union** of two sets.

• In this table, note that the overlap cannot exceed 3, because a BOTH value greater than 3 would give us a TOTAL for Y that exceeds 3! This is impossible since the question states that probability of event Y is 1/4, and 1/4 of 12 = 3.

➢ In the first table, the sum of the "UNION slots" gives us a total of 4 + 0 + 3 = 7, so the probability of the union of X and Y would equal 7/12.

• (Remember, our TOTAL slot = 12.)

• In the second table, the sum of the "UNION slots" gives us a total of 1 + 3 + 0 = 4, so the probability of the union of X and Y would equal 4/12, or 1/3.

➢ Thus, the probability that X or Y, or both, will occur can be any value from 1/3 to 7/12.

• As before, our answer can be any value from 1/3 to 7/12, so (B) and (C) are the correct answers, since 1/3 and 2/5 are the only answer choices that fall within this range.

(12) "Of Phrases" – Imagine a deck of cards in which one half of the cards are red and the other half are blue.

• If 3 cards are to be drawn at random from the deck, and each card is to be replaced immediately upon selection, what is the probability that exactly 2 of the 3 cards will be red?

➢ If you're like many test-takers, you might think that the answer should be 1/4, since there are only 4 possible outcomes: no reds, 1 red, 2 reds, or all reds.

• Unfortunately, this is incorrect because the extreme outcomes – no reds and all reds – are less likely to occur than outcomes with 1 or 2 heads.

• If we write out the ALL possible combinations by hand, we can see that the correct answer is actually 3/8, since 3 of the 8 possible outcomes have exactly two red cards:

RRR   <u>RRB</u>   <u>RBR</u>   RBB
BBR   BRB   <u>BRR</u>   BBB

➢ Now imagine that 5 cards are to be drawn at random from the deck. What is the probability that exactly 3 of the 5 cards will be red?

• This is a more difficult question, since it is hard to write out ALL the possible outcomes, especially in 2 minutes or less.

• To solve a problem like this, we need to use COMBINATORICS. Notice that we want "3 of the 5" cards to be red. Well, there are 10 ways to select a COMBINATION of 3 cards from a group of 5, as:

$$\frac{5!}{3!2!} = \frac{5 \times 4 \times \cancel{3}}{\cancel{3} \times 2 \times 1} = 10$$

➢ Likewise, every time we choose a card, there are 2 options: red or blue. Thus, choosing 5 cards has 32 possible outcomes, since $2 \times 2 \times 2 \times 2 \times 2 = 32$.

• The probability that 3 of the 5 cards are red is therefore 5/16, since:

$$\frac{\text{ways that 3 of 5 cards are red}}{2 \times 2 \times 2 \times 2 \times 2} = \frac{10}{32} = \frac{5}{16}$$

> ➤ Probability questions that require Combinatorics are easy to spot: they almost always contain an "OF PHRASE" such as "2 _of_ 3 cards" or "3 _of_ 5 women".

• To solve them, first treat the "of phrase" as a COMBINATION, as we did in the question above. Then place the outcome over the total number of possible outcomes.

• Consider the following:

A certain family is planning to have 4 children. If each child is equally likely to be a boy or a girl, what is the probability that 2 of the 4 children will be girls?

$$\text{(A) } \frac{1}{8} \quad \text{(B) } \frac{3}{16} \quad \text{(C) } \frac{1}{4} \quad \text{(D) } \frac{3}{8} \quad \text{(E) } \frac{1}{2}$$

Answer. D. According to the problem, we want "2 of the 4" children to be girls. Because the children are equally likely to be boys or girls, each child has TWO possible outcomes: boy or girl. The 4 children can therefore turn out 16 possible ways, since:

$$2 \times 2 \times 2 \times 2 = 16$$

Of these, there are exactly 6 ways in which "2 of the 4" children are girls, as:

$$\frac{4!}{2!2!} = \frac{4 \times 3 \times \cancel{2!}}{\cancel{2!} \times 2 \times 1} = 6$$

The probability that 2 of the 4 children are girls is therefore 3/8, since $6/16 = 3/8$:

> ➤ In some cases, you may need to pick from SEPARATE POOLS. For example, imagine selecting 3 students from a class of 8, 5 of whom are boys.

• To determine the probability that "2 of the 3" students are boys, you would first need to calculate the number of ways to select 2 boys from a pool of 5 and 1 girl from a pool of 3:

$$\frac{5!}{2!3!} = \frac{5 \times 4 \times \cancel{3!}}{2 \times 1 \times \cancel{3!}} = 10 \qquad \frac{3!}{1!2!} = \frac{3 \times \cancel{2!}}{1 \times \cancel{2!}} = 3$$

• You would then need to determine the number of ways to select any 3 students from a pool of 8:

$$\frac{8!}{3!5!} = \frac{8 \times 7 \times 6 \times \cancel{5!}}{3 \times 2 \times 1 \times \cancel{5!}} = \frac{8 \times 7 \times 6}{3 \times 2} = 8 \times 7 = 56$$

• Thus, the probability that 2 of the 3 students are boys would be 30/56, or 15/28, since there are $10 \times 3 = \textbf{30 ways}$ to select 2 boys and 1 girl, and **56 ways** to select any 3 students.

- Let's practice:

A certain box has 7 balls, of which 4 are black and 3 are white. Four balls are to be selected at random from the box.

Quantity A	Quantity B
The probability that 2 of the 4 balls are black	$\frac{1}{2}$

Answer: A. To determine the probability that "2 of the 4" balls are black, we first need to calculate the number of ways to select 2 black balls from a pool of 4 and 2 white balls from a pool of 3:

$$\frac{4!}{2!2!} = \frac{4 \times 3 \times \cancel{2}}{\cancel{2} \times 2 \times 1} = 6 \qquad \frac{3!}{2!1!} = \frac{3 \times \cancel{2}}{\cancel{2} \times 1} = 3$$

➤ Next, we need to determine the number of ways to select any 4 balls from a pool of 7:

$$\frac{7!}{4!3!} = \frac{7 \times 6 \times 5 \times \cancel{4!}}{\cancel{4!} \times 3 \times 2 \times 1} = \frac{7 \times 6 \times 5}{3 \times 2} = 7 \times 5 = 35$$

- Since there are $6 \times 3 =$ **18 ways** to select 2 black balls and 2 white balls, and **35 ways** to select any 4 balls, the probability that exactly 2 of the 4 balls are black must therefore be 18/35.

- According to the "Comparison Trick", 18/35 is a larger fraction that 1/2, since 36 is greater than 35. The correct answer is therefore (A).

$$\begin{array}{cc} 36 & 35 \\ \frac{18}{35} & \frac{1}{2} \end{array}$$

(13) "At Least Twice or More" – Earlier, we saw that the probability that an event occurs "at least once" equals "1 – the probability that it never occurs".

• Determining the probability that an event occurs "at least twice" is a little bit trickier.

➢ Imagine flipping a fair coin 4 times. If the coin lands tails up on EITHER 2, 3, or 4 of those flips, it lands tails up "AT LEAST TWICE".

• Thus, to determine the probability that the coin lands tails up "at least twice", we need to determine the probability that it does so <u>2 times or 3 times or 4 times</u>.

• Every time a coin is flipped, there are 2 possible outcomes: heads or tails. Flipping a coin 4 times therefore has 16 possible outcomes, since $2 \times 2 \times 2 \times 2 = 16$.

➢ The number of outcomes in which "2 of 4", "3 of 4", or "4 of 4" flips land tails up can be determined as follows (remember, $0! = 1$):

Tails on "2 of 4" Flips	Tails on "3 of 4" Flips	Tails on "4 of 4" Flips
$\dfrac{4!}{2!2!} = \dfrac{4 \times 3 \times \cancel{2!}}{\cancel{2!} \times 2 \times 1} = 6$	$\dfrac{4!}{3!1!} = \dfrac{4 \times \cancel{3!}}{\cancel{3!} \times 1} = 4$	$\dfrac{4!}{4!0!} = \dfrac{\cancel{4!}}{\cancel{4!} \times 1} = 1$

• Thus, the probability that the coin lands tails up at least twice is 11/16, since there are $6 + 4 + 1$ ways to get 2 or more tails and 16 possible outcomes.

➢ If we needed to determine the probability that the coin lands tails up "at least THREE times", we would simply add the probabilities that it does so 3 times or 4 times.

• Likewise, if we needed to determine the probability that the coin lands tail up "no more than twice", we would simply add the probabilities that it does so 1 time or 2 times.

• To ensure that you've got the hang of it, let's work through a second example together. Consider the following:

On any winter day in city X, there is a 50 percent chance that it snows. What is the probability that it snows on at least 3 of any 5 winter days in city X?

(B) $\frac{1}{4}$ (B) $\frac{3}{8}$ (C) $\frac{1}{2}$ (D) $\frac{3}{5}$ (E) $\frac{5}{8}$

Answer. C. According to the problem, city X has a 50 percent chance of snow on any winter day.

• Because the chance that it snows is equal to the chance that it doesn't, each day has TWO equally weighted outcomes: snow or no snow. Five days, therefore, have 32 possible outcomes, since:

$$2 \times 2 \times 2 \times 2 \times 2 = 32$$

➤ For it to snow on "at least three" of those days, it can snow <u>3 times or 4 times or 5 times</u>.

• The number of COMBINATIONS in which it snows on "3 of 5", "4 of 5", or "5 of 5" days can be determined as follows:

Snow on "3 of 5" Days	Snow on "4 of 5" Days	Snow on "5 of 5" Days
$\frac{5!}{3!2!} = \frac{5 \times 4 \times \cancel{3!}}{\cancel{3!} \times 2 \times 1} = 10$	$\frac{5!}{4!1!} = \frac{5 \times \cancel{4!}}{\cancel{4!} \times 1} = 5$	$\frac{5!}{5!0!} = \frac{\cancel{5!}}{\cancel{5!} \times 1} = 1$

• The probability that it snows on at least 3 of any 5 winter days in city X is therefore 16/32, or 1/2, since there are $10 + 5 + 1$ ways to get 3 or more days of snow and 32 possible outcomes. Thus, the correct answer is (C).

(14) Problem Sets – The following questions have been arranged into three groups: fundamental, intermediate, and rare or advanced.

• Whether you're aiming for a perfect score or a score closer to average, mastery of the concepts in the FUNDAMENTAL questions is absolutely essential.

➤ As you might expect, the INTERMEDIATE questions are more difficult but are essential for test-takers who need an above-average score or higher.

• Finally, the RARE or ADVANCED questions test concepts that are very sophisticated or seldom encountered on the GRE. Mastery of such questions is required only if you need a math score above the 90th percentile.

• As always, if you find yourself confused, bogged down with busy work, or stuck, don't be afraid to fall back on your "Plan B" strategies!

Fundamental

A certain jar contains 10 coins, 2 of which are pennies. One of the coins is to be selected at random from the box.

Quantity A	Ⓒ	Quantity B

1. The probability that the coin selected is not a penny $\qquad$ $\dfrac{4}{5}$

2. In a bag of 12 tennis balls, 3 are orange. If two balls are to be chosen at random from the bag, without replacement, what is the probability that both are orange?

(A) $\dfrac{1}{28}$ (B) $\dfrac{1}{24}$ (C) $\dfrac{1}{22}$ (D) $\dfrac{1}{18}$ (E) $\dfrac{1}{12}$

3. The probability that event E will occur is x, and the probability that event E will <u>not</u> occur is y. Which of the following can equal 1?

Select <u>all</u> possible options.

$\boxed{A}$ $x + y$ $\boxed{B}$ $x - y$ $\boxed{C}$ xy $\boxed{D}$ $\dfrac{x}{y}$

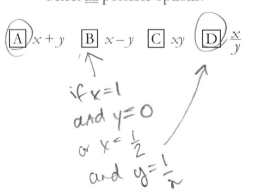

if x=1
and y=0
or x=½
and y=½

4. Events A and B cannot occur together. If the probability that event A or event B occurs is 0.6, and the probability of event A is 0.2, what is the probability of event B?

.4

The probability that both events F and G will occur is 0.38.

	Quantity A	Quantity B
5.	The probability that event F will occur	0.52

$P(F) \cdot P(G) = .38$
F could be 1 or .38

6. The probability that Lucia passes her entrance exam is 1/4. The probability that Lucia and Elias both pass their entrance exams is 1/6. What is the probability that Elias passes his entrance exam?

(A) $\frac{1}{4}$ (B) $\frac{1}{3}$ (C) $\frac{1}{2}$ (D) $\frac{2}{3}$ (E) $\frac{3}{4}$

7. A change purse contains 5 quarters, 4 dimes, and 3 pennies. What is the probability of picking a coin other than a dime three times in a row if each coin is selected at random?

Give your answer as a fraction.

$$\frac{14}{55}$$

remember to remove from pool after selection

8. Set A contains the numbers 1, 2, 3, and 4. Set B contains the numbers 5, 6, and 7. If one number is to be drawn from each set, what is the probability that the product of the two numbers is odd?

(A) $\frac{1}{12}$ (B) $\frac{1}{3}$ (C) $\frac{1}{2}$ (D) $\frac{2}{3}$ (E) $\frac{3}{4}$

zero is not odd!

The probability that event E will occur is three times the probability that it won't.

	Quantity A	Quantity B
9.	$P(E)$	0.75

C

Intermediate

10. A fair coin is to be tossed 3 times. What is the probability that the coin lands tails up at least once?

$$\text{(A) } \frac{1}{8} \text{ (B) } \frac{3}{8} \text{ (C) } \frac{1}{2} \text{ (D) } \frac{5}{8} \text{ (E) } \frac{7}{8}$$

A box contains x red blocks, $4x + 12$ white blocks, 3 blue blocks, and nothing else.

Quantity A		Quantity B
	(D)	

11. The probability of selecting a red block or a blue block at random   0.2

keep going with algebra

12. In a certain board game, a spinner has 4 equal sectors. If randomly spun 3 times, what is the probability that the spinner does not land on the same sector each time? Assume the spinner cannot land between sectors.

4 scenarios in which spinner lands on same sector so need to add

$$\text{(A) } \frac{7}{8} \quad \text{(B) } \frac{8}{9} \quad \text{(C) } \frac{11}{12} \quad \text{(D) } \frac{15}{16} \quad \text{(E) } \frac{63}{64}$$

A certain bowl has 20 marbles, of which 12 are red, 6 white, and 2 are blue. 8 of the marbles are large, 12 are small, and 7 of the red and white marbles are large.

Quantity A		Quantity B
	(C)	

13. The probability of randomly drawing a marble that is either large or blue $\frac{1}{2}$

✳ need to subtract overlap – large + blue

14. A bag contains only red, blue, and yellow marbles. The odds of randomly selecting a red marble from the bag are 1/7. If the odds of randomly selecting a blue marble are 1/3, and the bag cannot contain more than 63 marbles, what is the maximum number of yellow marbles that the bag can contain?

(A) 21   (B) 33   (C) 41   (D) 43   (E) 44

15. On a certain lot, 1/7 of the vehicles are wagons, and 1/4 of the other vehicles are sedans. If Paul buys a vehicle on this lot at random, what is the probability that he buys a sedan?

Round your answer to the nearest hundredth.

0.21

There are two decks of cards. The first has five cards labeled 1, 2, 3, 4, and 5, and the second six cards labeled A, B, C, D, E, and F. One card is to be selected at random from each deck.

Quantity A   Quantity B

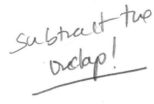

subtract the overlap!

16.   The probability of selecting a card labeled $\frac{1}{3}$
       with the number "3" or the letter "C"

17. From a box containing 12 identical baseballs, x identical softballs, and nothing else, one ball will be removed at random. If the probability is less than 2/5 that the removed ball will be a baseball, what is the least number of softballs that must be in the box?

(A) 12   (B) 15   (C) 16   (D) 18   (E) 19

2/5

to make probability less than 2/5 add softballs

18. A jar contains 30 red marbles, 40 blue marbles, and nothing else. 35 of the marbles are glass, and 5/7 of the glass marbles are blue. What are the odds of randomly drawing a red marble made of glass?

(A) $\frac{1}{7}$ (B) $\frac{1}{5}$ (C) $\frac{2}{7}$ (D) $\frac{1}{3}$ (E) $\frac{5}{14}$

Chapter 4: Probability

An experiment has events A, B, and C, for which the probability of each event is 0.25, 0.40, and 0.20, respectively. Events A and B can occur together, but events B and C cannot.

Just need to subtract overlap

	Quantity A	Quantity B
19.	The probability of event A or event B.	The probability of event B or event C.

20. At a certain magnet school, 30% of the students in the French club are girls. If the French club has 20 students, and 3 of its members are selected at random, what is the probability that at least one of those students is a boy?

(A) $\frac{56}{57}$ (B) $\frac{53}{55}$ (C) $\frac{50}{53}$ (D) $\frac{47}{51}$ (E) $\frac{44}{49}$

In a certain experiment, x and y are independent events.

$x + y - \left(\begin{smallmatrix} x \, y \\ x \, but \\ also \, y \end{smallmatrix}\right)\left(\begin{smallmatrix} x \, y \\ y \, but \, also \\ x \end{smallmatrix}\right)$

	Quantity A	Quantity B
21.	The probability that either event will occur, but not both.	$x + y - 2xy$

22. A symposium has 80 invitees, of which 30 are male and the rest are female. Among the invitees are 5 married couples consisting of 1 man and 1 woman. If a committee is to select 1 man and 1 woman from the invitees to be keynote speakers, what is the probability that the two keynote speakers will be a married couple?

(A) $\frac{1}{300}$ (B) $\frac{1}{60}$ (C) $\frac{1}{5}$ (D) $\frac{3}{16}$ (E) $\frac{15}{64}$

$P(\text{married male}) = \frac{5}{30} \rightarrow \text{select Jeff}$

$P(\text{Jeff's wife}) = \frac{1}{50}$

$\frac{5}{30} \cdot \frac{1}{50} = \frac{1}{300}$

Rare or Advanced

23. A jar contains 10 jellybeans, of which 4 are white, 3 are red, 2 are blue, and 1 is green. If 2 jellybeans are removed from the jar at random, what is the probability of selecting 1 red jellybean and 1 blue jellybean?

$$\text{(A)} \frac{1}{18} \quad \text{(B)} \frac{1}{15} \quad \text{(C)} \frac{1}{12} \quad \text{(D)} \frac{1}{6} \quad \text{(E)} \frac{2}{15}$$

A fair coin is flipped 5 times.

Quantity A	Quantity B
24. The probability of getting more heads than tails	0.5

25. A certain jar has red balls, green balls, and nothing else. The probability of drawing a red ball at random is 1/2. If that ball is not replaced, and the probability of drawing another red ball at random is 3/7, how many red balls does the jar initially contain?

$$\text{(A) 4} \quad \text{(B) 6} \quad \text{(C) 8} \quad \text{(D) 10} \quad \text{(E) 14}$$

A string of lights has 4 bulbs, each of which is equally likely to be on or off.

Quantity A	Quantity B
26. The probability that 2 of the 4 bulbs are off	0.5

27. A company has 8 employees, of whom 3 are men and 5 are women. A 3-person committee is to be selected at random from these employees. What is the probability that at exactly 2 of the committee members are women?

$$\text{(A)} \frac{3}{14} \quad \text{(B)} \frac{3}{8} \quad \text{(C)} \frac{1}{2} \quad \text{(D)} \frac{15}{28} \quad \text{(E)} \frac{4}{7}$$

28. A shelf holds 10 books, half of which are green and half of which are red. 5 of the books are dictionaries, and the other 5 are travel guides. If one of these books is to be selected at random, which of the following could be the probability that the book selected is either red or a dictionary?

Indicate <u>all</u> such values.

$\boxed{\text{A}}$ $\frac{1}{4}$ $\boxed{\text{B}}$ $\frac{2}{5}$ $\boxed{\text{C}}$ $\frac{1}{2}$ $\boxed{\text{D}}$ $\frac{3}{4}$ $\boxed{\text{E}}$ $\frac{4}{5}$

A fair coin is flipped 5 times.

<u>Quantity A</u>	<u>Quantity B</u>

29. The probability that no less than 4 of the flips land tails up

$\frac{1}{5}$

30. In a random experiment, 12 seeds are to be planted. For the experiment to succeed, every seed must sprout within 5 days, or the experiment is considered a failure. If for each individual seed the probability of not sprouting during the 5-day period is 0.08, what is the probability that the experiment will fail?

(A) 0.08   (B) $(0.08)^{12}$ (C) $1 - (0.08)^{12}$ (D) $(0.92)^{12}$ (E) $1 - (0.92)^{12}$

From a class of 3 boys and 3 girls, 4 students are to be randomly selected.

<u>Quantity A</u>	<u>Quantity B</u>

31. The probability of selecting more boys than girls

0.2

32. A team of 3 people is to be chosen from 5 pairs of siblings. What is the probability that everyone on the team will be unrelated?

(A) $\frac{1}{4}$ (B) $\frac{1}{2}$ (C) $\frac{2}{3}$ (D) $\frac{3}{4}$ (E) $\frac{4}{5}$

(15) Solutions – Video solutions for each of the previous questions can be found on our website at **www.sherpaprep.com/videos**.

- BOOKMARK this address for future visits!

  ➢ To view the videos, you'll need the LOGIN and PASSWORD that you created upon registering your copy of Statistics & Data Interpretation.

- If you have yet to register your book yet, please go to **www.sherpaprep.com/activate** and enter your email address, last name, and shipping address.

- Be sure to provide the SAME last name and shipping address that you used to purchase your copy of Master Key to the GRE or to enroll in your GRE course with Sherpa Prep!

  ➢ When checking your answers, we encourage you to watch the solution for any problem that you answered INCORRECTLY

- The same goes for any problem that took you MORE than TWO MINUTES to solve.

- After digesting the explanation, REVISIT your mistake a couple of days later to ensure that the problem no longer poses issues to you.

  ➢ If you struggle to solve the problem a SECOND time, add it to your "LOG of ERRORS" and redo it every few weeks.

- Solving tricky questions MORE THAN ONCE is the best way to learn from your mistakes and to avoid similar difficulties on your actual exam.

Fundamental	Intermediate		Rare or Advanced
1. C	10. E	20. A	23. E
2. C	11. C	21. C	24. C
3. A, B, D	12. D	22. A	25. A
4. 0.4	13. B		26. B
5. D	14. B		27. D
6. D	15. 0.21		28. C, D, E
7. 14/55	16. C		29. B
8. B	17. E		30. E
9. C	18. A		31. C
	19. B		32. C

Chapter 5

Data
Interpretation

Data Interpretation

To be discussed:

Fundamental Strategies

Whether you're aiming for a perfect score or a score closer to average, the following strategies will make Data Interpretation questions easier for you.

1 Introduction

2 Before Answering the Questions

3 Digesting the Diagrams

4 Tackling the Questions

5 Approximation

Math Concepts

Data Interpretation questions feature a variety of math concepts. You'll find a proper review of those concepts here.

6 Conversions

7 Taking the Percent of a Number

8 Percent Changes

9 Percent Relationships

10 Ratios, Averages & Medians

11 Overlapping Sets

12 Probability

13 Math Drills

Traps & Tricks

Familiarizing yourself with the graphs that you'll encounter on the GRE, and the classic "traps" and "tricks" that come with them, is vital for mastering Data Interpretation questions.

14 Bar Graphs

15 Pie Charts

16 Line Graphs

17 Data Tables & Rare Diagrams

18 Multi-Figure Data Sets

Practice Questions & Summary

There's no substitute for elbow grease. Practice your new skills to ensure that you internalize what you've studied.

19 Summary

20 Problem Sets

21 Solutions

Fundamental Strategies

(1) Introduction – Roughly 15% of all quantitative questions on the GRE involve graphs and charts.

• Such questions are commonly known as Data Interpretation questions.

> ➤ Data Interpretation questions come in sets. Each set has THREE questions and anywhere from one to three diagrams.

• Since every GRE exam has two Quantitative sections (excluding research sections), and each of these sections has one Data Interpretation set, your exam will contain SIX Data Interpretation questions.

• Every now and then, the GRE will include a seventh Data Interpretation question that is NOT part of a set, but this is fairly uncommon.

> ➤ Mathematically, most Data Interpretation questions involve PERCENTS, FRACTIONS, DECIMALS, and RATIOS.

• From time to time, you may also encounter questions involving STATISTICS, PROBABILITY, OVERLAPPING SETS, or GEOMETRY.

• If you've worked through all five volumes of <u>Master Key to the GRE</u>, you already know all the MATH necessary to solve any Data Interpretation question. If you haven't, don't worry: we'll review everything shortly.

> ➤ As you'll see in the sections to come, Data Interpretation questions are rarely sophisticated.

• Conceptually, most are fairly straightforward and, in many cases, the arithmetic involved with such questions is easily handled with the onscreen calculator.

• For most people, the difficulty of Data Interpretation lies in solving the problems quickly and avoiding careless mistakes.

> ➤ If that's you, we've got good news: there are a number of ways we can help.

• Finally, we encourage you to FAMILIARIZE yourself thoroughly with the types of graphs and charts found on the GRE. Each comes with a unique set of classic "TRICKS" and "TRAPS". The "traps" are easily avoided IF you've mastered the "tricks" ahead of time.

(2) Before Answering the Questions – There are many keys to improving your ability to solve Data Interpretation questions.

- The first of them, in many ways, is the most important as well as the easiest:

   ➢ BEFORE tackling a Data Interpretation question set, we want you to take as much TIME as you need to MASTER the graphs and charts.

- If you're like many test-takers, you may not feel that there is enough time for you to do so. We understand that concern.

- The truth of the matter, however, is that it takes most people less than 30 seconds to carefully read through and understand the Data Interpretation diagrams.

   ➢ And even if you happen to require a little more time, slowing down to master the graphs and charts BEFORE answering the questions remains a great time investment.

- After all, if you attack the questions before you perfectly UNDERSTAND what the graphs are about, what's going to happen when you try to solve them?

- For one thing, it's going to be HARDER to find the information you need, since you won't know where to find it.

   ➢ Worse still, answering questions about a graph you don't really understand is going to make the questions SEEM harder than they actually are.

- And wrestling with this added confusion will only slow you down further.

- In other words, if you rush into the questions, all of the time that you think you're saving will be LOST once you struggle to solve them. In fact, we would argue that you will actually SAVE time when you invest it up front.

   ➢ Yes, you may lose 30 or so seconds before answering the questions, but you'll likely save MORE than that over the course of a typical three-question set.

- Just as importantly, you'll be more likely to answer the questions CORRECTLY.

➢ To help you internalize this point, answer the following question BEFORE taking the time to understand the graph.

• Give yourself exactly ONE MINUTE to do so:

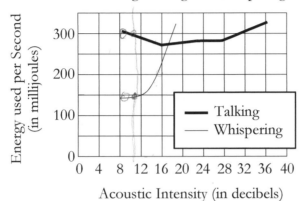

Energy Used Per Second Versus Acoustic Intensity During Talking and Whispering

If *I* is the acoustic intensity, in decibels, at which the energy used per second during talking is twice the energy used per second during whispering, then, according to the graph above, *I* is between

(A) 10 and 12   (B) 12 and 14   (C) 14 and 16   (D) 16 and 18   (E) 18 and 20

• If you weren't able to do so, now take the time to familiarize yourself with the graph's labels, headings, and content.

➢ The BOLD line represents the energy spent while TALKING, and the thin line represents the energy spent while WHISPERING.

• Using the answer choices, we can see that at 12 decibels, a little less than 300 millijoules are spent talking and roughly 150 millijoules are spent whispering.

• We can also see that this ratio DECREASES as the acoustic intensity rises above 12 decibels.

➢ For example, at 16 decibels, roughly 275 millijoules are spent talking, but nearly 225 millijoules are spent whispering.

• The correct answer must therefore be (A), since the energy spent talking at any intensity above 12 decibels is considerably LESS than TWICE the energy spent whispering at that same intensity.

(3) Digesting the Diagrams – More than anything, Data Interpretation questions test your ability to be CAREFUL and PRECISE.

• In our experience, careless mistakes are BY FAR the most common reason that test-takers get Data Interpretation questions wrong.

> ➢ In part, such mistakes stem from the fact that most people rush into the questions before reading the diagrams.

• In many cases, however, careless mistakes are the result of reading the diagrams POORLY.

• If you want to significantly improve your proficiency with Data Interpretation questions, you need to adopt GOOD HABITS.

> ➢ When reading a graph or a chart, take the time to UNDERSTAND what each diagram means.

• This means slowing down to examine each LABEL and HEADING carefully.

• **It also means asking yourself questions**. "Does the information make sense?" "Does the data show any TRENDS?" "Are there any numbers?" If so, "are the numbers PERCENTAGES or CONCRETE VALUES?"

> ➢ If you have TWO diagrams, ask yourself whether you understand the DISTINCTION between the two.

• Likewise, make sure that you understand how they relate to another.

• Finally, TAKE NOTES. If your graph provides any TOTAL values, write them down and what they refer to. If your graph has two diagrams, abbreviate the KEY WORD or phrase that defines each diagram.

> ➢ Taking such notes will FORCE you to identify any significant numbers and help you INTERNALIZE the central ideas.

• Yes, jotting down a few numbers and abbreviations will slow you down. However, an extra five seconds to ensure that you are aware of the important values and distinctions is a great investment of your time.

- In short, you need to be an ACTIVE reader.

   ➤ If you're content to let the information "wash over" you, you're not going to understand the graphs well enough to protect yourself against careless errors.

- To give you a better sense of what we mean by all this, consider the following diagrams:

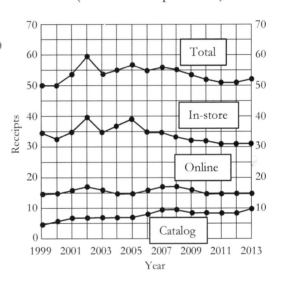

The Retail and Wholesale Revenue of Company *X*, 1999-2013 (in billions of dollars) (1 billion = 1,000,000,000)

Receipt of Company *X*'s Retail Revenue, by Source, 1999-2013 (in millions of purchases)

- BEFORE tackling the questions of a set like this, you should be thinking: "Okay, this set is about a company's revenues and receipts from the years 1999 to 2013, a 15-year period."

   ➤ "The graph on the LEFT compares the retail and wholesale REVENUE of company *X*."

- "The revenue from both increases over time, but retail revenue increases more dramatically. The graph on the RIGHT compares the RECEIPT of company *X*'s <u>retail</u> revenue by source: in-store, online, and catalog. For all three, the number of purchases generally hold steady."

- **Your NOTES should look like this**: "Rev. = billions ($), Rec. = millions (purch.). Real #'s, not %."

(4) Tackling the Questions – When tackling Data Interpretation problems, it's just as important to read the questions PRECISELY as it is to digest the diagrams.

• Solving for the WRONG thing is a common reason that test-takers get Data Interpretation problems wrong.

> ➢ To prevent yourself from misreading the questions, we encourage you to WRITE DOWN the KEY WORDS as you read.

• Taking notes will FORCE you to identify what the question's after and FOCUS your attention on what's critical. Take the following question:

In 1976, what percent of part-time students were born in countries other than the United States?

(A) 20   (B) 25   (C) 30   (D) 35   (E) 40

• This question asks you to identify the <u>percent</u> of <u>part-time</u> students from countries <u>other than</u> the United States in <u>1976</u>.

> ➢ Thus, while reading it, you might jot down the notes "1976", "percent", "p/t", and "<u>other</u> than U.S.".

• As with the diagrams, jotting down a few numbers and abbreviations will slow you down.

• During your exam, if you're tempted to skip taking notes, just remember that an extra 5 seconds to ensure that you answer the RIGHT question is always a GREAT investment of your time.

> ➢ When answering the questions, it's also important that you READ the MEASUREMENTS as PRECISELY as possible.

• IMPRECISE readings are another common reason that test-takers get Data Interpretation questions wrong.

• To get a sense of whether you are prone to measuring values imprecisely, consider the graph on the following page. Determine the value of all donations apportioned to overhead and operational expenses for Charity *X* in the 1987-1988 financial year:

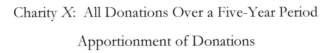

Charity X: All Donations Over a Five-Year Period

Apportionment of Donations

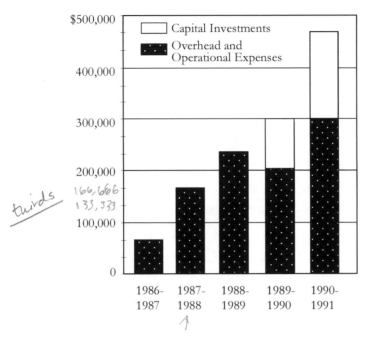

• As you will see in the sections to come, if your response was anything other than $166,666 (or $167,000), there are questions in which your reading would lead to a WRONG answer.

> We know that the apportionment to overhead and operational expenses in the 1987-88 financial year was exactly $166,667 for TWO reasons.

• First, the tick marks on the side of the graph reveal that the contributions between $100,000 and $200,000 are demarcated in THIRDS (count the intervals between the two amounts):

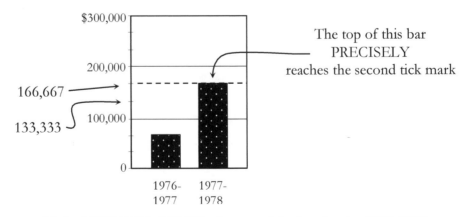

• Second, since one-third of $100,000 is $33,333, the top of the bar for the 1987-1988 school year exactly reaches the $166,667 mark.

• So, don't get lazy with your measurements. ALWAYS determine them as precisely as possible.

➢ Should a question ask you to determine an APPROXIMATE value, you can always round the value later — once you know the exact value and whether it's safe to round.

• If you find it difficult to measure something precisely, use your SCRATCH PAPER as a make-shift RULER, like so:

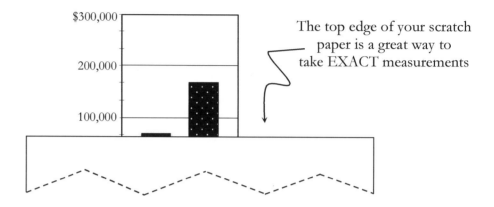

The top edge of your scratch paper is a great way to take EXACT measurements

• The edge of a sheet of paper is a straight line, so it can always help you compare two measurements precisely.

➢ Finally, when performing SIMPLE VISUAL TASKS (such as counting the number of points that exceed a certain limit), do so as CAREFULLY as possible.

• It's easier than you think to miscount dots on a computer screen! Don't rush through such tasks just because they seem simple.

• Even the most mathematically-gifted test-takers get such questions wrong. So, SLOW DOWN. "Simple visual task" questions should be money in the bank. Remember: when solving a Data Interpretation problem, investing an extra 5 seconds to avoid a careless mistake is ALWAYS worth the time.

(5) Approximation – Finally, to save time, you'll need to be comfortable approximating fractions, decimals, and percents.

• Roughly a third of all Data Interpretation questions involve approximation in one form or another. In many of these cases, you'll be tempted to use the on-screen calculator.

> ➤ In general, we ENCOURAGE you to use the calculator if (but only if) you NEED to.

• Data Interpretation questions are more likely to require a calculator than any other type of Quantitative Reasoning question.

• Approximation, however, is often FASTER than the calculator — particularly in questions that involve a SERIES of calculations.

> ➤ To start, it's important to know when you SHOULD approximate and when you SHOULDN'T.

• As you may recall from our chapter on "Plan B" Strategies, most problems that contain phrases such as "approximately", "nearest to", and "closest to" can be solved through approximation.

• This is especially true if a problem contains **DIFFICULT numbers <u>AND</u> a phrase that means APPROXIMATELY**!

> ➤ When approximating, always ROUND your numbers as LITTLE as possible.

• You want to round just enough to make the arithmetic easy, but not so much as to distort the information significantly. Consider the following:

In a recent school year, college *C* received $467,000 in alumni contributions. Of these contributions, 12 percent were allocated to campus upkeep. Approximately what amount of those contributions was NOT allocated to campus upkeep?

(A) $4,000   (B) $50,000   (C) $352,000   (D) $410,000   (E) $500,000

Answer: D. According to the question, 12% of the allocations were allocated to campus upkeep.

• Thus, to determine how much of the contributions were NOT allocated to campus upkeep, we simply need to remove 12% from the total contributions.

- Because the college received $467,000 in contributions, we can say:

$$\$467,000 - 12\% \text{ of } \$467,000 = \text{Amount NOT for Upkeep}$$

> ➤ Since the question contains the word "approximately" AND it's difficult to calculate 12% of 467,000 quickly, the best way to solve this problem is to round the numbers.

- In general, **if you need to round two numbers, try to round them in the same direction.** Rounding numbers in opposite directions can exaggerate the effects of rounding. Thus, let's round 12% down to 10% and 467,000 down to 460,000.

- Since 10% of 460,000 is 46,000 (remember, to get 10% of a number, slide its decimal one space to the left), answer choice (D) must be the correct answer: $410,000 is the only answer close to our approximation of $414,000.

$$\$460,000 - \$46,000 = \$414,000$$

> ➤ But be careful: **if a problem contains numbers that CAN be easily handled, do NOT round.** Even if it contains a phrase that means "approximately".

- Rounding in such cases will always produce the wrong answer. Consider the following problem:

Which of the following is most nearly equal to the quotient of 3.2 ÷ 2?

(A) $\frac{2}{3}$ (B) $\frac{13}{10}$ (C) $\frac{3}{2}$ (D) $\frac{8}{5}$ (E) $\frac{5}{2}$

Answer. D. Because this question contains the phrase "most nearly equal to", we may be tempted to round 3.2 to 3. Doing so would lead us to choose (C) as the correct answer, since 3 ÷ 2 is another way of saying $\frac{3}{2}$.

> ➤ However, doing so would also be a mistake: this problem does not contain difficult numbers. 3.2 ÷ 2 is easy to work with.

- Since 3.2 ÷ 2 = $\frac{3.2}{2.0}$, we can "slide" each decimal point one space to the right and reduce the fraction as follows:

$$\frac{3.2}{2.0} = \frac{32}{20} = \frac{4(8)}{4(5)} = \frac{8}{5}$$

- Thus, the correct answer is (D).

> ➢ Finally, **beware of the "Rounding Trap"**. Exam-makers know that some test-takers will round.

• From time to time, therefore, they design questions that are intended to confuse test-takers who do. Consider the following:

10 units of commodity X cost \$14.29. At this rate, how much do 79 units of commodity X cost, in dollars?

(A) 56   (B) 82   (C) 91   (D) 110   (E) 130

Answer. D. To start, notice that this question does not contain a word or phrase that means "approximately". However, note that its answer choices are fairly dispersed.

> ➢ If your problem contains answer choices that are spread apart AND numbers that are difficult to work with, it's SAFE to round.

• You never want to approximate if the answers are tightly bunched.

• For example, answer choices such as (A) 56, (B) 58, (C) 59, (D) 60, (E) 62 would be TOO CLOSE together to consider rounding. Answer such as (A) 56, (B) 82, (C) 91, (D) 110, (E) 130, however, have sufficient space between them to consider doing so.

> ➢ To solve this problem, let's round \$14.29 up to \$15 and 79 up to 80. If 10 units of commodity X cost \$15, then each unit costs \$1.50.

• Thus, 80 units of commodity X should cost \$120, since:

$$80 \text{ units} \times \$1.50 \quad \rightarrow \quad 80(1+0.5) \quad \rightarrow \quad 80+40 = \$120$$

• Notice that our answer, 120, put us right in the middle of answer choices (D) 110 and (E) 130. **We've fallen right into the "Rounding Trap": our rounding has put exactly between two answer choices**.

> ➢ To climb out, we simply need to understand HOW our rounding AFFECTED our answer.

• Looking back, notice that we INCREASED the rate of the commodity AND increased the number of units purchased.

• Thus, our rounding INFLATED the total cost. Therefore, (D) is the correct answer, since the correct answer must be slightly SMALLER than our approximated answer of \$120.

Math Concepts

(6) Conversions – As mentioned at the outset of this chapter, Data Interpretation questions feature a variety of math topics.

• If you've worked through our previous books on Word Problems and Arithmetic, Number Properties, & Algebra, all of these topics will be familiar to you.

> ➤ Before exploring the classic "tricks" and "traps" that you'll find among GRE graphs and charts, however, let's take a moment to REVIEW them.

• In one way or another, most Data Interpretation questions involve fractions, decimals, or percents.

• This is particularly true of percents. MORE than HALF of all Data Interpretation questions feature percents.

> ➤ Since, a proper understanding of percents is essential for success on the Data Interpretation portions of the GRE, let's start our review there.

• As you may recall from the Percents chapter of our book on Word Problems, any percent can be CONVERTED to a fraction or a decimal.

• To convert **a percent to a fraction**, simply DIVIDE it by 100. To convert **a percent to a decimal**, SHIFT its decimal point TWO places to the left:

$$17\% = \frac{17}{100} = 0.17 \qquad 123\% = \frac{123}{100} = 1.23 \qquad 300\% = \frac{300}{100} = 3.00$$

> ➤ Conversely, any fraction or decimal can be converted to a percent by REVERSING these steps.

• Thus, to convert **a decimal into a percent**, SHIFT the decimal point TWO spaces to the right:

$$0.27 = 27\% \qquad\qquad 0.003 = 0.3\% \qquad\qquad 10.00 = 1,000\%$$

• Likewise, to **convert a fraction into a percent**, MULTIPLY it by 100:

$$\frac{2}{5} \rightarrow \frac{2}{5} \times 100 = \frac{2}{5} \times (20) = 40\% \qquad\qquad \frac{9}{4} \rightarrow \frac{9}{4} \times 100 = \frac{9}{4} \times (25) = 225\%$$

> ➢ From time to time, you need to convert TRICKY FRACTIONS into percents to solve a Data Interpretation problem.

- There are two ways to do so. One way is to use the on-screen calculator.

- Thus, if you needed to convert $\frac{3}{8}$ into a percent, you could type **3** $\boxed{\div}$ **8** $\boxed{=}$ into the calculator and multiply the result by 100 .

> ➢ In many cases, however, the FASTER way is to use the "Conversion List" we introduced in the Arithmetic chapter of our book on <u>Number Properties & Algebra</u>.

- Here's the list:

$$\frac{1}{2} = 0.5 \qquad \frac{1}{5} = 0.2 \qquad \frac{1}{8} = 0.125 \qquad \frac{1}{11} = 0.\overline{09}$$

$$\frac{1}{3} = 0.\overline{3} \qquad \frac{1}{6} = 0.1\overline{6} \qquad \frac{1}{9} = 0.\overline{1} \qquad \frac{1}{99} = 0.\overline{01}$$

$$\frac{1}{4} = 0.25 \qquad \frac{1}{7} \approx 0.14 \qquad \frac{1}{10} = 0.1 \qquad \frac{1}{100} = 0.01$$

> ➢ To get a sense of how this list works, imagine that you needed to convert $\frac{3}{8}$ or $\frac{6}{7}$ into percents.

- If you know that $\frac{1}{8} = 0.125$, then you can deduce that $\frac{3}{8} = 37.5\%$, since $\frac{3}{8}$ is simply $3 \times \frac{1}{8}$:

$$\frac{3}{8} \;\rightarrow\; 3 \times \frac{1}{8} = 3 \times 0.125 \;\rightarrow\; 0.375 \times 100 = 37.5\%$$

- Likewise, if you know that $\frac{1}{7} \approx 0.14$, then you can deduce that $\frac{6}{7} \approx 86\%$, since $\frac{6}{7}$ is $1 - \frac{1}{7}$:

$$\frac{6}{7} \;\rightarrow\; 1 - \frac{1}{7} \approx 1 - 0.14 \;\rightarrow\; 0.86 \times 100 = 86\%$$

> ➢ The "Conversion List" is also really useful for APPROXIMATING tricky percents as fractions — something the on-screen calculator CAN'T help you with!

- Imagine that you needed to determine the approximate fractional value of 28%.

- If you divide 28 by 100, you get $\frac{28}{100}$, which reduces to $\frac{7}{25}$. Unfortunately, $\frac{7}{25}$ is not a useful answer. Not only is it not an approximation, it's too large and unwieldy to identify a simple equivalent. However, if you know that $\frac{1}{7} \approx 14\%$, then it's fairly easy to recognize that $28\% \approx \frac{2}{7}$, since $2 \times 14\% = 28\%$.

(7) Taking the Percent of a Number – To solve Data Interpretation questions involving percents, you'll need to perform a host of other operations, too.

- Most importantly, you must be able to TAKE a PERCENT of a number.

  ➢ In most cases, the FASTEST way to take a percent of a number is with the $\boxed{\textbf{``10\% Shortcut''}}$ that we introduced in our book on <u>Number Properties & Algebra</u>.

- As you may recall, if you can get 10% of a number, you can get other percents of that number (e.g. 5%, 15%, 20%, 30%, etc.) very easily.

  ➢ To get 10% of a number, simply SLIDE the decimal point ONE space to the left. Thus:

$$10\% \text{ of } 82 = 8.2 \qquad 10\% \text{ of } 230 = 23 \qquad 10\% \text{ of } 0.05 = 0.005$$

- To get 5% of a number, therefore, simply take HALF of 10%:

$$5\% \text{ of } 270 = \tfrac{1}{2} \text{ of } 27 = 13.5 \qquad\qquad 5\% \text{ of } 38 = \tfrac{1}{2} \text{ of } 3.8 = 1.9$$

- Likewise, to get 20%, 30%, or 40% of a number, get 10% of that number and double, triple, or quadruple it:

$$\underline{20\% \text{ of } 180} \qquad\qquad\qquad \underline{60\% \text{ of } 110}$$
$$2 \times (10\% \text{ of } 180) = 2 \times 18 = 36 \qquad 6 \times (10\% \times 110) = 6 \times 11 = 66$$

  ➢ If you can get 1% of a number, the "10% shortcut" can also be used to determine more complicated percents, such as 6%, 11%, or 29%.

- To get 1% of a number, simply SLIDE its decimal spot TWO spaces to the left:

$$1\% \text{ of } 82 = 0.82 \qquad 1\% \text{ of } 230 = 2.3 \qquad 1\% \text{ of } 0.05 = 0.0005$$

- Thus, to get 11% of a number, add 10% and 1% together:

$$11\% \text{ of } 120 = (10\% \text{ of } 120) + (1\% \text{ of } 120) = 12 + 1.2 = 13.2$$

- Likewise, to get 29% of a number, subtract 1% from 30%:

$$29\% \text{ of } 40 = 3 \times (10\% \text{ of } 40) - (1\% \text{ of } 40) = (3 \times 4) - 0.4 = 11.6$$

➢ Another great way to "take a percent of a number" is to convert a percent to a FRACTION.

• In math, the word OF typically means "MULTIPLY". Therefore, statements such as "40% of 30" and "70% of 200" can be thought of as:

$$\frac{40}{100} \times 30 \qquad\qquad \frac{70}{100} \times 200$$

• Once a percent is in fraction form, any ZEROES in common to the tops and bottoms of the fraction and number can be CANCELED. Thus:

$$\frac{40}{100} \times 30 = \frac{4\cancel{0}}{1\cancel{0}\cancel{0}} \times \frac{3\cancel{0}}{1} = 4 \times 3 = 12 \qquad\qquad \frac{70}{100} \times 200 = \frac{70}{1\cancel{0}\cancel{0}} \times \frac{2\cancel{0}\cancel{0}}{1} = 70 \times 2 = 140$$

➢ The ⟨"**Fraction Approach**"⟩ to percents is particularly effective with more complicated percents.

• Imagine that you needed to determine "14% of 350" or "22% of 30":

$$\frac{14}{100} \times 350 \qquad\qquad \frac{22}{100} \times 30$$

• After canceling the zeroes, you would only need to BREAK DOWN the remaining numbers to determine the percentages. Thus:

$$\frac{14}{10\cancel{0}} \times 35\cancel{0} = \frac{\cancel{2}(7)}{\cancel{2}(\cancel{5})} \times \cancel{5}(7) = 49 \qquad\qquad \frac{22}{10\cancel{0}} \times 3\cancel{0} = \frac{22}{10} \times 3 = 2.2 \times 3 = 6.6$$

➢ We highly recommend that you know BOTH strategies.

• Although the "10% Shortcut" is often the faster strategy (and the strategy that you should use more frequently), the "Fraction Approach" is a great complement to the "10% Shortcut".

• Some problems yield more easily to one approach than the other. Knowing both strategies is a huge help, especially when the numbers get funky.

➢ Finally, you can always use the on-screen CALCULATOR. We recommend this approach ONLY if you're working with extremely AWKWARD numbers.

• Thus, if you needed to determine 18% of 173, you could type **0.18** ⨯ **173** = into the calculator. We think that using a calculator in a situation like this would be a smart choice.

(8) Percent Changes – To solve Data Interpretation questions, you also need to be able to work with percent changes.

• To CALCULATE a percent change, first place the difference between the new and original values over the original value.

> ➤ Then, MULTIPLY the result by 100 in order to CONVERT the fraction into a percent:

$$\text{Percent Change} = \frac{\text{Difference}}{\text{Original}} \times 100$$

• Thus, if the number of students enrolled in school S was 240 in 1976 and 300 in 1978, the enrollment INCREASED by 25%, since:

$$\frac{\text{Difference}}{\text{Original}} \times 100 \quad \rightarrow \quad \frac{300-240}{240} \times 100 \quad \rightarrow \quad \frac{6\cancel{0}}{24\cancel{0}} \times 100 = \frac{1}{4} \times 100 = 25\%$$

> ➤ Just remember that the ORIGINAL value is always the value that is CHRONOLOGICALLY earlier.

• Hence, if store T had $60,000 in sales in 1984 and $40,000 in sales in 1983, the store experienced a 50% INCREASE in sales, since 1983 chronologically precedes 1984.

• Thus:

$$\frac{\text{Difference}}{\text{Original}} \times 100 \quad \rightarrow \quad \frac{60,000-40,000}{40,000} \times 100 \quad \rightarrow \quad \frac{20,000}{40,000} \times 100 = \frac{1}{2} \times 100 = 50\%$$

> ➤ If a question involves a percent change GREATER than 100 percent, take care not to make assumptions. Such questions are easy to misconstrue.

• Treat them as you would any other question involving a percent change.

• Thus, if the price of a certain book increases from $10 to $30, the percent increase is 200%, NOT 300%, since:

$$\frac{\text{Difference}}{\text{Original}} \times 100 \quad \rightarrow \quad \frac{30-10}{10} \times 100 \quad \rightarrow \quad \frac{20}{10} \times 100 = 2 \times 100 = 200\%$$

➢ From time to time, Data Interpretation questions will also ask you to APPLY a percent change.

• For example, a problem may tell you that a $120 stock increased its value by 30%, or that a "40% off" sale lowered the value of a sweater to $60.

• When the value of an object increases or decreases, the relationship between its ORIGINAL value and its NEW value can be stated as:

$$\textbf{Original} \times (1 \pm \textbf{\% Change}) = \textbf{New}$$

➢ If the percent change is an INCREASE, the value of that increase should be ADDED to 1. Conversely, if it's a decrease it should be subtracted from 1.

• Hence, if the price of a $90 tennis racket increases by 20%, the **new price** of the tennis racket will equal the **original price** × **1.2**, or $108, since:

$$\$90(1 + 0.2) = 90(1.2) = \$108$$

• Conversely, if the price of a sweater is $63 after a 30% discount, the **original price** of the sweater will equal $90, since:

$$\text{original} \times (1 - 0.3) = \$63 \quad \rightarrow \quad \text{original} = \frac{\$63}{0.7} = \frac{\$630}{7} = \$90$$

➢ To simplify the arithmetic of certain calculations, think of your original value as "**10 × something**". You can then "transfer" this 10 to slide away the decimal point.

• For example, if the price of a $50 pair of shoes increases by 20%, the **new price** of the shoes will equal the **original price** × **1.2**, or $60, as:

$$\$50(1.2) = 5\underbrace{(10)(1.2)}_{\text{multiply}} = 5(12) = \$60$$

• Likewise, if a $130 dress is marked down 70%, the **new price** of the dress will equal the **original price** × **0.3**, or $39, since:

$$\$130(0.3) = 13\underbrace{(10)(0.3)}_{\text{multiply}} = 13(3) = \$39$$

Remember:
30% off = 70% *of*

(9) Percent Relationships – Finally, when it comes to percents, there are two basic relationships that you need to know.

- The first is between $\boxed{\textbf{a PART and its WHOLE}}$. Imagine that you needed to determine "what percent of 250 is 45".

  ➤ A simple way to solve such questions is to compare the part to the whole through the following PROPORTION:

$$\frac{\text{Part}}{\text{Whole}} = \frac{\text{"Percent"}}{100}$$

- For example, to determine "what percent of 250 is 45", we need to determine the **percent**. We've been given the **part** and the **whole**, so we can set up the relationship as:

$$\underset{\text{whole}}{\overset{\text{part}}{\frac{45}{250}}} = \frac{x}{100} \quad \text{"percent"}$$

- Thus, 45 is $\boxed{18 \text{ percent}}$ of 250, since cross-multiplication gives us:

$$45(100) = 250x \quad \rightarrow \quad \frac{45(100)}{250} = x \quad \rightarrow \quad \frac{45(100)}{5(5)} = 9(2) = 18 = x$$

  ➤ If you're confused about which value is the "part" and which the "whole", simply remember that "IS = PART" and "OF = WHOLE".

- In other words, any "part-to-whole" relationship can also be thought of as:

$$\frac{\text{Part}}{\text{Whole}} = \frac{\text{Is}}{\text{Of}} = \frac{\text{Percent}}{100}$$

- For example, to determine "what percent 64 is of 40", we need to determine the **percent**. We've been told "64 **is**" some percent "**of** 40", so the relationship between 64 and 40 is:

$$\underset{\text{of}}{\overset{\text{is}}{\frac{64}{40}}} = \frac{x}{100} \quad \text{percent}$$

- Thus, 64 is $\boxed{160 \text{ percent}}$ of 40, as:

$$64(100) = 40x \quad \rightarrow \quad \frac{64(100)}{40} = x \quad \rightarrow \quad \frac{64(100)}{8(5)} = x \quad \rightarrow \quad 8(20) = 160 = x$$

- The second relationship that you need to know is the percent by which one value is
  $\boxed{\text{Greater Than or Less Than}}$ another.

  ➤ "Greater than or less than" questions are a lot like "calculating a percent change" questions.

- To solve them, first place the DIFFERENCE between the two values over the "GREATER or LESS THAN" value. Then, multiply the result by 100 to convert the fraction into a percent:

$$\frac{\text{Difference}}{\text{"Greater or Less Than" Amount}} \times 100$$

- For example, imagine that you needed to determine the percent by which 140 is greater than 80.

  ➤ To do so, you would simply need to place the difference between 140 and 80 over the "greater than" number, which is 80.

- We know that 80 is the "greater than" number since the PHRASING of the information states that "140 is (some percent) **greater than 80**".

- Thus, 140 is 75% greater than 80, since the difference between 140 and 80 is 60:

$$\frac{\text{Difference}}{\text{Greater Than}} \times 100 \quad \rightarrow \quad \frac{60}{80} \times 100 \quad \rightarrow \quad \frac{3}{4} \times 100 = 75\%$$

  ➤ Likewise, imagine that the revenue of company *C* was $80,000 is June and $70,000 in May.

- To determine the percent by which the revenue in May was less than that in June, you would place the difference between the revenues over the revenue in June, since the phrasing states that "the revenue in May was **less than that in June.**"

- Hence, the revenue in May was 12.5% less than that in June, since the difference between the two revenues was $10,000 and the revenue in June was $80,000:

$$\frac{\text{Difference}}{\text{Less Than}} \times 100 \quad \rightarrow \quad \frac{10,000}{80,000} \times 100 \quad \rightarrow \quad \frac{1}{8} \times 100 \quad \rightarrow \quad 0.125 \times 100 = 12.5\%$$

(10) Ratios, Averages & Medians – From time to time, Data Interpretation questions also involve ratios, averages, and medians.

• As you may recall from the Ratios & Proportions chapter of our book on Word Problems, there are three ways to express a ratio:

    1. By use of the word "to".
    2. As a fraction.
    3. With a colon.

• For example, if a bowl contains 2 red apples for every 3 green apples, the relationship between the number of red apples and the number of green apples can be expressed as:

2 red apples to 3 green apples $\dfrac{2 \text{ red apples}}{3 \text{ green apples}}$ 2 red apples : 3 green apples

> ➤ When expressing relationships as ratios, always express the elements in the ORDER that they are GIVEN.

• For example, if a grocer sells 5 apples for every 2 pears, that ratio would properly be expressed as 5 : 2 or $\dfrac{5}{2}$.

• If the ratio were represented as 2 : 5 or $\dfrac{2}{5}$, the expression would erroneously indicate that 2 apples were sold for every 5 pears.

> ➤ In most instances, the best way to simplify a ratio is to EXPRESS the terms as a FRACTION.

• Once a ratio is expressed in fraction form, its terms can be reduced with the same techniques that are used to simplify all fractions.

• Thus, the ratio of 3.6 to 4.2 is equal to $\dfrac{6}{7}$, since $\dfrac{3.6}{4.2}$ can be simplified by "sliding" both decimal points one space to the right:

$$\frac{3.6}{4.2} \rightarrow \frac{36}{42} \rightarrow \frac{6(6)}{6(7)} = \frac{6}{7}$$

> ➤ Likewise, the ratio of $\dfrac{14}{9}$ to $\dfrac{21}{12}$ is equal to $\dfrac{8}{9}$, since dividing $\dfrac{14}{9}$ by $\dfrac{21}{12}$ yields:

$$\frac{\frac{14}{9}}{\frac{21}{12}} \rightarrow \frac{14}{9} \div \frac{21}{12} \rightarrow \frac{14}{9} \times \frac{12}{21} \rightarrow \frac{2(\cancel{7})}{3(3)} \times \frac{\cancel{3}(4)}{\cancel{7}(\cancel{3})} = \frac{2(4)}{3(3)} = \frac{8}{9}$$

- If you've read the Statistics chapter on our book on <u>Word Problems</u>, you may also recall that there are several ways to gauge the "centrality" of a number set.

  ➤ The most common way is to take its AVERAGE, a term also known as the ARITHMETIC MEAN.

- The average of a number set is simply the SUM of its terms divided by the NUMBER of terms within the set. Formally, this relationship can be represented as follows:

$$\frac{S(\text{um of terms})}{N(\text{umber of terms})} = A(\text{verage})$$

- Thus, the average of 3, 6, 7, 8, and 11 is 7, since the sum of the 5 terms is 35, and $35 \div 5 = 7$. Likewise, if a set of numbers has an average of 9 and adds to 72, there are 8 numbers in the set, since:

$$\frac{S}{N} = A \;\rightarrow\; \frac{72}{N} = 9 \;\rightarrow\; 72 = 9N \;\rightarrow\; N = \frac{72}{9} = 8$$

  ➤ Another common way to gauge the "centrality" of a number set is to take its MEDIAN.

- The median of a group of numbers is the number in the MIDDLE of the set, when the data is arranged in ASCENDING order.

- Hence, the number set {9, 3, 1, 7, 5} has a median of 5, since 5 is the middle term when the set is arranged from least to greatest: {1, 3, 5, 7, 9}.

  ➤ If a set of data has an EVEN number of terms, the median is the AVERAGE of the two MIDDLE terms.

- Thus, the number set {11, 1, 3, 9, 7, 5} has a median of 6, since 5 and 7 are the middle terms when the set is arranged in ascending order: {1, 3, 5, 7, 9, 11}.

- Likewise, the data set below has a median of 3.5, since there are $4 + 9 + 2 + 6 + 9 = 30$ terms in the set, and the 15th largest of the numbers is a 3 while the 16th largest of the numbers is a 4:

Number	1	2	3	4	5
Frequency	4	9	2	6	9

(11) Overlapping Sets – From time to time, Data Interpretation questions will also involve Overlapping Sets.

• Overlapping Sets questions involve TWO or more groups of people (or objects), wherein some members belong to MORE THAN ONE group.

➢ For example, imagine a school with 100 students, of whom 65 study French, 43 study German, 17 study both languages, and 9 study neither language.

• This school contains two groups of students: those who study French and those who study German. Because some of the students who study French also study German, the two groups OVERLAP.

➢ Whenever two groups overlap, every member can always be categorized as EITHER:

1. IN the first group or NOT IN the first group
2. IN the second group or NOT IN the second group

• For example, every student in the school above can be categorized as someone who (1) **studies French** or (2) **does not**. Likewise, every student in the school above can be categorized as someone who (3) **studies German** or (4) **does not**.

• Thus, a TABLE can be drawn whose rows and columns correspond to these four possibilities.

➢ As you may recall from our chapter on Overlapping Sets (Word Problems), drawing a TABLE is generally the SUREST way to solve an overlapping sets problem.

• In addition to the rows and columns mentioned above, every Overlapping Sets Table should also contain a **total row** and a **total column**, giving it a total of NINE slots. Hence, a table for the school above would look like this:

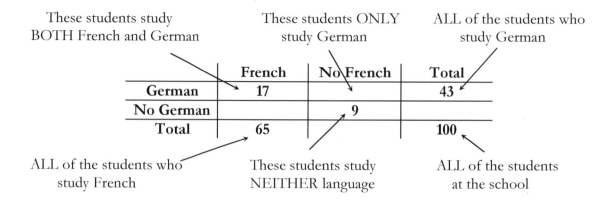

	French	No French	Total
German	17		43
No German		9	
Total	65		100

These students study BOTH French and German

These students ONLY study German

ALL of the students who study German

ALL of the students who study French

These students study NEITHER language

ALL of the students at the school

➢ As you can see, each slot in an Overlapping Sets Table represents a DISTINCT group.

• For example, the **upper-left** slot represents the intersection of the "French" and "German" categories, and thus indicates the number of student who study **both languages.**

• Likewise, the **center** slot represents the intersection of the "No French" and "No German" categories, and thus indicates those students who study **neither** language.

➢ Once the data supplied by an Overlapping Sets problem has been inserted into the table, the problem can be solved by ADDING each row and column to its TOTAL.

• For example, our table about the school on the previous page can be completed as follows:

48 students ONLY study French,
since 17 + 48 = 65

26 students ONLY study German,
since 17 + 26 = 43

	French	No French	Total
German	17	**26**	43
No German	**48**	9	**57**
Total	65	**35**	100

35 students do NOT study French,
since 65 + 35 = 100

57 students do NOT study German,
since 43 + 57 = 100

• Hence, if we needed to determine the number of students at the school that ONLY study German, the answer would be 26, since the **upper-center** slot of our table represents the intersection of the "German" and "No French" categories (thus representing the students who **only study German**).

➢ Alternatively, you can solve some overlapping sets questions with the Overlapping Sets formula:

$$\text{Group } A + \text{Group } B + \text{Neither} - \text{Both} = \text{Total}$$

• In general, the formula is FASTER than the table. Unfortunately, it's not very helpful when a question involves "ONLY groups".

• By "only groups", we mean the group of people or objects that are in "Group *A* but not Group *B*" or in "Group *B* but not Group *A*".

> ➤ Thus, problems in which some people are "in one group but not another" or are "only in one particular group" would NOT be great candidates for the formula.

• To get a sense of how the formula works, imagine a school of 70 students, in which 30 study French, 50 study Spanish, and 10 study neither.

• To determine the number of the students who study both French and Spanish, we can simply plug this information into the formula as follows:

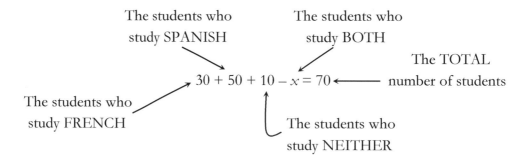

> ➤ Hence, 20 of the 70 students at this school study both French and Spanish, since:

$$30 + 50 + 10 - x = 70$$
$$90 - x = 70$$
$$x = 20$$

• If we were to use an Overlapping Sets Table to solve this problem, our table would initially look like this:

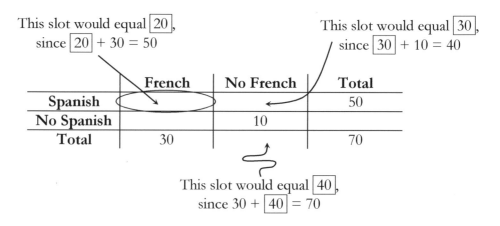

(12) Probability – Finally, on very rare occasions, Data Interpretation questions will involve Probability.

• In general, Data Interpretation questions that involve Probability are pretty EASY. In fact, all of the examples we've seen boil down to a FEW basic concepts.

> ➤ The most important of these concepts is simply the definition of probability. As you likely know, probability measures the likelihood that something will occur.

• Formally, the chance that something may happen can be stated as:

$$\frac{\text{The Number of Ways it } \mathbf{CAN} \text{ Happen}}{\text{The } \mathbf{Total} \text{ Number of Outcomes}}$$

• For example, the probability of rolling a "2" with a fair six-sided die is 1/6, since a six-sided die has 6 total outcomes, and only 1 of those outcomes is a "2".

> ➤ Of course, for a probability to be accurate, the likelihood of its outcomes must be EQUALLY WEIGHTED.

• For instance, one might think that there's a 1/2 chance of picking the ace of spades from a deck of cards, since picking a card can result in 1 of 2 things: getting the ace or not getting it.

• However, the actual probability is 1/52, since a full deck of cards has 52 cards, each of which has an EQUAL chance of being selected if chosen at random (and there's only one ace of spades).

> ➤ You should also be able to determine the probability that "one event AND another occurs", or that "one event OR another occurs".

• If you've read through the Probability chapter of our book on Word Problems, you may recall that we call such scenarios "AND probabilities" and "OR probabilities".

• To determine the probability that one event AND another BOTH occur ("AND probability"), simply MULTIPLY their individual probabilities together.

> ➤ For example, if the probability of Event A is 3/5 and the probability of event B is 2/3, the probability that Events A and B both occur is 2/5, since $3/5 \times 2/3 = 2/5$.

• Just BE CAREFUL if you're selecting items from a COLLECTION. Unless items are REPLACED upon selection, you will have ONE LESS choice after every selection.

• To solve "OR probabilities", you always want to ASK yourself ONE question: "Are BOTH events POSSIBLE?"

> **If the answer is <u>NO</u>, simply <u>ADD</u> the probabilities of each event.**

• For example, if a jar has 10 marbles, of which 5 are red, 3 are blue, and 2 are green, the probability of selecting a red marble is 5/10 and the probability of selecting a blue marbles is 3/10.

• The probability of selecting a marble that is red <u>or</u> blue is therefore 4/5 (or 0.8), since you CANNOT select a red and blue at the same time if you only select one marble:

$$\frac{5}{10} + \frac{3}{10} = \frac{8}{10} = \frac{4}{5}$$

> **If the answer is <u>YES</u>, you still <u>ADD</u> the probabilities, but you must <u>SUBTRACT the OVERLAP</u>.**

• For example, if a hamper has 10 articles of clothing, of which 6 are shirts, 4 are blue, and 1 is a blue shirt, the probability of selecting a shirt is 6/10 and the probability of selecting something blue is 4/10.

• However, 1 of the 10 items is a blue shirt. Because a "blue shirt" is the overlap between "shirts" and "clothing that is blue", the probability of selecting a shirt or something blue is 9/10 (or 0.9), since:

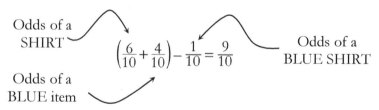

> We subtract the overlap because we are essentially DOUBLE-COUNTING the item(s) that belong to both groups.

• For instance, in the hamper problem, we're counting the blue shirt both as a "shirt" and as "something blue", so we've counted it twice.

• By subtracting the probability of getting the blue shirt, we're removing the over-count.

(13) Math Drills – Solutions can be found on the pages that follow.

1. Convert each of the following to a decimal _and_ a fraction:

   (a) 60% $= .6$ or $3/5$ (b) 55% $.55$ or $11/20$
   (c) 180% $= 1.8$ or $9/5$ (d) 12.5% $.125$ or $1/8$

2. Convert each of the following to a percent:

   (a) 0.05 $= 5\%$ (b) $\frac{7}{5}$ $= 140\%$

3. Which of the following is the closest approximate value of 42%?

   $.36 \quad .38 \quad .4 \quad .43 \quad .44$
   (A) $\frac{4}{11}$ (B) $\frac{3}{8}$ (C) $\frac{2}{5}$ (D) $\frac{3}{7}$ (E) $\frac{4}{9}$

4. Calculate each of the following:

   (a) 35% of 120 $\frac{35}{100}(120)= 42$ (b) 22% of 150 $= 33$

5. Determine the following:

   (a) In 1981, stock S was worth $400 in June and $300 in May. By what percent did the value of the stock change? 33%
   (b) The cost of a meal is $48 after a 20% tip. What is cost of the meal before the tip? original $\times 1.2 = 48$
   (c) 45 is what percent of 225? 20% original $= \frac{48}{1.2} = 40$
   (d) What percent less than 80 is 60? 25%

6. Calculate each of the following:

   (a) The ratio of 3.2 to 2.4 $4:3$ (b) The ratio of $\frac{2}{3}$ to $\frac{3}{8}$ $16:9$

7. Determine the arithmetic mean and median for the following data set: median 3 mean 3

Value	1	2	3	4	5
Frequency	5	3	5	1	6

8. School S has 10 students, of whom 4 study Chemistry, 3 study Physics, and 2 study both.

   (a) How many students at school S study Physics but not Chemistry? 1
   (b) If two students are selected at random, what is the probability that each studies both Physics and Chemistry? 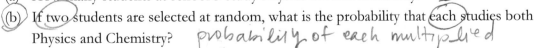 probability of each multiplied
   (c) If one student is selected at random, what is the probability that he or she studies Chemistry or Physics? $1/2$

| Solutions |

1. To convert a percent into decimal, SHIFT its decimal TWO spaces to the left:

(a) $60\% = 0.60 = 0.6$
$\underset{\sim}{}$

(b) $55\% = 0.55$
$\underset{\sim}{}$

(c) $180\% = 1.80 = 1.8$
$\underset{\sim}{}$

(d) $12.5\% = 0.125$
$\underset{\sim}{}$

Likewise, to convert a percent into a fraction, DIVIDE it by 100:

(a) $60\% = \dfrac{60}{100} = \dfrac{6}{10} = \dfrac{3}{5}$

(b) $55\% = \dfrac{55}{100} = \dfrac{5(11)}{5(20)} = \dfrac{11}{20}$

(c) $180\% = \dfrac{180}{100} = \dfrac{18}{10} = \dfrac{2(9)}{2(5)} = \dfrac{9}{5}$

(d) $12.5\% = \dfrac{12.5}{100} = 0.125 = \dfrac{1}{8}$

2. To convert a decimal or fraction into a percent, simply REVERSE the steps above. Thus, to convert a decimal into a percent, shift its decimal two places to the RIGHT. Likewise, to convert a fraction into a percent, MULTIPLY it by 100:

(a) $0.05 \rightarrow 05.0 = 5\%$
$\underset{\sim}{}$

(b) $\dfrac{7}{5} \rightarrow \dfrac{7}{5} \cdot 100 = \dfrac{7}{\cancel{5}} \cdot \cancel{5}(20) = 140\%$

3. From the "Conversion List", we know that: $\dfrac{1}{5} = 0.2$, $\dfrac{1}{7} \approx 0.14$, $\dfrac{1}{8} = 0.125$, $\dfrac{1}{9} = 0.\overline{1}$, and $\dfrac{1}{11} = 0.\overline{09}$. Thus, (D) is the correct answer, since:

(A) $\dfrac{4}{11} = 4 \times \dfrac{1}{11} = 4 \times 0.\overline{09} = 0.\overline{36} = \boxed{36.36\%}$

(B) $\dfrac{3}{8} = 3 \times \dfrac{1}{8} = 3 \times 0.125 = 0.375 = \boxed{37.5\%}$

(C) $\dfrac{2}{5} = 2 \times \dfrac{1}{5} = 2 \times 0.2 = 0.4 = \boxed{40\%}$

(D) $\dfrac{3}{7} = 3 \times \dfrac{1}{7} \approx 3 \times 0.14 = 0.42 \approx \boxed{42\%}$

(E) $\dfrac{4}{9} = 4 \times \dfrac{1}{9} = 4 \times 0.\overline{1} = 0.\overline{4} = \boxed{44.4\%}$

Alternatively, we can divide each answer choice with a calculator, but doing so would cost valuable time.

4. Using the "10% Shortcut", we get:

(a) 35% of 120: 10% of 120 = 12, so 5% = 6. Thus:

$$35\% = (3 \times 10\%) + 5\% = (3 \times 12) + 6 = 36 + 6 = 42.$$

(b) 22% of 150: 10% of 150 = 15, so 1% = 1.5. Thus:

$$22\% = (2 \times 10\%) + (2 \times 1)\% = (2 \times 15) + (2 \times 1.5) = 30 + 3 = 33.$$

Using the "Fraction Approach", we get:

(a) 35% of 120: $\dfrac{35}{10\cancel{0}} \times 12\cancel{0} \;\rightarrow\; \dfrac{35}{10} \times 12 \;\rightarrow\; \dfrac{\cancel{5}(7)}{\cancel{5}(\cancel{2})} \times \cancel{2}(6) = 42.$

(b) 22% of 150: $\dfrac{22}{10\cancel{0}} \times 15\cancel{0} \;\rightarrow\; \dfrac{22}{10} \times 15 \;\rightarrow\; \dfrac{\cancel{2}(11)}{\cancel{2}(\cancel{5})} \times 3(\cancel{5}) = 33.$

5a. To calculate a PERCENT CHANGE, first place the difference between the new and original values over the original value. Then MULTIPLY the result by 100 in order to CONVERT the fraction into a percent.

Since May precedes June, the original value of the stock is $300. Thus, the value of the stock increased by 33.3%, since:

$$\frac{\text{Difference}}{\text{Original}} \times 100 \;\rightarrow\; \frac{400 - 300}{300} \times 100 \;\rightarrow\; \frac{100}{3\cancel{00}} \times 1\cancel{00} = \frac{100}{3} = 33.3\%$$

5b. When the value of an object increases or decreases, the relationship between its ORIGINAL value and NEW value can be stated as:

$$\text{Original} \times (1 \pm \% \text{ Change}) = \text{New}$$

Here, the cost of the meal after the 20% tip is $48, so we need to determine its ORIGINAL cost. Since a 20% tip is an increase, the percent change is ADDED to 1:

$$\text{original} \times (1 + 0.2) = \$48$$

Thus, the cost of the meal before the tip was $40, since dividing both sides by 1.2 gives us:

$$\text{original} \times (1 + 0.2) = \$48 \;\rightarrow\; \text{original} = \frac{\$48}{1.2} = \frac{\$480}{12} = \$40$$

5c. To solve "Part-to-Whole" questions, simply compare the part to the whole through the following proportion:

$$\frac{\text{Part}}{\text{Whole}} = \frac{\text{"Percent"}}{100}$$

Here, we've been given the **part** and the **whole**, so we can establish the relationship between them as:

$$\overset{\text{part}}{\underset{\text{whole}}{\frac{45}{225}}} = \overset{\text{"percent"}}{\frac{x}{100}}$$

Thus, 45 is $\boxed{20 \text{ percent}}$ of 225, since cross-multiplication gives us:

$$45(100) = 225x \quad \rightarrow \quad \frac{45(\cancel{100})}{9(\cancel{25})} = x \quad \rightarrow \quad 5(4) = 20 = x$$

Remember, if you're confused about which value is the "part" and which is the "whole", "IS = PART" and "OF = WHOLE". Thus, the statement "**45 is** what percent **of 225**" indicates that "is" = 45 and "of" = 225.

5d. To determine the percent by which one value is "GREATER or LESS THAN" another, place the difference between the values over the "greater or less than" value. Then multiply the result by 100 to convert the fraction into a percent. Thus, 60 is 25% less than 80, since the difference between 60 and 80 is 20:

$$\frac{\text{Difference}}{\text{Less Than}} \times 100 \quad \rightarrow \quad \frac{20}{80} \times 100 \quad \rightarrow \quad \frac{1}{4} \times 100 = 25\%$$

We know that 80 is the "less than" number since the PHRASING of the question asks "what percent **less than 80** is 60?"

6a. To simplify ratios, express them as FRACTIONS. Thus, the ratio of 3.2 to 2.4 is equal to $\frac{4}{3}$, since $\frac{3.2}{2.4}$ can be simplified by "sliding" both decimal points one space to the right:

$$\frac{3.2}{2.4} \quad \rightarrow \quad \frac{32}{24} \quad \rightarrow \quad \frac{4(8)}{3(8)} = \frac{4}{3}$$

6b. Likewise, the ratio of $\frac{2}{3}$ to $\frac{3}{8}$ is equal to $\frac{16}{9}$, since dividing $\frac{2}{3}$ by $\frac{3}{8}$ yields:

$$\frac{\frac{2}{3}}{\frac{3}{8}} \quad \rightarrow \quad \frac{2}{3} \div \frac{3}{8} \quad \rightarrow \quad \frac{2}{3} \times \frac{8}{3} = \frac{16}{9}$$

7. The average, or arithmetic mean, of a number set is simply the SUM of its terms divided by the NUMBER of terms within the set.

Value	1	2	3	4	5
Frequency	5	3	5	1	6

This set has $5 + 3 + 5 + 1 + 6 = 20$ terms. The sum of these terms is 60, since:

$$5(1) + 3(2) + 5(3) + 1(4) + 6(5) \quad \rightarrow \quad 5 + 6 + 15 + 4 + 30 = 60$$

Thus, the average of the set is $\frac{60}{20} = 3$.

The median of a group of numbers is the number in the MIDDLE of the set, when the data is arranged in ASCENDING order. If a set of data has an EVEN number of terms, the median is the AVERAGE of the two MIDDLE terms.

The median of this set is also 3, since there are 20 numbers in the set, and the 10th and 11th largest numbers both equal 3.

8a. There are two ways to determine how many students at school S study Physics but not Chemistry. We can set up the following Overlapping Sets Table:

	Chemistry	No Chem.	Total
Physics	2		3
No Physics			
Total	4		10

1 student studies Physics but NOT Chemistry,
since $2 + \boxed{1} = 3$

Alternatively, we can recognize that certain students are being double-counted. If 3 of the 10 students study Physics, and 2 of these students study both Physics and Chemistry, then only 1 of the 3 studies Physics but not Chemistry.

8b. If two students are selected at random, the odds that the first student studies Physics and Chemistry are 2/10, since school S has 10 students, of whom only 2 study both.

Likewise, the odds that the second student studies Physics and Chemistry are 1/9, since only 1 of the remaining 9 students studies both.

To determine the probability that one event AND another BOTH occur ("AND probability"), MULTIPLY the individual probabilities together. The probability that the first student AND the second student study Physics and Chemistry is therefore 1/45, since:

$$\frac{2}{10} \times \frac{1}{9} \quad \rightarrow \quad \frac{1}{5} \times \frac{1}{9} = \frac{1}{45}$$

8c. If one student is selected at random, the probability that he or she studies Physics is 3/10, since only 3 of 10 students at school S study Physics. Likewise, the probability that he or she studies Chemistry is 4/10, since only 4 of the 10 students study Chemistry.

To determine the probability that one event OR another occurs ("OR probability"), always ASK yourself: "Are BOTH events POSSIBLE?"

If the answer is "YES", you ADD the probabilities but SUBTRACT the OVERLAP. Here, the answer is "yes", since some of the students at school S who study Physics also study Chemistry.

Because 2 of the students who study Physics also study chemistry, the probability of selecting a student who studies one OR the other is 1/2, since:

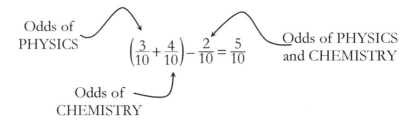

$$\text{Odds of PHYSICS} \quad \left(\frac{3}{10} + \frac{4}{10}\right) - \frac{2}{10} = \frac{5}{10} \quad \text{Odds of PHYSICS and CHEMISTRY}$$

Odds of CHEMISTRY

Traps & Tricks

(14) Bar Graphs – On the GRE, there are four types of graphs and charts that you can encounter: bar graphs, pie charts, line graphs, and data tables.

• Of these four types, bar graphs are the most common.

➢ Bar Graphs shows amounts as VERTICAL or HORIZONTAL bars and are typically used to display information over a period of TIME.

• In many cases, the trickiest aspect of working with bar graphs is simply reading the graphs correctly.

• For starters, bar graphs rarely provide EXACT numerical values. Instead, many bars extend above or below a specified quantity line, so their values can only be determined with a careful guesstimate:

The Average Annual Expenses for Education in City *C*, Per Family, 1981-1985

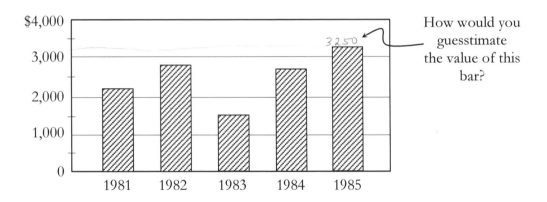

How would you guesstimate the value of this bar?

➢ When GUESSTIMATING the value of a bar, you must be as PRECEISE as possible.

• As mentioned in the section on "Tackling the Questions", lazy guesstimation will result in misreadings and incorrect answers.

• For example, in the graph above, your reading for the <u>Average Annual Expenses for Education</u>, per family, in <u>1985</u> should be approximately $3,250. **Readings such as $3,000 or $3,500 are NOT precise enough** and could result in incorrect answers.

- If you find it difficult to measure something precisely, remember to use your SCRATCH PAPER as a make-shift RULER, like so:

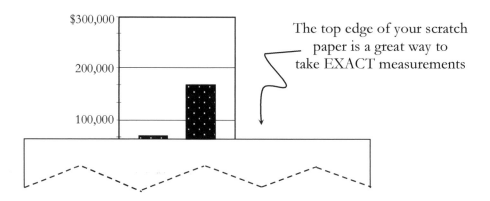

The top edge of your scratch paper is a great way to take EXACT measurements

> ➤ A second reason that bar graphs can be tricky to work with is that the bars are often STACKED.

- Stacked bars graphs allow readers to see the COMPOSITION of a TOTAL amount. For example, in the graph below, notice that the average yearly expenses are composed of fees for Tuition and fees for Supplies.

The Average Annual Expenses for Education in City *C*, Per Family, 1981-1985

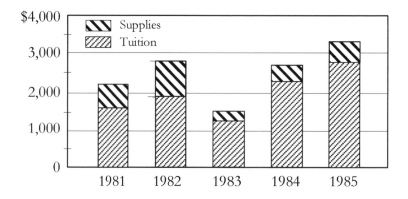

> ➤ Stacked bar graphs are easily MISREAD. To determine the value of a section, remember that the SUM of the SECTIONS equals the TOTAL.

- Thus, to determine the average expenses spent per family on <u>Supplies</u> in <u>1982</u>, you CANNOT simply look at the top of the Supplies section.

- You have to **SUBTRACT the amount spent on Tuition from the Total Expenses**. Hence, roughly $900 was spent on Supplies in 1982, since Total Expenses for the year were approximately $2,850 and Tuition was about $1,950.

> ➤ Finally, in the most complicated bar graphs, the bars are both STACKED and BUNCHED.

• Such graphs are especially easy to misread, since they contain so many different pieces of information:

The Average Annual Expenses for Education in City *C*, Per Family, 1981-1985

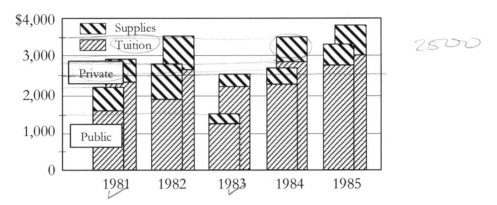

• Thus, in the graph above, average annual educational expenses in City *C*, per family, can be analyzed by year, source, or domain, or by any combination of these categories.

> ➤ When working with bar graphs, there are several CLASSIC "TRAP" questions that you should be FAMILIAR with.

• These questions show up repeatedly, since test-takers commonly get them wrong. For each example that follows, be sure to refer back to the graph directly above.

1. "Repetitive Calculation" questions.

• The most important of these trap questions invite you to perform a SERIES of simple, but tedious calculations. Here's an example:

For which of the following years were the total expenses at private institutions no more than $500 greater than the total expenses at public institutions?

Indicate all such years.

A 1981   **B** 1982   **C** 1983   **D** 1984   **E** 1985

Answer. E. This question asks us to determine the years in which total expenses at private institutions were no more than $500 greater than those at public institutions. The key words have been underlined.

• To answer such a question, it appears that we need to get the difference between total expenses for private and public institutions for EACH of the years shown.

> ➢ It isn't so. **Any question that requires a series of tedious calculations can ALWAYS be solved with a VISUAL or LOGICAL approach**.

• Remember, the GRE is testing your ability to find a smart, simple solution to problems that seem complicated or time-consuming.

• They will never design a question that can only be solved through a series of laborious calculations.

> ➢ For a problem like this, rather than calculate the difference in expenses for all five years, first <u>mark off "$500" on the edge of your scratch paper</u>.

• Like so:

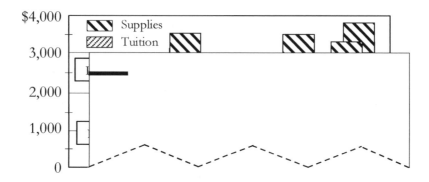

• Then, measure that difference VISUALLY against the difference between private and public expenses for each of the years shown.

> ➢ If done correctly, you should find that 1985 is the only year in which total expenses at private institutions could be no more than $500 greater than those at public ones.

• Although it may be hard to determine the exact difference in 1985, we know that it cannot exceed $500, since "Select One or More" questions MUST have at least one answer that satisfies the question. Thus, the correct answer is (E) only.

2. "Count the Bars" questions.

• "Count the Bars" questions ask you to count the number of bars that exceed (or fail to exceed) a certain value. Consider the following:

In how many of the years shown did tuition expenses at private institutions fail to exceed $2,500?

(A) One   (B) Two   (C) Three   (D) Four   (E) Five

Answer. B. This question asks us to determine the number of years in which <u>tuition</u> at <u>private</u> institutions <u>failed</u> to <u>exceed $2,500</u>. The key words have been underlined.

> ➢ To answer "Count the Bars" questions, **use a piece of PAPER to form a straight line at the specified value.**

• Then, count the bars that do or don't exceed the amount. Doing so here gives us the following:

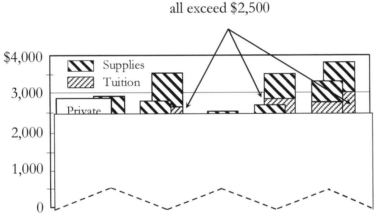

• As you can see, the expense of private tuition EXCEEDS $2,500 in three years: 1982, 1984, and 1985. If we SUBTRACT this total from the five years shown, we're left with two years that did not exceed $2,500. Thus, the correct answer is (B).

> ➢ Alternatively, we can directly count the bars that fail to exceed $2,500: 1981 and 1983.

• In most cases, however, you'll find the "subtraction strategy" to be faster, particularly if a graph has numerous possibilities to consider.

3. "Top Section" questions.

• "Top Section" questions ask you to determine the value of the top section of a stacked bar. Here's an example:

In 1984, the average annual expense in city *C*, per family, for supplies at private institutions most nearly equals which of the following?

(A) $600 (B) $750 (C) $1,400 (D) $2,800 (E) $3,500

Answer: A. This question asks us to determine the expense for supplies at private institutions in 1984. The key words have been underlined.

• As mentioned in our discussion of STACKED bars, "Supplies" are the TOP SECTION of the stacked bars in our graph.

> ➤ Thus, to determine how much was spent on supplies in a given year, we have to subtract "Tuition" from "Total Expenses".

• We CAN'T just look at the tops of the bars.

• In 1984, the average annual expense at private institutes totaled a little bit more than $3,500, and tuition was roughly $2,900.

> ➤ Thus, supplies must have approximately cost $600, since $3,500 − $2,900 = $600. The correct answer is therefore (A).

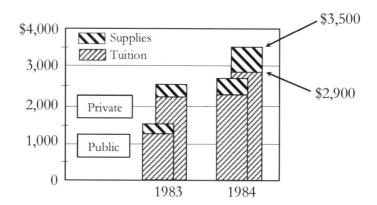

• Note that supplies did not cost $3,500 (the commonly chosen incorrect answer) because the top of the bar represents the total expenses for the year, not the amount spent on supplies.

(15) Pie Charts – A pie chart represents information as sections of a circle.

• Pie charts lend themselves to questions involving percentages and proportions. There are two reasons for this:

1. Each section of a circle represents a percentage of that circle.

2. Pie charts display "part-to-whole" relationships. Each section of a circle also represents a part of the entire circle.

• When working with pie charts, always LOOK for a CONCRETE VALUE given somewhere outside the circle.

➢ Pie charts almost always test your ability to determine a percent of a number, so you'll need a real number that you can get a percentage of.

• If the pie chart itself has been broken into real numbers, rather than percentages, expect at least one proportion question.

➢ Like bar graphs, pie charts feature several "TRAP" questions. Make sure that you are FAMILIAR with them.

• These questions show up repeatedly on the GRE, since test-takers commonly get them wrong. For the question that follows, refer to the graph below:

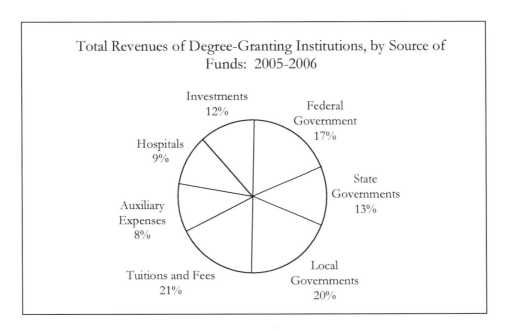

Total Revenues = $246.2 billion

1. "Add the Percentages" questions.

• The most important of these trap questions ask you to CALCULATE a SERIES of percentages. Here's an example:

Approximately what amount, in billions of dollars, of the total revenues of degree-granting institutions came from the federal government, investments, and tuition and fees?

Round your answer to the nearest <u>whole number</u>.

Answer. 123. This question asks us to determine the <u>approximate</u> amount of total revenue from the <u>federal government</u>, <u>investments</u>, and <u>tuition and fees</u>. The key words have been underlined.

• Because the exam provides a calculator, it's tempting to type out these percentages one by one, like this:

Federal Government = 17% of 246 = | 0.17 | × | 246 | = | 41.8
Investments = 12% of 246 = | 0.12 | × | 246 | = | 29.5
Tuition and Fees = 21% of 246 = | 0.21 | × | 246 | = | 51.7

• Of course, you'd also have to type | 41.8 | + | 29.5 | + | 51.7 | = | into the calculator, since 41.8, 29.5, and 51.7 are not easily added.

> **Like all questions that ask for a SERIES of calculations, however, questions like this have an easy shortcut.**

• We call these sorts of questions "Add the Percentages" questions, since you can solve them MUCH more quickly if you simply ADD the percentages before you calculate anything.

• Notice that **if we add 17% + 12% + 21%, we get 50%.** Thus, the correct answer must be 123, since 50%, or half, of 246.2 is approximately 123.

2. "Get the Angle" questions.

• From time to time, you will encounter pie chart questions that ask you to determine the angle measurement of a SECTION of the pie. Here's an example:

The areas of the sectors in the graph have been <u>drawn in proportion</u> to the percentages shown. What is the approximate <u>measure, in degrees</u>, of the sector representing the percent of <u>total revenues from investments</u>?

Round your answer to the nearest <u>integer</u>.

43

Answer. 43. This question asks us to determine the <u>approximate</u> angle measurement of the <u>investments</u> section of the graph. The key words have been underlined.

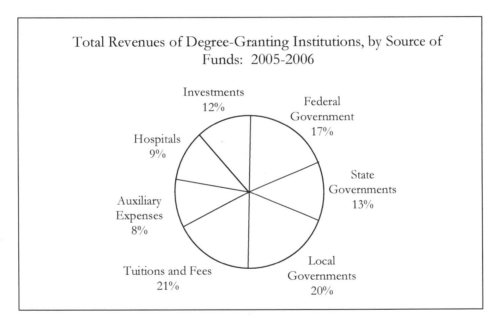

Total Revenues of Degree-Granting Institutions, by Source of Funds: 2005-2006

Investments 12%
Federal Government 17%
Hospitals 9%
State Governments 13%
Auxiliary Expenses 8%
Local Governments 20%
Tuitions and Fees 21%

Total Revenues = $246.2 billion

• As you may recall, **there are 360° in a circle.**

• In the chart above, INVESTMENTS represent 12% of our circle graph. Thus, the angle measurement of the investments sector is approximately 43°, since:

$$12\% \text{ of } 360° = \boxed{0.12} \boxed{\times} \boxed{360} \boxed{=} 43.2°$$

3. "Altered Amount" questions.

• "Altered Amount" questions ask you to determine the "part-to-whole" relationship between a section and the circle AFTER the circle has been <u>altered</u>. Here's an example:

If total revenue from the federal government were to decrease by $6 billion in the 2006-2007 school year, and all other revenues and funding sources were to be identical to those of 2005-2006, what percentage of the total revenues in 2006-2007 would come from the federal government?

(A) 10%   (B) 12%   (C) 14%   (D) 15%   (E) 16%

Answer: D. This question asks us to determine the percentage of <u>total revenue</u> from the <u>federal government</u> in <u>2006-2007</u> if the federal government were to decrease funding by $6 billion. The key words have been underlined.

➤ To answer such a question, we first have to realize that revenue from the federal government in 2005-2006 was approximately $42 billion, since:

$$17\% \text{ of } \$246 \text{ billion} = \boxed{0.17} \boxed{\times} \boxed{246} \boxed{=} \$42 \text{ billion}$$

• If this amount were to DECREASE by $6 billion, and all other amounts were to be held CONSTANT, two things would happen:

1) Revenue from the federal government would decrease from $42 to $36 billion.
2) Total revenue would decrease from $246 to $240 billion. (Remember, revenue from the federal government is PART of the total revenue!)

• Thus, the "part-to-whole" relationship between revenue from the federal government and total revenue would be:

$$\frac{\text{part}}{\text{whole}} = \frac{\$36}{\$240} = \frac{\cancel{6}(6)}{\cancel{6}(40)} = \frac{3}{20}$$

➤ The revenue from the federal government would therefore represent 15% of the total revenue, since:

$$\frac{3}{\cancel{20}} \times 10\cancel{0} = \frac{30}{2} = 15\%$$

• Hence, the correct answer is (D).

(16) Line Graphs – A line graph shows amounts as a series of points that are connected by a continuous line.

• Like bar graphs, line graphs are usually used to display information over a period of time.

> ➢ Because the line that runs between the points is uninterrupted, line graphs always display information over a CONTINUOUS period of time.

• In this regard, line graphs differ from bar graphs, which can display information over a period of time that is not continuous.

• Most line graphs contain multiple lines. Usually these lines diverge, converge, and intersect, creating a host of potential questions. Thus, **many line graph questions are VISUAL in nature** and require <u>careful</u> observation.

> ➢ Like bar graphs and pie charts, line graphs feature several "TRAP" questions. Make sure that you are FAMILIAR with them.

• These questions show up repeatedly on the GRE, since test-takers commonly get them wrong. For the question that follows, refer to the graph below:

State *X*'s Total Milk Exports Compared to its Milk Exports
to Florida, 1983-1993

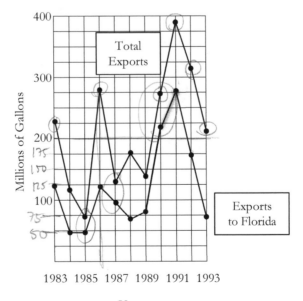

1. "Count the Dots" questions.

• "Count the Dots" questions ask you to count the number of data points that EXCEED, or fail to exceed, a certain measurement. Here's an example:

**For how many of the years shown did State X export more than
<u>200 million gallons of milk?</u>**

(A) 3   (B) 4   (C) 5   (D) 6   (E) 7

Answer. D. This question asks us to determine the number of years in which State X exported <u>more than 200 million gallons</u> of milk. The key words have been underlined.

➤ To answer "Count the Dots" questions, **TRACE the relevant lines with your finger** to count the number of points that exceed the specified amount.

• And take your time! "Simple visual task" questions are easy to miss if you work too quickly. An extra 5 seconds to avoid a careless mistake is ALWAYS a worthwhile investment.

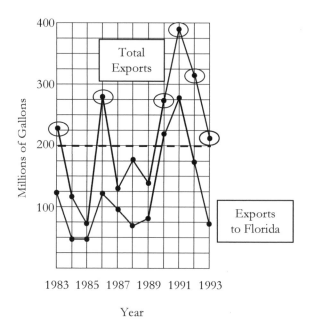

➤ In the graph above, the <u>total exports</u> line <u>exceeds</u> $200 million in 6 years: 1983, 1986, 1990, 1991, 1992, and 1993. Thus, the correct answer is (D):

• We DISCOURAGE you from using the edge of a piece of paper to solve such questions.

• Most line graphs have multiple lines, so it is easy to count the dots on the WRONG line if you cover the graph with a piece of paper. Save the "paper trick" for bar graphs.

2. "Busy Work" questions.

• Like bar graphs and pie charts, line graphs commonly feature questions that involve a lot of busy work. Here's an example:

The amount of milk that State X exported to states other than Florida was greatest in which of the following years?

(A) 1984   (B) 1986   (C) 1988   (D) 1991   (E) 1993

Answer. B. This question asks us to determine the year in which the volume of milk exported to <u>states other than Florida</u> was <u>greatest</u>. The key words have been underlined.

  ➢   Remember, **any Data Interpretation question that requires tedious busy work can always be solved with a VISUAL or LOGICAL approach**.

• To determine the volume of exports to <u>other</u> than Florida, we have to SUBTRACT the volume of milk exported to Florida from that exported in total.

• One way we could do so would be to determine the volume of exports, both to Florida and in total, for each of the years given and then to calculate the differences. As you can imagine, however, such an approach would be fairly time-consuming.

  ➢   A much easier way to solve a problem like this is to COUNT the BOXES between the two export lines, like so:

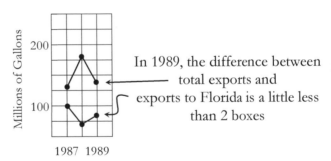

• Counting the boxes for each answer choice approximately gives us:

  (A) 1984 = a little less than 3 boxes   (D) 1991 = less than 6 boxes
  (B) 1986 = a little more than 6 boxes   (E) 1993 = less than 6 boxes
  (C) 1988 = slightly more than 4 boxes

• Thus, the correct answer must be (B), since no other answer choice shows a difference of more than 6 boxes between the export lines.

3. "Maximization" questions.

• "Maximization" questions ask you to identify the year in which the DIFFERENCE between two lines is as LARGE (or as small) as POSSIBLE. Here's an example:

For the year in which total milk exports and milk exports to Florida were most nearly equal, how many million gallons of milk did State X export?

(A) 150   (B) 130   (C) 90   (D) 75   (E) 50

Answer. D. This question asks us to determine the <u>total exports</u> of the year in which the <u>total milk exports</u> and <u>milk exports to Florida</u> were <u>most nearly equal</u>. The key words have been underlined.

• Maximization questions often involve VISUAL TRICKERY.

  ➢ The task of identifying the highest point on a graph, or the smallest distance between two points, is generally a relatively a simple task.

• As a result, exam-makers often DESIGN line graphs in a manner that promotes CARELESS errors.

• Take the graph below. The export lines converge noticeably in 1987, which lies at the CENTER of the graph, so MANY test-takers select (B) as the correct answer:

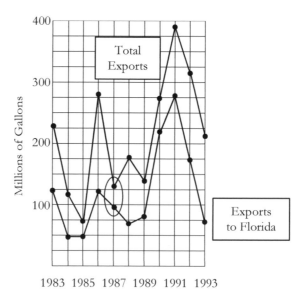

• Remember, when working with data interpretation questions that involve SIMPLE, VISUAL tasks, SLOW DOWN.

> **If you find what you're looking for in less than 10 seconds, give yourself another 10 seconds to be sure that you haven't missed something!**

• Investing the extra time to avoid a careless mistake is ALWAYS worth it.

• For example, in this question, if we take the time to check the difference between the export lines for EACH year on the graph, we might notice that in 1985, which lies at the PERIPHERY of the graph, the difference between the lines is just a single box:

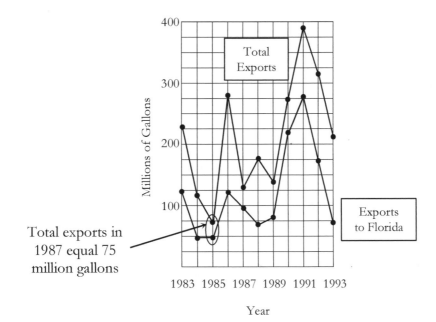

> Because the difference between the lines in 1987 is a little over 1 box, the year in which total exports and exports to Florida were most nearly equal was actually 1985.

• The correct answer must therefore be (D), since <u>total</u> milk exports in 1985 were roughly 75 million gallons.

(17) Data Tables & Rare Diagrams – Data tables are the last sort of diagram that you will encounter on the GRE.

• On rare occasions Data Interpretation sets will feature unique or exotic diagram types such as scatter plots, floor plans, or Venn diagrams.

> ➤ However, such sets are extremely uncommon and the questions that accompany them are generally straightforward.

• Data tables present information in the form of a chart or spreadsheet.

• In general, such tables are useful because they can arrange information in a manner that is easy to read. However, they don't allow readers to make visual estimations or observe patterns easily.

> ➤ As a result, data table questions contain little visual trickery. Rather, they tend to be more math "heavy" than those that come with bar graphs, pie charts, or line graphs.

• Data table questions also tend to involve rarer math concepts such as Overlapping Sets, Averages, Medians, and Probability more frequently.

• Because of their emphasis on math, data tables generally feature fewer "TRAP" questions than bar graphs, pie charts, and line graphs.

> ➤ Of course, you should still be wary of questions that seem to require a lot of busy work.

• There may not be a simple VISUAL solution that you can apply, but there will almost surely be some sort of way to do the work quickly.

• In some cases it may be approximation, in others it may be adding a series of percentages together before calculating each one individually (recall "Add the Percentages" questions from the section on pie charts).

> ➤ There is, however, one sort of "TRAP" question that the GRE frequently employs with data tables.

• We call them "Not Enough Information" questions.

1. "Not Enough Information" questions.

• "Not Enough Information" questions are easy to spot, since they always have "It cannot be determined from the given information" as answer choice (E). Here's an example:

**Percent of the 200 People in Group 1 and the 300 People
in Group 2 Who Have Selected Traits**

Physical Traits	Percent of People in Group 1 Who Have Trait	Percent of People in Group 2 Who Have Trait
Ambidextrous	2%	3%
Blonde Hair (natural)	15%	12%
Blonde Hair (non-natural)	21%	18%
Green Eyes	6%	10%
Left-Handed	8%	11%
Perfect Eyesight (natural)	22%	18%
Perfect Eyesight (non-natural)	43%	38%

For group 1 only: if everyone who is green-eyed and everyone who is left-handed have naturally blonde hair, how many other people in the group have naturally blonde hair?

(A) 16
(B) 8
(C) 2
(D) 1
(E) It cannot be determined from the information given.

Answer. E. This question asks us to determine how many <u>other</u> people <u>in group 1</u> have <u>naturally blonde hair</u> if all the people in that group who are <u>green-eyed</u> and who are <u>left-handed</u> are naturally blonde. The key words have been underlined.

- "Not Enough Information" questions typically involve the OVERLAP of two sets of information.

  ➢ To solve such questions, consider using an Overlapping Sets Table if you are UNSURE whether you have enough information!

- To answer this question, for example, **we need to know how many people in group 1 are BOTH left-handed AND green-eyed.**

- After all, if the 6% of people who are green-eyed was also part of the 8% who are left-handed, there would be fewer people with either quality than if the 6% of people who are green-eyed were completely distinct from the 8% who are left-handed.

  ➢ To prove it, let's plug the information we've been provided into an Overlapping Sets Table.

- As you can see, the portion of our grid that displays the intersection of people who are **green-eyed and left-handed** cannot be filled in:

	Green-eyed	Not Green	Total
Left-handed		?	8%
Not Lefty	?	?	2%
Total	6%	**94%**	100%

- Thus, the correct answer must be (E): since we don't know how many people are both green-eyed and left-handed (and since people with either trait have naturally blonde hair), we can't determine how many <u>other</u> people in group 1 have naturally blonde hair.

  ➢ Note that answer choice (C) is the TRAP answer, since it fails to acknowledge the potential OVERLAP.

- After all, if 15% of group 1 has naturally blonde hair, and if NONE of the people who are left-handed (8%) have green eyes (6%), then 1% of the OTHER people in the group would have naturally blonde hair, since:

$$15\% \text{ of "Total"} - (8\% \text{ "Lefty"} + 6\% \text{ "Green Eyes"}) = 1\% \text{ "Other"}$$

- Thus, group 1 would have two other people with naturally blonde hair, because the group has 200 people and 1% of 200 = 2.

(18) Multi-Figured Data Sets – Up until now, we've only looked at graphs and charts with a single diagram.

• On the GRE, however, Data Interpretation sets often feature TWO or THREE different figures.

  ➢ For example, a set might include two pie charts or a mixture of diagrams, such as a bar graph and a data table or two line graphs and a pie chart.

• The questions that accompany multi-figure sets are no different than the questions that accompany a set consisting of a single diagram.

• They test the same mathematical concepts and feature the same types of questions that we've discussed in the sections above.

  ➢ That said, multi-figure sets are typically more confusing, since they display a lot of information.

• Worse still, such sets sometimes contain questions that require the use of information from more than one figure.

• When working with multi-figure sets, there are TWO things you can do to reduce confusion.

  ➢ First, **take MORE time** than you usually would to read the graphs. Slowing down will help you digest what you need to.

• Second, **LABEL each graph** with a single word.

• For example, imagine a Data Interpretation set with three figures: one figure displays information on tariffs, another on imports, and a third on exports. On your scratch paper, you should label those figures "Tariffs", "Imports", and "Exports", respectively.

  ➢ Taking the time to organize and clarify information will dramatically increase the speed and ease with which you handle multi-figure Data Interpretation sets.

• Remember, **CONFUSION equals wasted time**. If you take the time to sort out information before you approach the questions you'll be better off for doing so.

• To get a sense of what it's like to work with a multi-figured Data Interpretation set, consider the following graphs:

Average Number of Dollars per Month Spent by Employed Persons on Various Categories, Sorted by Age and Gender

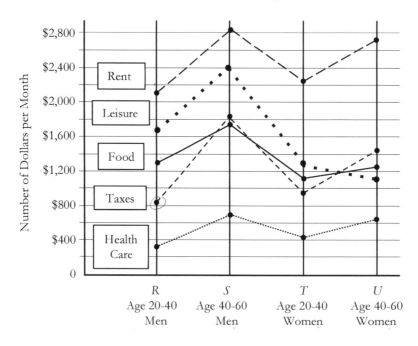

Average Number of Dollars Per Month Spent by Employed Persons on Types of Food, Sorted by Age and Gender

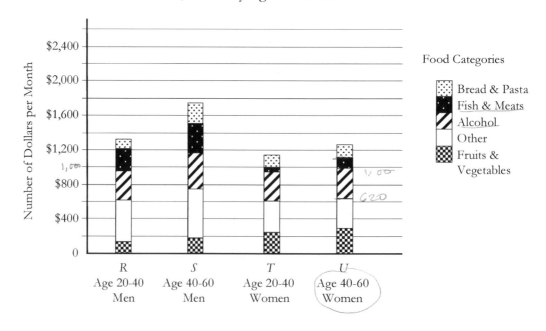

> ➢ For most multi-figure question sets, you'll find that one question will require you to combine information from both graphs AT ONCE.

• The other questions will be typical bar graph or line graph questions, like the one below:

Approximately what is the average number of dollars per month that employed women ages 40-60 spend on food that is either fish or meat?

(A) $50   (B) $100   (C) $500   (D) $1,000   (E) $1,100

Answer: B. This question asks us to determine the approximate number of dollars per month that employed women ages 40-60 spend on food that is either fish or meat. The key words have been underlined.

• Since the top graph features information on "various categories" and the bottom graph features information on "types of food", we need to check the bottom graph to find information on foods such as fish and meat.

> ➢ In the bottom graph, fish and meat are represented by the portions of each bar that are black with white dots.

• Thus, to calculate the number of dollars spent by women ages 40-60 on fish or meat, we need to read the top and bottom of the bar circled below as PRECISELY as possible:

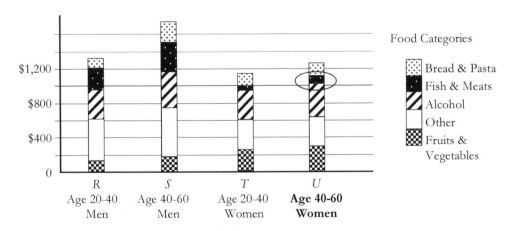

• Since the top of this bar is a little over the $1,100 mark and the bottom is a little over the $1,000 mark, women ages 40-60 spend approximately $100 per month on fish or meat. Thus, the correct answer is (B).

Which of the following lists the four groups from least to greatest with respect to the average number of dollars per month that each spends on taxes?

(A) R, S, T, U　**(B)** R, U, T, S　**(C)** R, T, S, U　**(D)** U, S, T, R　**(E)** R, T, U, S

Answer. E. This question asks us to rank the four groups from least to greatest with respect to the dollars per month that each spends on taxes. The key words have been underlined.

• The top graph features information on "various categories" and the bottom graph features information on "types of food".

> ➤ Thus, to find information on a category that doesn't involves a "type of food", such as taxes, we need to check the top graph.

• If we read the top graph carefully, we find that each group spends the following amount on taxes:

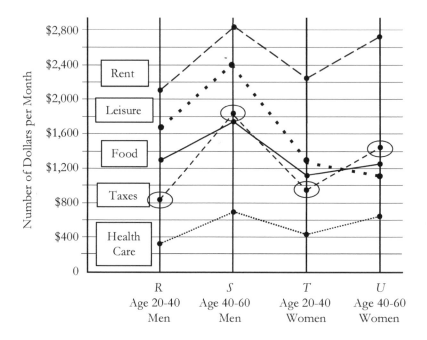

> ➤ As we can see, group R spent the least on taxes and group S spent the most, so the correct answer must begin with an R and end with an S

• Thus, only choices (B) and (E) can be correct.

• We can also see, however, that group T spent less than group U, so the order of the four groups, from least to greatest, must be R, T, U, S. The correct answer is therefore (E).

The ratio of the average number of dollars spent per month by employed women ages 20-40 on health care to the average number of dollars spent per month on alcohol is most nearly equal to

(A) $\frac{4}{5}$ (B) $\frac{6}{5}$ (C) $\frac{4}{3}$ (D) $\frac{3}{2}$ (E) 1

Answer. B. This question asks us to determine the <u>ratio</u> of money spent monthly on <u>health care</u> by employed <u>women ages 20-40</u> to that spent on <u>alcohol</u>. The key words have been underlined.

• To answer this question, we need to know two things about women ages 20-40:

    1. The number of dollars they spend monthly on health care.
    2. The number of dollars they spend monthly on alcohol.

• The top graph features information on "various activities" and the bottom graph features information on "types of food".

    ➤ Thus, we need to check the top graph for information on a "non-food" item such as health care <u>and</u> the bottom graph for a food-related item such as alcohol.

• If we read the top graph carefully, we can see that employed <u>women ages 20-40</u> spend roughly $425 per month on health care.

• Likewise, if we read the top bottom graph carefully, we can see that employed women ages 20-40 spend roughly $350 per month on alcohol, since the top of their alcohol bar is approximately $950 and the bottom is just a hair over $600.

    ➤ Thus, the ratio of money spent monthly on health care by employed women ages 20-40 to that spent on alcohol is roughly $425 to $350.

• Since the question asks us to identify the answer that is "most nearly equal" to the ratio between these two amounts, we can round the amount spent on health care to $420 to make the math easier:

$$\frac{\$425}{\$350} \quad \rightarrow \quad \frac{\$420}{\$350} = \frac{42}{35} = \frac{6(7)}{5(7)} = \frac{6}{5}$$

• Thus, the correct answer is (B).

(19) Summary – Roughly 15% of the Quantitative questions on the GRE involve graphs and charts.

• Before tackling a Data Interpretation question set, take as much TIME as you need to MASTER the graphs and charts.

> ➤ Read each label and heading carefully, and be sure that you UNDERSTAND exactly what each diagram means.

• While examining the graphs, ask yourself the following questions:

• "Does the information make sense?" "Does the data show any TRENDS?" "Are there any numbers?" If so, "are the numbers PERCENTAGES or CONCRETE VALUES?" Being an active reader will protect you from careless errors.

> ➤ If you have TWO diagrams, ask yourself whether you understand the DISTINCTION between the two and how they relate to another.

• While you read, TAKE NOTES. If your graph provides any TOTAL values, write them down and what they refer to. If your graph has two diagrams, abbreviate the KEY WORD or phrase that defines each diagram.

• Jotting down information will FORCE you to identify any significant numbers and help you INTERNALIZE the central ideas.

> ➤ When tackling the questions, ABBREVIATE the KEY WORDS and phrases as you read.

• Solving for the WRONG thing is a common reason that test-takers get Data Interpretation problems wrong.

• Remember, investing an extra five seconds to ensure that you answer the RIGHT question is always a GREAT use of your time.

> ➤ When taking measurements, be sure that you do so as PRECISELY as possible.

• IMPRECISE readings are another common reason that test-takers get Data Interpretation questions wrong. If a line lies somewhere between $475 and $500, it's NOT okay to measure it as either $475 or $500. Your reading must be accurate.

- If you find it difficult to measure something precisely, use the edge of your SCRATCH PAPER as a make-shift ruler.

  ➢ Watch out for phrases such as "approximately", "closest to", and "nearest to", or problems whose answer choices are SPACED far apart.

- While the on-screen calculator is sometimes necessary for Data Interpretation questions (and we encourage to use it when it is), approximation is often FASTER.

- Before rounding, make sure that it's safe to do so. Rounding difficult numbers when a question doesn't say "approximately" or rounding simple numbers when a question does say "approximately" can lead to incorrect answers.

  ➢ Although Data Interpretation questions can involve ANY math concept covered in our books, such questions tend to feature only a handful of math operations.

- In particular, be sure that you can:

  ☑ Convert percents to fractions and decimals (and vice versa)
  ☑ Take a percent of a number
  ☑ Calculate and apply a percent change
  ☑ Set up a ratio
  ☑ Figure out "What percent of A is B?"
  ☑ Determine "What percent greater" one quantity is than another
  ☑ Calculate an average (arithmetic mean) and a median
  ☑ Set up and use an Overlapping Sets Table

  ➢ If you've yet to do so, be sure to go through our discussion of the charts and graphs that you'll encounter on the GRE.

- Each has a small number of CLASSIC "traps" and "tricks" that you should be FAMILIAR with.

- Finally, always remember two things:

  1. If a question requires a lot of busy work, look for an easy solution. Such questions almost always have a VISUAL or LOGICAL shortcut, or yield to approximation.

  2. If a question involves a simple VISUAL task (such as counting points), SLOW DOWN. It's easier than you think to misread graphs on a computer screen, especially under test conditions!

(20) Problem Sets – Each of the following Data Interpretation sets has three groups of questions: fundamental, intermediate, and advanced.

• Whether you're aiming for a perfect score or a score closer to average, mastery of the concepts in the fundamental questions is absolutely essential.

➤ As you might expect, the intermediate questions are more difficult. The ability to solve such questions is crucial for test-takers who need above-average scores.

• Finally, the advanced questions test rare or sophisticated concepts, or involve a confusing wrinkle or subtle deception.

• Mastery of such questions is required only if you need a math score above the 90th percentile.

➤ As always, if you find yourself confused, bogged down with busy work, or stuck, don't be afraid to fall back on your "Plan B" strategies!

• Questions 1-6 are based on the following data:

The Financial Performance of Corporation *X*, 1974-1990
(in United States dollars)

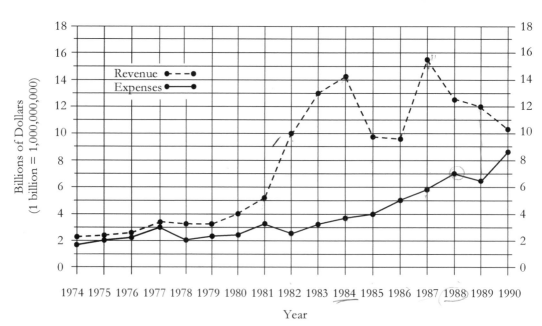

Note: Drawn to scale.

Fundamental

1. For which year shown on the graph did revenue exceed the previous year's revenue by the greatest dollar amount?

misread - question - exceed previous year, not expenses

5   5   1

    (A) 1982 (B) 1983 (C) 1984 (D) 1985 (E) 1987

2. By what percent did the expenses of Corporation X increase from 1978 to 1985?

    (A) 50% (B) 75% (C) 100% (D) 200% (E) 250%

Intermediate

3. Which of the following is closest to the amount, in billions of dollars, by which the increase in revenue from 1981 to 1982 exceeds the increase in revenue from 1982 to 1983?

    (A) 1.9 (B) 3.9 (C) 5.0 (D) 6.1 (E) 8.0

4. For how many years shown on the graph did revenue exceed expenses by more than 5 billion dollars?

7

5. In 1984, the dollar value of expenses was approximately what percent of the dollar value of revenue?

    (A) 4% (B) 17% (C) 27% (D) 79% (E) 367%

Advanced

6. If it were discovered that the dollar value of expenses shown for 1988 was incorrect and should have been $5.3 billion instead, then the average (arithmetic mean) dollar value of expenses per year for the 17 years would be how much less, in millions of dollars?

mistake averaged over years

100 million dollars

Chapter 5: Data Interpretation

Questions 7-12 are based on the following data:

Professors Classified by Category in 1997

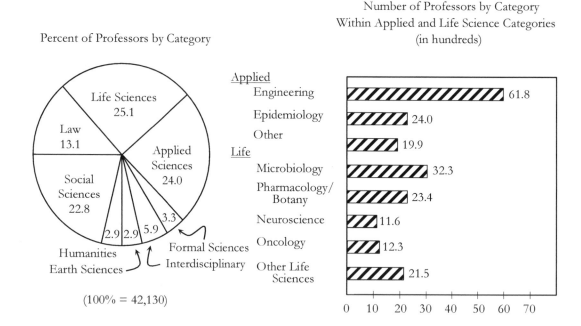

Percent of Professors by Category

Number of Professors by Category
Within Applied and Life Science Categories
(in hundreds)

(100% = 42,130)

Fundamental

7. Approximately what was the ratio of professors in the social sciences category to professors in earth sciences?

   (A) 10 to 1   (B) 8 to 1   (C) 7 to 1   (D) 5 to 6   (E) 4 to 5

8. The number of professors that were interdisciplinary was approximately how much greater than the number of professors that were in humanities?

   (A) 300   (B) 630   (C) 1,260   (D) 2,480   (E) 3,700

Intermediate

9. Approximately how many of the professors in the applied sciences category were <u>not</u> in epidemiology?

   (A) 6,180   (B) 7,600   (C) 8,970   (D) 9,360   (E) 10,110

---

10. In 1997, if twice as many professors in the formal sciences category as professors in oncology were on sabbatical, and 10 percent of the professors in oncology were on sabbatical, approximately what percent of the professors in the formal sciences category were on sabbatical?

    (A) 5%   (B) 9%   (C) 18%   (D) 22%   (E) 25%

11. In the left graph, if the areas of the sectors have been drawn in proportion to the percentages shown, for which of the following categories is the approximate measure of the sector between 10 and 20 degrees?

    Indicate all such categories.

    A   Humanities
    B   Earth Sciences
    C   Formal Sciences
    D   Interdisciplinary
    E   Law

Advanced

12. If there was a total of 32,900 professors in 1990, the fraction by which the number of professors increased from 1990 to 1997 was closest to which of the following?

    (A) $\frac{3}{20}$ (B) $\frac{1}{6}$ (C) $\frac{2}{9}$ (D) $\frac{3}{11}$ (E) $\frac{2}{7}$

Questions 13-18 are based on the following data:

The Retail and Wholesale Revenue
of Company *X*, 1999-2013
(in billions of dollars)
(1 billion = 1,000,000,000)

Receipt of Company *X*'s Retail Revenue,
by Source, 1999-2013
(in millions of purchases)

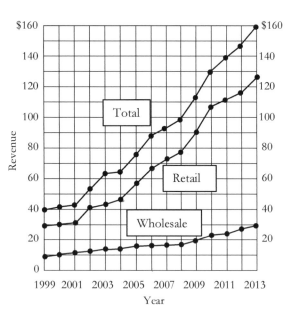

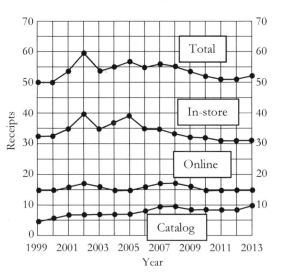

Fundamental

13. Of the following years, which showed the least difference between retail revenue and wholesale revenue?

(A) 1999   (B) 2004   (C) 2008   (D) 2012   (E) 2013

14. In 2004, approximately how many billions of dollars were received from in-store retail operations?

(A) 37
(B) 50
(C) 60
(D) 87
(E) It cannot be determined from the information given.

Intermediate

15. Which of the following periods showed a continual increase in the total number of purchases for Company *X*?

(A) 2001-2003   (B) 2003-2005   (C) 2005-2007   (D) 2007-2009   (E) 2009-2011

16. Which of the following totals were within the range of total purchases from in-store, online, and catalog operations for each year from 1999 to 2013, inclusive?

Indicate all such totals.

A   52 million

B   54 million

C   55 million

D   60 million   — doesn't quite touch 60 million

E   64 million

F   65 million

G   67 million

17. In 2006, retail revenue was approximately what percent of the total revenue for that year?

(A) 20%   (B) 60%   (C) 70%   (D) 80%   (E) 90%

Advanced

18. For which of the following years was the number of purchases from online operations most nearly equal to $\frac{3}{7}$ of that from in-store operations?

(A) 1999   (B) 2002   (C) 2005   (D) 2007   (E) 2009

imprecise — did not test rest of answers

Questions 19-24 are based on the following data:

Percent of Total Male Physicians and Percent of Total Female Physicians at Hospital X by Field

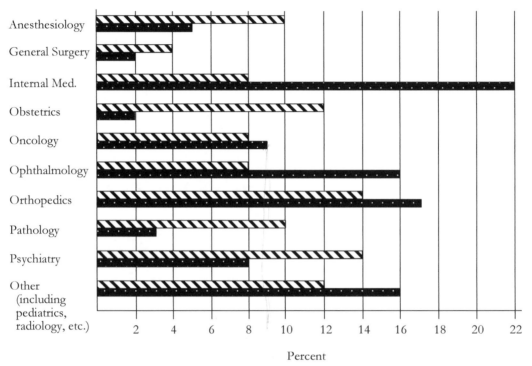

Note: Drawn to scale.

19. For how many of the categories is the <u>percent</u> of total male physicians at Hospital X greater than 11 percent?

    (A) Two   (B) Three   (C) Four   (D) Five   (E) Six

20. How many female physicians are there in oncology?

    (A) 14   (B) 16   (C) 17   (D) 18   (E) 20

Intermediate

21. Approximately what percent of the physicians practicing orthopedics is male?

(A) 35%   (B) 38%   (C) 41%   (D) 45%   (E) 51%

22. If the number of female physicians in psychiatry were to increase by 75 percent, how many female physicians would there be in psychiatry?

$$\boxed{28}$$

23. If there are 141 residents practicing obstetrics at Hospital X, what is the approximate ratio of the number of residents practicing obstetrics to the number of physicians practicing obstetrics?

(A) 20 to 3   (B) 19 to 4   (C) 9 to 2   (D) 17 to 4   (E) 8 to 3

4.5   4.25

Advanced

24. At Hospital X, the number of female physicians practicing internal medicine is approximately what percent greater than the number of female physicians practicing orthopedics?

(A) 18%   (B) 20%   (C) 28%   (D) 33%   (E) 36%

Questions 25-30 are based on the following data:

Monthly Health Care Costs and Hourly Wages*

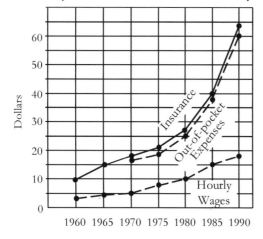

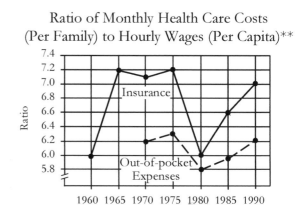

*Median Monthly Health Care Costs and
Median Hourly Wages, Per Family

$$**\text{Ratio} = \frac{\text{Median Family Health Care Costs (Per Family)}}{\text{Median Hourly Wages (Per Capita)}}$$

Note: Graphs drawn to scale.

Fundamental

25. In 1985, what was the approximate median cost, per family, for monthly out-of-pocket health care expenses?

(A) $15   (B) $35   (C) $36   (D) $38   (E) $40

26. In 1990, what was the approximate difference, per family, between the median cost for monthly out-of-pocket health care expenses and the median hourly wage?

(A) $42   (B) $45   (C) $46   (D) $46.50   (E) $47.50

Intermediate

27. By approximately what percent did the median monthly cost for health insurance, per family, increase from 1965 to 1985?

(A) 26%   (B) 38%   (C) 63%   (D) 167%   (E) 267%

28. For which of the following years was the ratio of the monthly median cost for health care insurance (per family) minus the monthly median cost for out-of-pocket expenses (per family) to hourly wages (per capita) the least?

(A) 1970 (B) 1975 (C) 1980 (D) 1985 (E) 1990

29. If in 1995 the hourly wage (per capita) was $8.00, and the ratio of the median cost for monthly out-of-pocket health care expenses (per family) to the hourly wage (per capita) was the same as in 1990, what was the median monthly cost for out-of-pocket health care expenses (per family) in 1995?

Round your answer to the nearest <u>integer</u>.

50

Advanced

30. In 1990, if the median monthly cost of health insurance, per family, had been $14.40 greater, the ratio of the median monthly cost of health insurance, per family, to the hourly wage, per capita, would have been 8.2. What was the hourly wage, per capita, in 1990?

(A) $9.56 (B) $10 (C) $11.25 (D) $12 (E) $14.75

Questions 31-36 are based on the following data:

Distribution of Population by Religious Denomination for State X in
1991 and Projected for 2015

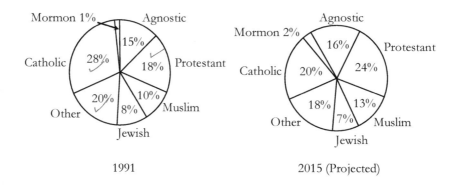

| Total Population: 15 Million | Total Population: 17.5 Million |

1991   2015 (Projected)

Fundamental

31. In 1991, approximately how many people in state X were agnostic?

Round your answer to the nearest <u>hundred thousand</u>.

2,300,000

32. In 1991, how many categories were comprised of more than <u>2.5 million</u> people?

(A) One   (B) Two   (C) Three   (D) Four   (E) Five

Intermediate

33. What is the ratio of the number of Protestants in 1991 to the projected number of
Protestants in 2015?

(A) $\frac{4}{9}$ (B) $\frac{5}{14}$ (C) $\frac{9}{14}$ (D) $\frac{3}{4}$ (E) $\frac{14}{9}$

34. Approximately what is the projected percent decrease in the <u>number</u> of Catholics in state *X* from 1991 to 2015?

(A) 42%   (B) 35%   (C) 20%   (D) 17%   (E) 7%

35. From 1991 to 2015, there is a projected increase in the number of people in which of the following categories?

Select <u>all</u> such categories.

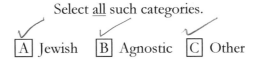

A Jewish   B Agnostic   C Other

Advanced

36. If the number of Catholics in state *X* were to increase by 5% from 1991 to 2030, then the number of Catholics in 2030 would approximately be what percent of the number projected in 2015?

(A) 96%   (B) 100%   (C) 112%   (D) 125%   (E) 133%

Questions 37-42 are based on the following data:

Average Quarterly Distribution for Magazine X

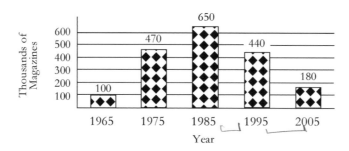

Total Yearly Revenue for Magazine X

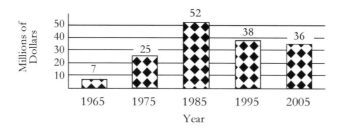

Average Number of Advertisements per Issue for Magazine X

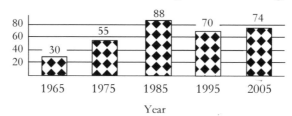

Fundamental

37. In how many of the years shown was the average number of advertisements per magazine at least twice as much as the average in 1965?

    (A) Four   (B) Three   (C) Two   (D) One   (E) None

38. In 1975, if the printing cost per magazine was $0.25, what would have been the total cost of printing the average quarterly distribution?

    did not convert into proper units

    thousands

    $117.50

    $117,500,000

Sherpa
Prep

Intermediate

39. In 2005 the number of dollars of revenue was how many times as great as the average quarterly distribution?

(A) 2,000   (B) 500   (C) 200   (D) 100   (E) 50

40. Which of the following statements can be inferred from the data?

Select all possible statements.

A   Of the years shown, the greatest increase in total revenue during any 10-year period was $27 million.

B   In each of the 10-year periods shown in which yearly revenue decreased, average quarterly distribution also decreased.

C   From 1995 to 2005 the average number of advertisements per issue increased by more than 5 percent.

41. The percent decrease in average quarterly distribution from 1985 to 1995 was approximately

$$\frac{diff}{original}$$

$$\frac{4}{70} = 5.7\%$$

(A) 10%   (B) 12%   (C) 20%   (D) 26%   (E) 32%

Advanced

42. In 1995, the average price, in dollars, per issue sold of magazine X was approximately

(A) 1.25
(B) 2.15
(C) 12.05
(D) 21.50
(E) It cannot be determined from the information given.

Questions 43-48 are based on the following data:

Three Types of Housing Units Available and
Sold in Cities *A*, *B*, and *C* Last Year

Number of Units Available

Number of Units Sold as a Percent
of Number of Units Available

City	Town Houses	Condos	Ranch Houses
A	75	55	40
B	90	40	35
C	80	25	50

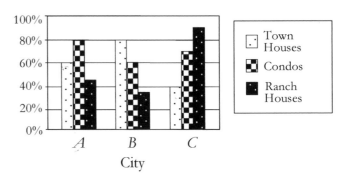

Fundamental

43. The total number of ranch houses available last year in City *C* was what fraction of
the total number of ranch houses available last year in all three cities?

(A) $\frac{3}{11}$ (B) $\frac{2}{7}$ (C) $\frac{3}{8}$ (D) $\frac{2}{5}$ (E) $\frac{3}{7}$

44. If the number of town houses sold this year in City *A* were to double the number sold
last year, the percent increase in the number of town houses sold in City *A* would
equal?

(A) 50% (B) 100% (C) 150% (D) 200% (E) 250%

Intermediate

45. The town houses sold in City *B* last year were sold at an average price of $119,950 plus
a 7 percent commission. What was the total revenue, including commission, for the
town houses sold in City *B* last year?

Round your answer to the nearest <u>hundred thousand</u>.

9,200,000

46. For which of the following categories did the number of units sold last year exceed 20?

Select all such categories.

☑ A Town houses sold in City *A*

☑ B Condos sold in City *B*

☑ C Town houses sold in City *C*

☐ D Ranch houses sold in City *B*

☐ E Condos sold in City *C*

47. Last year, the number of town houses sold in City *B* was what percent greater than the number of town houses sold in City *C*?

(A) 45%   (B) 56%   (C) 108%   (D) 120%   (E) 125%

Advanced

48. If the median price for a condo sold in City *B* last year was $60,000, and the average (arithmetic mean) price was $50,000, which of the following must be true?

misread question

Select all possible statements.

☐ A Exactly two condos in City *B* sold for $60,000.   *(doesn't have to be true)*

☑ B No condo in City *B* sold for more than $1.08 million.

☐ C The number of condos in City *B* that sold for $70,000 or more did not exceed the number that sold for $30,000 or less.

(21) Solutions – Video solutions for each of the previous questions can be found on our website at **www.sherpaprep.com/videos**.

• BOOKMARK this address for future visits!

> ➤ To view the videos, you'll need the LOGIN and PASSWORD that you created upon registering your copy of Statistics & Data Interpretation.

• If you have yet to register your book yet, please go to **www.sherpaprep.com/activate** and enter your email address, last name, and shipping address.

• Be sure to provide the SAME last name and shipping address that you used to purchase your copy of Master Key to the GRE or to enroll in your GRE course with Sherpa Prep!

> ➤ When checking your answers, we encourage you to watch the solution for any problem that you answered INCORRECTLY

• The same goes for any problem that took you MORE than TWO MINUTES to solve.

• After digesting the explanation, REVISIT your mistake a couple of days later to ensure that the problem no longer poses issues to you.

> ➤ If you struggle to solve the problem a SECOND time, add it to your "LOG of ERRORS" and redo it every few weeks.

• Solving tricky questions MORE THAN ONCE is the best way to learn from your mistakes and to avoid similar difficulties on your actual exam.

> Questions 1-6

    1. E
    2. C
    3. A
    4. 7
    5. C
    6. 100

Questions 7-12

7. B
8. C
9. B
10. C
11. A, B, C
12. E

Questions 13-18

13. A
14. E
15. B
16. A, B, C
17. D
18. B

Questions 19-24

19. C
20. D
21. E
22. 28
23. D
24. C

Questions 25-30

25. D
26. A
27. D
28. C
29. 50
30. D

Questions 31-36

31. 2,300,000
32. C
33. C
34. D
35. A, B, C
36. D

Questions 37-42

37. B
38. 117,500
39. C
40. A, B, C
41. E
42. E

Questions 43-48

43. D
44. B
45. 9,200,000
46. A, B, C
47. E
48. B

Sherpa Prep

Master Key to the GRE

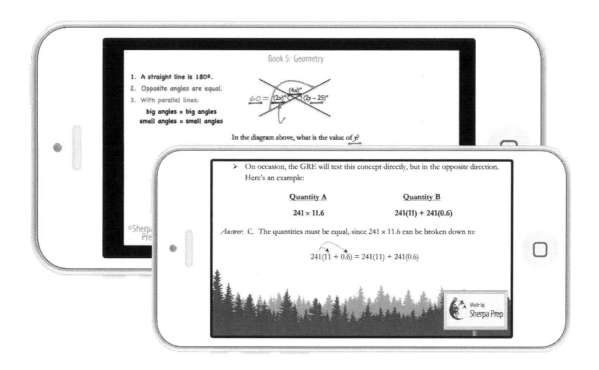

Made in the USA
Middletown, DE
10 June 2017